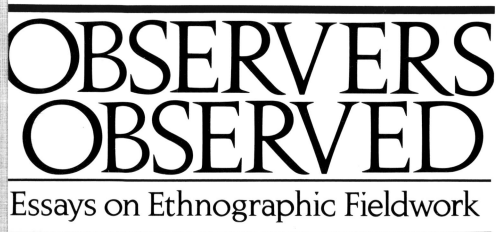

OBSERVERS OBSERVED

Essays on Ethnographic Fieldwork

Edited by George W. Stocking, Jr.

Observers Observed

HISTORY OF ANTHROPOLOGY

EDITOR
George W. Stocking, Jr.
Department of Anthropology, University of Chicago

EDITORIAL BOARD
Talal Asad
Department of Sociology and Social Anthropology, University of Hull

James Boon
Department of Anthropology, Cornell University

James Clifford
Board of Studies in the History of Consciousness,
University of California, Santa Cruz

Donna Haraway
Board of Studies in the History of Consciousness,
University of California, Santa Cruz

Curtis Hinsley
Department of History, Colgate University

Dell Hymes
Graduate School of Education, University of Pennsylvania

Henrika Kuklick
Department of History and Sociology of Science,
University of Pennsylvania

Bruce Trigger
Department of Anthropology, McGill University

Observers Observed

ESSAYS ON ETHNOGRAPHIC FIELDWORK

Edited by

George W. Stocking, Jr.

HISTORY OF ANTHROPOLOGY
Volume 1

THE UNIVERSITY OF WISCONSIN PRESS

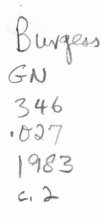

Published 1983

The University of Wisconsin Press
114 North Murray Street
Madison, Wisconsin 53715

The University of Wisconsin Press, Ltd.
1 Gower Street
London WC1E 6HA, England

Printings 1983, 1985

Printed in the United States of America

Library of Congress Cataloging in Publication Data
Main entry under title:

Observers observed.
(History of anthropology; v. 1)
Includes bibliographies and index
1. Ethnology—Field work—Addresses, essays, lectures.
2. Participant observation—Addresses, essays, lectures.
3. Ethnology—History—Addresses, essays, lectures.
I. Stocking, George W., 1928–   . II. Series.
GN346.O27 1983   306'.0723   83-47771
ISBN 0-299-09450-2
ISBN 0-299-09454-5 (pbk.)

Contents

Observers Observed

HISTORY OF ANTHROPOLOGY

Whence/Whither

At a time when bookshelves bulge with journals ever-more-costly and ever-less-often read, the launching of a new volume-series demands a brief self-explaining introduction. What is the audience whose unserved needs we address? What is the subject of our discourse? How do we intend to pursue it? And why do we begin with a particular aspect of it?

Although there has been occasional interest in the history of anthropology throughout the century since the emergence of the modern academic discipline, a more systematic concern may be traced to the Conference on the History of Anthropology stimulated by A. I. Hallowell and sponsored by the Social Science Research Council in 1962 (cf. Hymes 1962). Two decades later, what was once for the most part the episodic effort of reminiscent elder anthropologists or roving intellectual historians has become something approximating a recognized research specialization. *The History of Anthropology: A Research Bibliography* includes 2,439 titles culled from over 5,000 collected by its editors (Kemper & Phinney 1977), and for the past decade each biannual issue of the *History of Anthropology Newsletter* has recorded a substantial number of articles, doctoral dissertations, and books by scholars who think of themselves as historians of anthropology (Stocking, ed. 1973–).

The impetus for this development has come from both history and anthropology. Historians have no doubt been impelled in part by the inherent expansionism of a profession whose rapidly multiplying apprentices must find still unplowed fields for their research. But historical interest is also motivated by more general professional and social concerns centering on issues of knowledge and power. The long-run trend towards the professionalization of intellectual life within academic disciplines often lately pervaded by a sense of crisis has made these disciplines themselves seem historically problematic; issues of racial and ethnic relations in the decolonizing world have turned historians' attention to the ideology of race and culture (cf. Hinsley 1981).

Although doubtless variously motivated, the heightened retrospective interest of anthropologists reflects the special sense of disciplinary crisis that

3

has developed since about 1960. With the withdrawal of the umbrella of European power that long protected their entry into the colonial field, anthropologists found it increasingly difficult to gain access to (as well as ethically more problematic to study) the non-European "others" who had traditionally excited the anthropological imagination—and who seemed finally about to realize, through cultural change, the long-trumpeted anthropological prediction of the "vanishing primitive." Some envisioned "the end of anthropology" along with its traditional subject matter (cf. Worsley 1970). Some wondered whether anthropology was a reversible and universal form of knowledge or merely the way Europeans had explained to themselves the "others" encountered during the centuries-long period of European overseas expansion (Stocking 1982b:419). Still others proposed the "reinvention" of the discipline. Calling into question its institutionalization within the academy, turning for the first time in its history toward Marxist and feminist theory, they advocated a more "reflexive" study of social groups within Euro-American societies, and an active political involvement on behalf of its subjects (Hymes, ed. 1973). Whether it is being reinvented, or simply being carried along by institutional inertia, anthropology in the early 1980s continues to face profound issues of disciplinary identity (Hoebel, ed. 1982). The development of self-study by post-colonial "native anthropologists" raises new ethical and methodological problems; reflexive study in the metropolis contributes to the centrifugal proliferation of "adjectival anthropologies" without providing a unifying substantive focus; epistemological and ethical doubts have weakened methodological resolution without yet resolving the problematic character of fieldwork method; the questioning of old concepts and the legitimation of new theoretical alternatives has not established the basis for a new integrative orientation; and despite a growing concern with increasing non-academic employment options for its surplus doctorates, the discipline remains essentially an academic one.

In this context, some anthropologists have become increasingly conscious of the historical character of their discipline. Not only are the problems and the data of anthropology once again seen to be essentially historical after a half-century of predominantly synchronic emphases, but anthropology itself is increasingly viewed as an historical phenomenon. In order to understand their present predicament and to find and/or to legitimate approaches that might lead them out of it, a number of anthropologists have turned to the history of anthropology (e.g., Augé 1979; Crick 1976; Harris 1968).

The founding of History of Anthropology (hereafter, HOA) is an outcome of this double disciplinary impulse. Until now, there has been no arena in which both anthropologists and historians might pursue historical problems of common concern before an informed and interested audience. Articles on various aspects of the history of anthropology have been scattered hither and yon, appearing now and then in anthropological journals little read by historians, but as often in historical journals scarcely seen by anthropologists. HOA will attempt to provide a single central forum for their mutual discourse.

The duality of our audience is not the only problematic issue suggested by our title. Despite anthropology's century as an academic discipline, its definition is in some respects more problematic today than at the time of its early institutionalization. Depending on national tradition, sub-disciplinary identification, and theoretical orientation, its external and internal boundary relations vary considerably (cf. Hannerz, ed. 1983; Diamond, ed. 1980). The embracive ("four-field") conception of anthropology has been most characteristic of the American and certain phases of the British tradition. On the European continent the term long referred primarily to the study of "man" as a physical being; and there are those in the United States today who would separate "socio-cultural" anthropology as sharply from biological anthropology as, for example, from psychology or economics.

One might resolve the issue by defining a fundamental problem-orientation underlying the historical diversity of disciplinary definition: the history we encompass is that of "the systematic study of human unity-in-diversity." Such a formula allows a place not only for biological anthropology (e.g., Haraway 1978), archeology (e.g., Trigger 1980), anthropological linguistics (e.g., Hymes, ed. 1974), and socio-cultural anthropology (e.g., Boon 1983), but for such historical or national variants as "ethnology" and *volkskunde*, as well as the "anthropological" aspects of psychology, aesthetics, economics, etc. It allows us also to consider as historically problematic the processes by which certain approaches to or aspects of human diversity are (or are not) incorporated into such systematic study (cf. Kuklick 1980)—for example, the changing fate of Marxist or feminist perspectives on social organization (e.g., Rosaldo & Lamphere, eds. 1974), or the exclusion of missionary ethnography in favor of "scientific" fieldwork (cf. Clifford 1982).

Nevertheless our formula—which is itself full of problematic concepts—tends still to suggest an orientation, however flexible, toward the history of a "discipline." No doubt much of our historiography will be thus construed—or constrained. But in principle we recognize no sharp borders surrounding the "discipline" of anthropology. It is not merely a matter of including western "folk anthropology" as part of the historical background from which "scientific anthropology" emerged (cf. Hallowell 1965). It is also one of recognizing that in every period the "systematic study of human unity-in-diversity" is itself constrained—some might say systematically structured—by the ongoing and cumulative historical experience of encounters and comprehensions between Europeans and "others." These comprehensions articulate closely with ideologies of European self-knowledge—as the evolutionary equation of savage/madman/peasant/child/woman suggests—and the often bloodily expropriative nature of these encounters gives them a special weighting of moral concern. The history of anthropology is thus the history of a "discipline" whose enmeshment in world-historical structures and processes especially compels attention.

From the broadest point of view, then, the history of anthropology we propose to encompass is that of the systematic study of human unity-in-diversity, against the background of historical experience and cultural assumption that has provoked and constrained it, and which it in turn has conditioned.

The launching of HOA takes place in the context of a more general rapprochement between the two inquiries. For just as anthropologists lately have turned to history, many historians (quite aside from the interest in the history of disciplines) have turned recently to anthropology for conceptual and methodological orientations (Gaunt 1982). Despite this rapprochement, and an underlying substantive and epistemological kinship, there nevertheless tend to be differences in the approaches that anthropologists and historians take to the history of anthropology. To borrow categories used elsewhere some years ago to describe motivation and style in historical inquiry, anthropologists are more likely to be "presentist" and historians more "historicist" in treating the history of issues currently debated within anthropology (Stocking 1965; cf. Stocking 1982a). To put the matter another way, anthropologists are more likely to be committed to one side or another, and historians to be (relatively) disinterested observers, and the histories they write are likely to reflect this fact. Each approach has advantages and disadvantages. If historians are less likely to be blinkered by theoretical bias, they are also more likely to suffer from a lack of technical sophistication and relevance; and if an anthropologist's commitment may inhibit understanding of the "losing" side, it can also illuminate issues that remain below the threshold of a more disinterested concern.

Drawing its editorial board from both disciplines, HOA will be receptive to a variety of historical and anthropological points of view. We favor studies grounded in concrete historical research, but we hope to rise well above anecdotal antiquarianism to contribute to the critical understanding of general issues of serious current anthropological concern. We hope to encourage the development of a disciplinary historiography that is both historically sophisticated and anthropologically knowledgeable.

It should be emphasized that we are not proposing a division in which anthropology provides subject matter and history methodological orientation. In this respect the history of anthropology differs significantly from that of certain other inquiries. For the historian of physics, the methods and concepts of that discipline do perhaps have relevance only as subject matter. For the historian of anthropology, they are not only the object of inquiry, but may provide also a means by which it is pursued. As Hallowell argued several decades ago, the history of anthropology should be approached as "an anthropological problem" (Hallowell 1965).

The history of anthropology, however, is not one but many such problems, each with many facets, which may be approached in a variety of particular ways. And each problem may engage not only particular groups of anthropologists and historians, but also sociologists of science and literary historians, as well as others with specific or general interests in the human sciences. With these constraints in mind, HOA has adopted a format of periodic book-length volumes organized around particular themes announced and developed in advance. In addition to substantive articles of varying length, documentary materials, personal reminiscences, critical essays, and essay reviews relating to the volume theme, each volume of HOA will include one or more "miscellaneous studies," in order to allow a place for high-quality research outside our chosen topics. Should the muses of our authors prove more generally resistant to coordination, we will not hesitate to publish an occasional miscellaneous volume. In this manner, we hope to bring together the best work being produced, and to stimulate research which, if it does not find a place in HOA, may enrich the pages of other journals that will retain an interest in the history of anthropology.

As theme for the inaugural volume of HOA, we have focussed on the development of ethnographic fieldwork in socio-cultural anthropology. Both for practitioners and outsiders, a distinguishing feature of modern anthropology is the commitment to fieldwork by "participant-observation." Entering as a stranger into a small and culturally alien community, the investigator becomes for a time and in a way part of its system of face-to-face relationships, so that the data collected in some sense reflect the native's own point of view. This style of inquiry is much more than a mode of data-gathering widely (although by no means universally) adopted in a particular discipline of the human sciences. At once setting anthropology apart from other such inquiries and linking it to a broader European tradition of participatory cultural exoticism, it is the basis for a most unlikely image of the academic intellectual: "the anthropologist as hero" (Sontag 1966). It is a kind of shared archetypical experience that informs, if it does not generate, a system of generalized methodological values or disciplinary ideology: the value placed on fieldwork itself as the basic constituting experience not only of anthropological knowledge but of anthropologists; the value placed on a holistic approach to the cultures (or societies) that are the subject of this form of knowledge; the value placed on the equal valuation of all such entities; and the value placed on their uniquely privileged role in the constitution of anthropological theory (Stocking 1982b; cf. Mandelbaum 1982). It has, in short, been the legitimizing basis for anthropology's claim to special cognitive authority (cf. Clifford 1983).

During the decades of socio-cultural anthropology's "classical period"— roughly 1925 to 1960 (cf. Stocking 1978)—fieldwork evoked relatively little systematic questioning or analysis (Nash & Wintrob 1972). Certain aspects of it were subject to a degree of formal elaboration that enabled them to be taught as technical skills (Epstein, ed. 1967). For the most part, however, fieldwork training was a matter of learning by doing, and this less in the tradition of apprenticeship than of "sink-or-swim." There was a certain amount of formal scholarly discussion of certain methodological issues, but there is little in the published record to suggest a serious consideration of the fundamental epistemological, psychological, or ethical issues involved in research where the investigator was expected—if archetype were to be realized—to become rather intimately involved in the processes he or she was studying. As befits the central methodological rite in a discipline whose national communities continued into the 1950s to resemble the face-to-face *gemeinschaften* they archetypically studied, fieldwork was enacted more than it was analyzed; part of the community's oral tradition, it was the subject of considerable mythic elaboration.

By 1960, this situation had begun to change. To some extent this may have been the result of the growth of anthropology itself. Especially in the United States, where there were substantial numbers of undergraduates taking anthropology courses, the community became large enough to provide a publishing market; and given its central role in the anthropological mystique, the field experience was bound eventually to become a marketable commodity. Field training, however, continued for the most part to be extremely informal, and the interest of publishers tended to lag behind a changing disciplinary consciousness, which by 1960 was beginning to respond to the changing circumstances of ethnographic inquiry in the era of decolonization. In that context, the publication of certain books did play a role in the emergence of the new consciousness—most notably Malinowski's *Diary in the Strict Sense of the Term* (1967). Suddenly there seemed to have been uncovered a long-repressed Conradian horror—what the culture-hero of the fieldwork myth had "actually" been feeling during his long and presumably empathetic immersion in the Trobriand *gemeinschaft*. Longing for white civilization and for white womanhood, he had relieved his frustration with outpourings of aggression against the "niggers" who surrounded him. In a political context in which anthropologists were being attacked for indirect or active complicity in the defense of colonial power (cf. Asad, ed. 1973), and even, despite the discipline's half-century critique of racial ideology, as themselves racialist, Malinowski's "niggers" were profoundly disturbing indeed.

Anthropologists have yet to come to terms with all the implications of Malinowski's diaries. But the years since 1967 have seen a considerable body of literature on the fieldwork process. The heightened consciousness of its problematic character has produced numerous discussions of the epistemological, methodological, psychological, ethical, and political implications of fieldwork, as well as a number of autobiographical accounts of varying length (cf. Agar 1980). Increasingly, ethnographies are accompanied by or even presented in the form of accounts of the fieldwork that produced them (cf. Cesara 1982). But while historians of the discipline have approached aspects of its development, there is as yet no general historical account of the modern anthropological fieldwork tradition. It is in this context that we have chosen our theme and subtitle for the first volume of *HOA*: "Observers Observed: Essays on Ethnographic Fieldwork."

Few if any themes in the history of anthropology can be systematically explored within the confines of a single 200-page volume of essays written by authors whose motivating interests are in fact quite varied. Since one of our purposes is to provoke further research, it may be useful to reflect briefly on some of the limitations of the history we have sketched. Granting that our choice of episodes was heavily conditioned by the circumstances of current work-in-progress, one can of course imagine a multitude of particular alternatives. We might have begun with Lewis Henry Morgan, whose kinship-terminology questionnaires and trans-Mississippi expeditions of the late 1850s were perhaps the earliest attempts systematically to collect data bearing on a specific ethnological problem; our failure even to mention Margaret Mead must surely strike many readers as anomalous.

The issue is perhaps better approached, however, in terms of certain limitations of the overall picture we have conveyed. Neglecting the development of fieldwork traditions in other areas of anthropology, we have shut off a wide range of reflective insights that might have been offered by contrasting, for instance, the modalities of archeological fieldwork with those of ethnography. Although we have included material from three major national ethnographic traditions, we have only touched upon their interaction, and comparisons between them have been for the most part implicit and juxtapositional (cf. Urry n.d.). More seriously, perhaps, our episodic approach has significantly distorted the presentation of the American ethnographic tradition. Skipping from Cushing in the Southwest and Boas in Baffinland forward to Barnett's disillusionment with summertime trait surveys, we have in fact omitted what many would consider the most characteristic manifestation

of Boasian ethnography: the style that produced Boas' "five-foot shelf" of
Kwakuitl texts. Building on the traditions of European humanistic scholarship, particularly on linguistic and folklore study, this approach saw ethnography as the construction of a body of textual material directly expressive of
the native mind, produced with the active and acknowledged assistance of
native ethnographic intermediaries like George Hunt. The contrast with the
British tradition is by no means absolute—Hocart, too, aspired to construct
his ethnographies in these terms. But if we characterize different ethnographic modes in terms of the forms of data that they privilege (such as
artifactual, textual, and behavioral), the contrast between the classic Boasian and Malinowskian modes is clear enough.

It is primarily the latter that undergirds the presently dominant disciplinary ideology; and it could be argued that, after all, our history has been
structured by a corresponding disciplinary myth-history of fieldwork. By focussing on developments since 1880, we have encouraged a de facto separation of modern ethnography from the long preceding experience of contact
between Europeans and "others." Furthermore, we have only briefly treated
what was lost (as well as gained) with the emergence of a scientistic academic
anthropology. At the same time, we have perhaps sustained a somewhat
backward-looking romantic image of the academic ethnographer: all our anthropologists are European, and if they did not all work alone, the "others"
that they studied were for the most part inhabitants of geographically distant
precincts of cultural exoticism. There is little reflection of the historical roots
of a more reflexive ethnography—nothing on European folklore or *volkskunde,* nothing on anthropological research in more complex societies. In
short, by limiting ourselves to the last century, by emphasizing its earlier
phases, by orienting ourselves toward academic anthropology, and by focussing on the critical role of individuals who figure prominently in the disciplinary myth, we have to some extent perpetuated a picture which, although
presented in more concretely historical terms, is in basic outline rather conventional.

But though this is in some ways a limitation, we make no apology for it.
If we focus on the familiar, it is our intention to defamiliarize it. To do this
need not always require recomposition from scratch. It may be a matter of
directing a brighter, fuller light on figures whose proportions have been distorted and whose surroundings have been cast into shadow—or of trying to
set their stereotyped postures once more in motion. No doubt other standpoints might have been adopted, other lamps held, other perspectives revealed. For anthropologists (prospective, certified, retired, or manqué) fieldwork is an endlessly engaging topic, which will surely appear again in HOA.
In the meantime, we will try to remain open to approaches that go beyond

explicit or implicit disciplinary definitions, in the hope that by defamiliarizing the past, we may perhaps help to open up the future.

ACKNOWLEDGMENTS

Aside from the editor, the editorial board, the contributors, and the production staff of the University of Wisconsin Press, several other individuals and organizations facilitated the preparation of this volume. The Wenner-Gren Foundation for Anthropological Research, Inc., provided a grant to underwrite editorial expenses. The staffs of the University of Chicago Department of Anthropology and of the Morris Fishbein Center for the Study of the History of Science and Medicine (especially Kathryn Barnes and Elizabeth Bitoy) provided necessary support. Kevin Mutchler served as editorial assistant, and Raymond Fogelson was ever-ready with helpful editorial advice. Our thanks to them all.

REFERENCES

Agar, M. 1980. *The professional stranger: An informal introduction to ethnography.* New York.
Asad, T., ed. 1973. *Anthropology and the colonial encounter.* London.
Augé, M. 1974. *The anthropological circle: Symbol, function, history.* Trans. M. Thom. Cambridge (1982).
Boon, J. 1983. *Other tribes, other scribes: Symbolic anthropology in the comparative study of cultures, histories, religions, and texts.* Cambridge.
Cesara, M. (K. Poewe). 1982. *Reflections of a woman anthropologist.* New York.
Clifford, J. 1982. *Person and myth: Maurice Leenhardt in the Melanesian world.* Berkeley.
———. 1983. On ethnographic authority. *Representations.* 1 (2).
Crick, M. 1976. *Explorations in language and meaning: Towards a semantic anthropology.* New York.
Diamond, S., ed. 1980. *Anthropology: Ancestors and heirs.* The Hague.
Epstein, A., ed. 1967. *The craft of social anthropology.* London.
Gaunt, D. 1982. *Memoir on history and anthropology.* Swedish Council for Research in the Humanities and Social Sciences. Stockholm.
Hallowell, A. 1965. The history of anthropology as an anthropological problem. In *Contributions to anthropology: Selected papers of A. Irving Hallowell,* ed. R. D. Fogelson, 21–35. Chicago.

Hannerz, U., ed. 1983. The shaping of national anthropologies. *Ethnos* 47.

Haraway, D. 1978. The past is a contested zone: Human nature and theories of production and reproduction in primate behavior studies. *Signs* 4:37–60.

Harris, M. 1968. *The rise of anthropological theory.* New York.

Hinsley, C. 1981. *Savages and scientists: The Smithsonian Institution and the development of American anthropology, 1846–1910.* Washington.

Hoebel, E., et al., eds. 1982. *Crisis in anthropology: View from Spring Hill, 1980.* New York.

Hymes, D. 1962. On studying the history of anthropology. *Items* 16:25–27.

Hymes, D., ed. 1973. *Reinventing anthropology.* New York.

———. 1974. *Studies in the history of linguistics: Traditions and paradigms.* Bloomington.

Kemper, R. V. & J. Phinney, eds. 1977. *The history of anthropology: A research bibliography.* New York.

Kuklick, H. 1980. Boundary maintenance in American sociology: Limitations to academic "professionalization." *J. Hist. Behav. Scis.* 16:201–19.

Malinowski, B. 1967. *A diary in the strict sense of the term.* New York.

Mandelbaum, D. 1982. Some shared ideas. In Hoebel et al., eds. 1982:35–50.

Nash, D., & R. Wintrob. 1972. The emergence of self-consciousness in ethnography. *Cur. Anth.* 13:527–42.

Rosaldo, M., & L. Lamphere, eds. 1974. *Women, culture and society.* Stanford.

Sontag, S. 1966. The anthropologist as hero. In *Claude Lévi-Strauss: The anthropologist as hero*, ed. E. N. & T. Hayes, 184–97. Paperback ed. Cambridge (1970).

Stocking, G. W., Jr. 1965. On the limits of "presentism" and "historicism" in the historiography of the behavioral sciences. *J. Hist. Behav. Scis.* 1:211–18.

———. 1978. Die geschichtlichkeit der wilden und die geschichte der ethnologie. Trans. W. Lepenies. *Geschichte und Gesellschaft* 4:520–35.

———. 1982a. Preface to the Phoenix edition. In *Race, culture, and evolution: Essays in the history of anthropology*, xi–xxi. Reprint ed. Chicago.

———. 1982b. Anthropology in crisis? A view from between the generations. In Hoebel et al., eds. 1982:407–19.

Stocking, G. W., Jr., ed. 1973–. *The history of anthropology newsletter.* Department of Anthropology, University of Chicago.

Trigger, B. 1980. *Gordon Childe: Revolutions in archaeology.* New York.

Urry, J. n.d. The history of field methods. In *The general conduct of field research*, ed. R. F. Ellen. London.

Worsley, P. 1970. The end of anthropology? *Trans. Sixth World Cong. Soc.* 3:121–29.

"THE VALUE OF A PERSON LIES IN HIS HERZENSBILDUNG"

Franz Boas' Baffin Island Letter-Diary, 1883–1884

DOUGLAS COLE

When Franz Boas was twenty-five years old, he travelled to Baffin Island to undertake anthropological and geographical research among the Eskimo. In view of his later eminence as reigning patriarch of American anthropology during the first third of the twentieth century, the letter-diaries that he kept during his *erstlingsreise* (Boas 1894:97) have a special interest for the history of the discipline.

Boas had secured his doctorate from Kiel University in the summer of 1881. Although his dissertation had been in physics, he had already chosen one of his minor fields, geography, as his future speciality. After pursuing for a time certain problems of the psychophysics of sense perception suggested by his doctoral studies, he began to focus his interests on the relationship between people and their natural environment. By April 1882, during the year of his required military service, he had begun planning "an investigation of the dependence of contemporary Eskimo migrations upon the physical relationships and forms of their land" (BPP: FB/A. Jacobi 4/10/82; cf. Kluckhohn & Prufer 1959, Stocking 1968).

Douglas Cole is Associate Professor of History at Simon Fraser University. He has published on the history of Canada and its art, including *From Desolation to Splendour: Changing Perceptions of the British Columbia Landscape*, and on the history of anthropology. He is currently finishing a book on museums and Northwest Coast anthropological collecting, and researching a study of Franz Boas' early years.

The reason for selecting the Eskimo (or Inuit) is not apparent at first glance. Boas seems to have felt that their environmental dependence was the most simple case with which to begin, though the paucity of information available upon the region and its natives weighed against the advantages of apparent simplicity. Perhaps the choice was a quite personal one, its roots lying far back in Boas' youth. As early as 1870, when he was but a boy of twelve, he wrote to his sister of undertaking an expedition to the north or south pole after completing university (BFP: FB/T. Boas 12/3/70). The probability that polar exploration was a long-standing idea and not a passing boyhood fantasy receives support from the course he took in 1878–79 at Bonn on the geography and research of polar areas.

Having decided to study the Inuit and their environment, Boas set about his preparations for an expedition. He moved to Berlin, where, among other things, he studied meteorological, astronomical, and magnetic observation with W. J. Förster of the Berlin Planetarium and anthropological measurement with Rudolf Virchow, as well as cartographic and topographical drawing. He also worked at both the Inuit and Danish languages, consulted Heymann Steinthal on linguistic points, examined the Arctic collections at the Berlin museum under the eye of Adolf Bastian, and learned photography. Through his developing Berlin acquaintances Boas was able also to organize the practical matters of launching the expedition. Bastian put him in touch with Georg von Neumayer, chairman of the German Polar Commission, which at that time was supporting scientific parties at Baffin and South Georgia islands. Neumayer promised transportation to Baffin Island with the Commission's ship and generously allowed Boas to have his pick of the returning station's instruments and supplies. Boas persuaded the editors of the *Berliner Tageblatt* to advance 3,000 marks against fifteen promised articles.

Much remained to be done, but the means for the expedition and its planned outline were clear. He would travel to Baffin Island's Cumberland Sound with the *Germania*, a ship built in 1869 for Arctic use. She would take him deep into Cumberland Sound to Kingawa, where Dr. Wilhelm Giese's scientific party had spent the International Polar Year of 1882–83. Should the Scottish station at Kikkerton Island seem more favorable as a base than the Kingawa hut, Boas had a letter from Crawford Noble, its Aberdeen owner, asking the resident master for his cooperation. Boas planned to take with him an assistant and a servant. Although Lieutenant von den Goltz, Neumayer's recommendation as assistant, backed out at the last moment, servant Wilhelm Weike, who had been in the Boas family service, remained. With the advice of old Arctic hands, Boas secured in Hamburg a large stock of provisions, guns, ammunition and trade goods, a thirteen-foot dinghy intended for the interior lakes, and a small steel sled.

His research strategy was developed from his rapid mastery of Arctic literature and honed by several contributions that he made to it during his preparatory year. The most important article, ostensibly about the homeland of the Netsilik Eskimo, partly described and partly postulated extensive routes of trade and travel between Inuit groups of the central and eastern Arctic (Boas 1883: 223–33). According to the article, these well-established routes extended from Ugulik, a settlement at the western tip of King William Island, eastward through Iglulik on Fury and Hecla Strait, and from there in two directions on Baffin Island—to Pond Inlet at the northern end, and down along the western coast, connecting eastwards to Cumberland Sound.

Boas fitted these interests and postulates into a plan for a one-year investigation based at Cumberland Sound. Aside from cartographic and meteorological research, his intention was to study Eskimo migration, hunting areas, trade routes, and the relationships of one group to another. He would travel in the summer and fall of 1883 to Lake Kennedy (Lake Nettilling), an inland sheet of fresh water, and from there attempt to reach the west coast of Baffin Island and follow it north to Iglulik. Returning to winter in Cumberland Sound, he would "collect ethnographic material and make a thorough study of the language, customs and habits of the Eskimo" (BFP: "Als Ausgangspunkt" n.d.). In the spring he would return to Iglulik and then, by the route postulated in his article, travel north to Pond Inlet, perhaps yet farther north to Devon Island. He would return to Cumberland Sound in July along the Davis Strait, and sail home in the fall aboard a whaler.

This ambitious itinerary and the tenacity to which Boas held to a trip to the west coast, despite overwhelming setbacks, indicates that he was exceedingly intent upon demonstrating that portion of the routes he had set out in his Netsilik article. There was probably more to it, too. An overland trip westward from Cumberland Sound would bring him to one of the largest unexplored regions of the Arctic and onto an apparently easy route north to Iglulik, Pond Inlet, and beyond. It would be a significant piece of geographic discovery.

Privately, Boas anticipated a different ending to his expedition. Knowing that vessels traded along Davis Strait, he hoped to be picked up by an American whaler. The reasons behind this desire to visit America were partly professional: for a number of reasons, including the recent upsurge of anti-Semitism, he was not convinced that his future lay in Germany. Another motive was personal and concerned Miss Marie Krackowizer.

Marie Krackowizer was the daughter of Dr. Ernst Krackowizer, an Austrian Forty-Eighter who became a prominent New York doctor before his death in 1875. The Krackowizers were close friends of another New York physician and German Forty-Eighter, Abraham Jacobi, who was Boas' uncle by marriage. When, in the summer of 1881, the Krackowizers and Jacobi holidayed together in the Harz mountains of Germany, they were joined by Boas, who had just finished sitting his doctoral exams at Kiel. He had only turned twenty-three, and Marie was not quite twenty. For three days they were almost constantly together, walking in the park at Wernigerode, looking down from the cliff of the Regenstein. They had an unforgettable early morning in the wild and picturesque Bodethal before all left for the Boas home in Minden, where Franz and Marie had two more days together. Although the Krackowizers settled temporarily in Stuttgart, the relationship lay dormant until Boas attended the Geographical Congress at Frankfurt in the spring of 1883 and feigned an appointment in Stuttgart as an excuse to call upon Marie. That April first afternoon, a beautiful spring Sunday, they stood under the old Schiller Oak "and told one another everything except what we really thought" (BFP: FB/MK 6/24/83). The omission was removed by a flurry of letters at the end of May. Less than three weeks before his departure for Baffin Island, they were quietly engaged. Her farewell letter, read as the *Germania* sailed down the Elbe, ended with "*Vorwärts! Ich warte dir!*"—"Onward, I wait for you!" (BFP: MK/FB 6/19/83). *Vorwärts* became a word repeated time and again by Boas to himself as he pursued his labors in the lonely barrens of Baffin Island.

The expedition meant a difficult separation for two such recently declared lovers. For twelve or more months any communication between them would be impossible. In the circumstances, they both kept diaries of unpostable letters. What matter if they could not be answered or even read for months?

These circumstances make Boas' letter-diary a very peculiar document. In a sense it is a single, 500-page letter composed over a fifteen-month period. Much of it is an outpouring of affection, an extended love letter, in which amorous effusions often overwhelm description of his field activities. The letter-diary served purposes which his simpler field journal could not. Like a letter, it provided an escape from present circumstances into indirect communication with someone dear and far away. Like a diary, it was a personal document where he could relieve himself of otherwise contained emotions—love, frustration, joy and despair. Under especially trying conditions, it sometimes ceased even to be a personal document and merely duplicated the sparse entries of his daily field journal. At other times, there are gaps of days, even longer, invariably followed by apologies and catch-up reports. While not a perfect way to reconstruct Boas' first field experience, it does allow considerable insight into his soul and travail.

The letter-diary is a very hard document to read. Iglus and tepiks possessed no writing desks and the letter diary went with him over the estimated 3,000 or so miles he travelled; by his own admission to Marie, his handwriting was often little more than "chicken-scratches" (*Krackelfüsse*—letter-diary 11/5/83). The extant document is not even "original" for the most part, but a carbon copy made on perforated 17.5 by 8.5 cm notepads. The original was mostly in pencil (there was a problem of keeping ink liquid) and the carbon is often smudged. Its legibility was a test even for the late Helene Boas Yampolsky, daughter of Boas, whose work in creating a translation cannot be praised too highly. While relying very much upon this translation, I have succeeded in filling some of her gaps and have made changes where I thought a better reading possible.

The poor legibility of the text and the necessity of turning German scribbled in the field into acceptable English make textual integrity impossible. Inuit personal names are given as accurate a rendering as possible, using *Baffin-Land* (Boas 1885) when they are mentioned there, but more often relying upon the most common or most clear form of the Boas manuscripts. Geographical names have been standardized, except Kikkerton and Kingawa, to Boas' list in *Baffin-Land* (90–94). Several other terms (e.g., Doctorā'dluk) have also been regularized—although it is important to note that Boas later insisted on the methodological significance of such "alternating" renditions (1889). As reproduced here, the letter-diary is rather severely abridged. The early shipboard sections, which occupy almost a third of the original manuscript, are almost entirely omitted; in all, the text is cut to about one quarter of the original. What remains, however, will perhaps convey the essence of Boas' ethnographic initiation.

––––––––––––

[The letter-diary opens three days after the *Germania* sailed from Hamburg on June 20, as it was passing from the Elbe into the North Sea. "My best beloved! Today I am beginning to write my diary to you and must tell you first of all how much I love you." Boas describes life on board, his cramped and smelly cabin, how he tried to give Wilhelm lessons in English ("He has a terribly thick head. Things don't penetrate very readily"), and how, by July 5, life had become "very monotonous." On his birthday, July 9, when the ship passed Greenland's Cape Farewell into the Arctic Ocean, he was so seasick that only in the afternoon could he even look at the letters and presents Weike had for him. Two days later, he ruminated on the purpose of the trip: "It is funny how everybody thinks I am making this trip for fame and glory. Certainly they do not know me and I would have a poor opinion of myself if that was a *goal* for which I put in work and effort. You know that I strive for a higher thing and that this trip is only a means to that goal. I suppose it is true that I want external recognition for my achievements, but only in so far as I wish to be known as a man who will carry out his ideas and act upon them. That is the only kind of recognition I can think of. Empty glory means nothing to me."

Cumberland Sound and Davis Strait on the east side of Baffin Island.

On July 15, the ship was in sight of Cape Mercy, the outermost point of the Cumberland Peninsula. Further progress, however, was impossible: "All we can see, looking landwards, is a desert of ice, shoal after shoal, field upon field, broken only by an occasional iceberg." Already he was having to revise his plans since it was becoming doubtful that they could break into the Sound before the middle of August. By July 27 he had given up his plan for a fall trip to Iglulik, and by August 7, Boas worried that the whole project might have to be abandoned: "How will my things get to Kikkerton and what shall I do in the fall if we get to land too late? And if we never get there, what then? I should be very sorry for the unfortunate north expedition" (the men at the German Polar Station). "And what a great disappointment it would be for me! But I will hope for the best. I have not been able to sleep for several nights for worry about these matters and I wish it would be settled in one way or another. Just think of it if I had lost four months for nothing. . . . I am really becoming depressed worrying about all this. The day after tomor-

row we shall have cruised about here for four weeks and have advanced scarcely
fifteen sea miles."

Although very depressed, Boas kept himself busy with photography, with
charting the coastline, and with taking samples of sea water and ice, until
finally August 28 brought a dramatic change: "Kikkerton in sight—the great
news of the day! It is just appearing through the fog and we are sailing on
under a favorable wind. It began to clear at five this morning and immediately all sails were hoisted to hurry us along. We are now at Miliaxdjuin
Island and hope to be in Kikkerton by noon. I do not know whether we shall
land, but I am glad to be this far. Onwards, onwards is the word now."]

September 2, Kikkerton   At last I find time to write to you, my Marie.
There has been so much work and fuss on shipboard and on shore that I had
not time to write. Now let me tell you what has happened. . . . We were
near Kikkerton and suddenly there was a shout "Ship ahead!" We could not
make out what boat it was, but soon noticed six Eskimo rowing the boat. Mr.
Alexander Hull [Hall], one of the Scots staying here, was in the back of the
boat steering towards us. Soon the boat was beside us and we exchanged
greetings. The captain and helmsman recognized him as an old acquaint-
ance, I as my new countryman. . . . The wind was diminishing rapidly and
the Scottish boat pulled our old Germania into the harbor. We pushed slowly
through the ice and saw the American station. They soon saw us and raised
their flag. We heard the dogs howling and saw some of the natives' tents and
soon the Scottish station waved their flag. . . . As we approached a boat
with Eskimo women came from the shore and helped pull our boat into the
harbor and we set out our own boat. At last ten minutes to three on August
28 we dropped anchor and had arrived happily and safely in the harbor of
Kikkerton. [The Scottish station consisted of living quarters and three storage buildings, the former the much-modified original house brought by William Penny in 1857. It possessed a large room for living and sleeping and
several smaller storage and service rooms. Closer to the shore was the American station owned by Williams & Co. of New London, Connecticut. Scattered nearby were Eskimo tents. Kikkerton was now the largest Inuit settlement on the Sound, though at this time most of the natives were hunting in
the interior and only a few, mostly women and those in the stations' employ,
were at Kikkerton.]

September 3, Kikkerton   . . . As everything is full of ice and there is no
chance that the Germania can get [to the German station] now, I offered to
go there with a boat full of Eskimo. . . . You can imagine that since everything is so unfortunate this year, there is much to consider and talk over. It
is really too bad. Nothing is as it should be here: the steamer is lying around
somewhere outside and cannot get in. The Scots see their provisions dwindle,
tobacco and matches are gone. We sit here and can get no farther. Captain

Kikkerton Harbor looking north. Lying at anchor, left to right, are the *Germania,* the *Catherine,* and the *Lizzie P. Simmons.* The main building of the Scottish station is on the left. Photograph by Boas, between September 10 and 16, 1883. Courtesy American Philosophical Society.

Roach is trapped near Kingawa and cannot get here, although he is expecting a ship. Our station is at Kingawa and they do not know whether they can get home or not.

September 4, Kikkerton If it is in any way possible, I shall go to Kingawa tomorrow. I shall borrow an Eskimo suit, as mine is not ready. This morning I visited an Eskimo hut for about two hours to collect vocabulary and I already have quite a number of words about implements, furnishing of the tepiks, parts of the human body, etc. This afternoon I want to collect plants. Now let me tell you what happened during the past days. After I showed Mr. Mutch, the director of the Scottish station, the letter from Mr. Noble, its owner, he was very kind and promised to be helpful in every way. My belongings were to be brought on land the next day. In the evening we visited all the tepiks (Eskimo tents) here, and they did not seem as bad as I had imagined. I cannot describe them now or I would be able to tell you nothing else. [The first day's encounter with the Inuit seems to have impressed Boas greatly, for it became the subject of three of his *Tageblatt* articles. In one he expressed a strong initial repulsion to their ugliness and to the horrifying stench that came from the hide tepiks. "Had someone then told me that in a short time I would be living without resistance in the same conditions, I would have denied such imputation with indignation. It was not long, however, before the force of circumstances had brought me to share the native caribou-hide dwelling and cook in the same kettle—though I usually took the precaution of having my own kettle" (Boas 1884b).] . . .

September 9, Kingawa   My first boat trip is behind me. I went to our station in Kingawa to bring them news of the Germania. . . . In the fjord lay Captain Roach's schooner, the Lizzie B. Simmons. I looked him up and went to Kingawa with him where we arranged that the station should return to Kikkerton with him. . . .

September 12, Kikkerton [The arrival of the Scottish station's steamer, the *Catherine,* under Captain Abernathy, brought mail from home, to which Boas responded]   At last, I hear from you again. I hear again that you love me, and I may kiss your golden curl. You cannot imagine how joyous, how happy I am. . . . A few days ago, on Friday, just as the ship that brought your letter arrived here, I was on my journey. It was evening and we landed at the foot of a steep cliff in a deep fjord. I had provided for my six Eskimo. I sat alone, the only person awake on the rocks, watching the ice. I had time and peace to think about my sweet love. The deep water was at my feet. Opposite me arose the steep and threatening black cliffs, the rapids we had crossed that afternoon rushed and roared at my side, and in the far distance shone the snow-covered mountains. But I saw only you, my Marie. You and the noble beauty of my surroundings made me conscious of the immensity of our separation. . . . [On the same day, he wrote reassuringly to his parents (BFP: FB/parents 9/12/83): "At home I imagined everything to be much more difficult than it is. Almost all the Eskimo understand English and I can deal with them very well. They are willing to work and good-natured, desiring only to be well-treated. On this first trip I heard no grumbling, although I had to drive them very hard. I did my own share, however, and ate no more than they received so that I could always say, I have it no better than you!"]

September 19, Kikkerton   . . . Tuesday I moved from the Germania and on Wednesday, the twelfth, I had finished all my letters excepting to you and to those at home. Thursday, the thirteenth, the Lizzie P. Simmons arrived from the station and I had enough to do to transfer all my things. I hear continually—Herr Dr. here, Herr Dr. there! Added to this everyone wished to show me a kindness and I had no peace until the Germania sailed away on Sunday morning, the 16th. Now I am alone here in Cumberland Sound, but I have found such a kind and friendly welcome here that I feel quite at home. I get along well in English and most of the Eskimo understand and talk English. I have engaged a man for the whole winter, whom I feed. He is to accompany me wherever I go, hunt for me, etc. He seems to be entirely reliable, as far as I know and according to his recommendations. I feel quite assured of succeeding here, so you must all feel likewise. . . .

[Because of the activity of loading and unloading the Scottish brig, almost all the Eskimo at the station were fully engaged. The release of Signa (or Jimmy), who was normally in Captain Roach's employ, was very important to Boas, the more so since "he knew the coast of Cumberland Sound in almost all its extensions and, what was the main thing to me, had spent much time at Lake Kennedy" (Boas 1885a:4). Still, until he could engage a full boat crew, he had to confine himself to the vicinity of the Kikkerton islands. His first excursion was a trip to Kingnait Fjord with Signa and Wilhelm, much of it strenuous walking along the irregular coast. Signa proved "a good soul; he does what I tell him without objecting and does not drink. . . ." Only after this short trip was the contract with Signa formally closed, as the field journal records on September 24: "Signa comes in the evening and we come to an agreement. He receives the Mauser. I think I may do this, since there is nothing else. Otherwise he receives bread, molasses and tobacco according to his wishes."] . . .

September 24, Kikkerton [Before the *Catherine* departed, Boas was able to write once more directly to Marie.] . . . As soon as the brig is gone, the house is to be repapered and I am to get my table and bed. Up to now I have to help myself as best I can and must sleep on the floor and have no place of my own. Then I shall make a frame of sealskin for your picture, or have it made by a skillful Eskimo woman. I have found glass for it and it shall hang above my table, you in the middle, my parents to the right and left. . . . There are two tiers of bunks, so that the three of us have four beds. There is a mirror between the two and my table will be placed under it. In the pantry are kept the provisions for daily use. My plans for the near future are to travel about in the vicinity of Kikkerton, as I have done up to now, then when it begins to freeze to stay here until about Christmas and to do ethnographical work. In January the Eskimo again start to travel. I shall go with them and probably to Lake Kennedy. Perhaps I can carry on from there, perhaps I shall be forced to come back here. I cannot say anything further with certainty. . . . I got everything from Kingawa that I needed. Mr. Mutch, who will remain alone at the station here, is a nice helpful person. Originally he was a servant in the home of Mr. Noble. . . . He never went to school, but has acquired quite a bit of knowledge by himself, much more than a man who comes out of a German public school. . . . He immediately promised to help me in every way and in the winter will take me with his sled and dogs to the sea, where an Eskimo he knows lives who will take me further. . . . I have bought furs now and all I need now is a sleeping bag. So you see I am *very* well taken care of in every way. I really enjoy the taste of seal meat and gulls, so I need have no fear of sickness. . . .

[On September 25 Boas left with Captain Abernathy on the *Catherine* to visit an oil cache on Warham Island. It was intended as a short trip, but the weather turned bad and the brig was forced to take shelter at Naujateling or Blacklead Island on the south coast. Only on October 4 was Boas able to return to Kikkerton, where he then took several short trips in Signa's whale-boat. With Wilhelm, Signa, Ututjak (or "Yankee," a nephew of Signa), and Nachajashi, he then travelled the length of Pangnirtung Fjord. It was during this trip that Boas first actually tasted raw seal liver: "It didn't taste bad once I overcame a certain resistance" (BFP: Field Journal 10/7/83). After returning to the fjord's entrance, the boat party turned northward.] . . .

October 11, north of Pangnirtung Fjord . . . Yesterday was an eventful day for us. When I stopped writing there was work to do and I attempted to mark down a survey of part of the coast on the back of my diary. We rowed northward along the coast and I intended if possible to go as far as American Harbor and finish the coastal survey from Kikkerton to Kingawa. At noon we stopped to rest on a plant-covered terrace and while dinner was being cooked, I climbed up and found three old well-preserved graves. I wanted very much to take the moss and lichen-covered skulls, but I did not dare on account of the Eskimo, whom I would have greatly offended. So I had to row on without saying anything about my discovery and at about 5:30 in the evening we reached our night quarters safely. It was a small, rocky spit of land which extends beyond the long stretched out islands. I had slept on one of these before at Augpalugtualung, on my way to Kingawa. We were busy arranging our things when we suddenly saw a sail coming in our direction. Soon my people recognized the Eskimo. One of them, Yankee, recognized his brother and ran down quickly to help them unload. You can have no idea of the load in such an Eskimo boat. They are thirty-feet-long whaling boats filled with men, women and children. In front and in back it was heaped with skins obtained during the summer's hunting, in the middle lie the dogs, who from time to time introduce bellowing music, and floating behind, the small kayak, the leather boat of the Eskimo. They quickly put up the tepiks (tents). There were two families. They then began to cook. Soon a second boat arrived that had travelled with them and now we had become a whole village on this small spit of land, which before this had been uninhabited—four Eskimo families and me with two tents! First I visited the natives and brought them tobacco, which they accepted with great pleasure because theirs had been used up during the summer's hunting. At the same time I bought twelve reindeer skins for our winter clothing. I am now really rid of a worry, because one of them brought a stone from Lake Kennedy which I also bought.

These people had spent the whole summer at the longed-for Lake Kennedy, where they hunted caribou. Had I not been detained on the old Germania so long I could have been there a long time ago! Well, I should be satisfied because during the fall I have surveyed the largest part of the coast of this sound. Later on the Eskimo came to visit me, they made themselves comfortable in my tent, which had never before seen so many guests. I [entertained?] with half a plug of tobacco and a glass of rum. I had guests until ten o'clock, men and women. . . .

[Fearing that unless he accompanied the Inuit back to Kikkerton, the hunters might sell the promised skins to the station, Boas discontinued his northern trip. After securing his hides, he again left the station with Signa for Salmon Fjord to the south. The weather was bad, and most of the time, when they were not sheltering from fog, snow and wind, was spent in surveying the shores; but Boas reported in his field journal on October 17 that Signa had "showed me Eskimo games and I observed attentively in order to record and learn everything." Only days after his return to Kikkerton on October 22, ice began to form on the Sound, and Boas was confined to Kikkerton until early December when it became strong enough to bear a sled. He set up a tent on the ice in which he could measure the tides, charted the island and its surroundings, and, "greatly helped by Mr. Mutch," pursued his study of the Inuit, focussing on their geographical knowledge. "Every night I spent with the natives who told me about the configuration of the land, about their travels, etc. They related the old stories handed over to them by their ancestors, sang the old songs after the old monotonous tunes, and I saw them playing the old games, with which they shorten the long, dark winter nights" (Boas 1884a:253).] . . .

November 5, Kikkerton   . . . The amiable Eskimo come and go continually. Almost the whole of Kikkerton is drawing maps for me so that I can find the clues to new problems. I have obtained a great deal already but you have no idea how difficult it is to drag it out of people. I really intended to put up my tent down below today but the weather is so bad that I gave it up until it improves. It is warm [−4° C] but it is stormy and snowing. If you only knew how comfortable I am in my house! I wonder whether you have read my letters by this time. Poor Marie, you must study all my chicken scratches. My poor handwriting makes me a true criminal and nothing can be done about it. . . .

November 18, Kikkerton   . . . [Tidal] observations and the talks with the Eskimo take a lot of time. I am . . . busy with questioning the natives who are giving me information on all parts of their homeland. . . . This morning I sat in a tiny, tiny snowhut at the deathbed of a poor little Eskimo boy. The Eskimo are so confident that the Doctorā'dluk, as they call me, can help them when they are sick, that I always go to them when they call me.

And I always feel so unhappy when I am with those poor people and cannot help them. There sat the mother and I in that small cold hut, the boy lay between us, wrapped in covers. The mother, with frightened looks, often asked me whether "the pikanini were pinker," and I only saw the small limbs grow colder and colder and how he gasped harder and harder for breath. And then it was all over. You do not know how often my heart is heavy because I am unable to help. This is already the second deathbed at which I have stood! I have another patient, a woman with pneumonia. Fortunately she is getting better, although for three or four days I expected her to die. The poor man and his wife were both sick at the same time, and even though the other Eskimo provided them with meat, it would have gone badly with them had I not brought them food and something to drink. I tell myself that it is not my fault that the child died but I feel it as a reproach that I could not help. And maybe that is why I am turning to my Marie today to find solace in her love! . . .

November 25, Kikkerton I am afraid that you will scold me when I come back because I write so seldom, my Marie. But I really cannot help it. During all these days I was so tired when I came back home that I did not want to move and evenings my good friends came to tell me something or sing to me. Whether I wished to or not I had to write down what they told me. . . . Marie, truly it is a rough life here among the Eskimo. I often painfully miss the voice of a friend, but you help me bear all this and I shall return to you as I left. . . . Daily now I see the little flag you made for me fluttering in the wind. Wilhelm or Signa carries it and some others to the places where I make my observations and I always think of you when I see it!

December 2, Kikkerton   . . . I was interrupted because a woman arrived who is making fur stockings for me and wants to be paid. Then another one came carrying her youngest child in her hood and leading the other one. This one, a little boy named Kŏ'kĕtsitū, is my good friend. As soon as he sees me he calls out Doctorā'dluk, Doctorā'dluk, hop, hop!, Doctorā'dluk, i.e. the big doctor, that is my name here, and I occasionally let him ride on my knee. He talks and tells me a great deal, but unfortunately I do not understand one word, or only very little, as the language is very difficult to learn. I am good friends with most of the children as I play with them often. Usually we sing together and play, whereby I always have the secret intention of learning their games. I wish you could see me among the Eskimo. It is not nearly as bad as you imagine. I am as comfortably warm in my fur clothes as I could wish to be. I took a two-hour walk today only for pleasure and in spite of the wind and [−23° C] cold I was as warm as in the house. I will be happy when I can show you photographs of all the places where I have been! I go about Kikkerton in order to take them and in the evenings I have important conversations with the Eskimo about customs, songs, religion, etc.

Mr. Mutch is very helpful as interpreter and gives me a great deal of information about all possible things. Now they are all busy making caribou clothing and I hope they will be finished this week. Then I can again think of travelling and hope first to go northward. In the next month I intend to set up a depot of provisions, etc. for Davis Strait and then to go to Lake Kennedy. . . .

December 4, Kikkerton   . . . It is strange how one's feeling for cold changes. At home yesterday I would have frozen miserably and here it seemed like a beautiful day in spring. A trip with a dog sled is very amusing. Imagine a small, low hand sled, such as one uses at home for trucking, only lighter. In front are twelve dogs all pulling at a rope to which their reins are attached. Signa, Wilhelm, and I each wrapped in our furs sit on the low sled. Signa drives the dogs with his twenty-foot-long whip. He must forever yell and call to them in order to keep them going and then they run and jump pell-mell, occasionally bite one another, and in half an hour or less, the reins are in such confusion that we must halt. Hopefully! I can leave here in a week, to start on my journey north. . . . Jimmy Mutch, my host, . . . is obliging in every way and helps me with his best knowledge of the Eskimo language whenever he can so that I am very much obligated to him for adding to my knowledge in this respect. He even lends me his dogs for trips. In short, I have to be thankful to him in every way. He is a very pious man, who allows no work to be done in the house on Sundays. I do not allow this to keep me from my own work, whatever it may be, excepting to desist from any noisy work, such as carpentry or repair work, etc. At home I believed I would have much free time in the winter, but I was mistaken, for I hardly have a minute to myself.

[It had become clear quite early from his conversations with the Eskimo that some of Boas' basic information about their travel and geographic knowledge was wrong. He had thought from reports in Europe that the Cumberland Sound Inuit often travelled to and along the western coast of Baffin Island. He found, however, that "there was not one man who knew anything about the country"; only a single native, and he born at Pond Inlet, had even heard of the Igluling of Fury and Hecla Strait (Boas 1884:256–57). Boas determined, nevertheless, to head west as soon as travel was possible: first to Lake Kennedy (Lake Nettilling) and then to Foxe Channel and the western coast. The arrival of two Eskimo from the northern part of the Gulf heralded the beginning of sled travel.] . . .

December 9, Kikkerton   Today we had visitors for the first time, Padloaping and Shorty, two Eskimo from Tikeraxdjuax. They arrived yesterday toward 10 p.m. in sleds with their wives and one child each. Unfortunately, there are again two children very sick with a diphtheria-like sickness, [and] both died. One belongs to Ssegdloaping, the other to Bob. This will cause an unpleasant disruption to the making of my caribou suit as the women will not work for three days. At the end of this time, which is not set definitely, they have to ask the mourning women whether there is any objection to them working. Padloaping and Shorty came in the morning to allow me to question them about Nettilling. I got quite valuable information from them. Padloaping saw near Tudron tracks of Adlen [a fabulous people with some animal features; cf. Boas 1888:637]. They were broken off at the tips. He thinks he walked on bearskin.

December 10, Kikkerton Padloaping and Shorty finished the maps of Nettilling. They wanted to go back this evening, not having accomplished what they wanted, namely to borrow dogs with which to get their fur skins down from Kangia (end of Tininixdjuax). The dogs in Kikkerton are not very numerous because the disease was very bad last fall. There are very few cases now. I get everything ready for my departure. At about 11 [p.m.] all is ready. My bird slippers will be finished, although I was afraid that they would also not work on these, but it is only sealskin and caribou skin which they are forbidden to make into *new* clothing. They are, however, permitted to mend anything and make new things of birds or European goods. Not all know these rules exactly; when in doubt, they usually turn to Nukhikarlin or Eisik or Kanterodoaping.

[In the fall a disease, apparently brought from Greenland by the first whalers to have wintered in the Sound and now endemic, struck every settlement, killing about half the dogs in the Sound by December. It was precisely from Padloaping's and Shorty's settlement on Nettilling Fjord that Boas had hoped to secure dogs to take him to the great inland lake. Under the circumstances, he could undertake only a survey of the northern part of the Sound, borrowing a few of Mutch's dogs for his light sled. On December 11, Boas, Wilhelm, and Signa left for Anarnitung.]

December 12, near Niuxtung Dear Marie! I am now two days distant from Kikkerton, at the same place where I was a long time ago in a boat and where I met the Eskimo who were returning from Nettilling. What great differences exist between now and then. . . . Although it is [−35° C] cold, I did not feel cold while I walked. My caribou clothing was almost too warm. I almost went off alone with Signa, because Wilhelm's clothing was not ready, but Mr. Mutch took pity on me and lent me his things. I hope they will send us the missing things next week. . . . Do you know that for a while I believed I had no heart, because I did not take things so much to heart as others did. But I know better now. You, my Marie, have taught me that I am still able to feel. How happy we will be! But I am wandering from my excursion to Augpalugtung. (You wrote me once I should not use logic in my letters— don't you do that in this case.) I believe that one can be really happy only as a member of humanity as a whole, if one works with all one's energy together with the masses towards his goals. I think if one always felt that way it would be much easier to bear hardships and one would be more thankful for every joy. But now good night! I only want to say once again that I always, always, love you immeasurably, that I only long for the moment that shall take me back to you and with longing I picture the time when nothing shall separate us. And now sleep well, dearest. Dream of your Franz.

December 13, near Niuxtung . . . Wilhelm and I will leave early and go farther north to make recordings of the coast. We shall soon come to the water holes which are kept open by the [tidal currents of the fjords] and will prevent us from proceeding further. . . . Fog hinders us considerably, but we get four miles further to the north. As we return Signa is busy chopping food for the dogs, i.e. first to saw frozen seal meat and then chop it up with an ax. . . . Itu is going back to Kikkerton so I shall give him a letter to take to Mutch. I want to ask him to send a lamp etc. . . . You see, my Marie, I am writing my journal and to you on the same pages. It is the only way I have of letting you too get a picture of my daily life. The iglu is so cold that I cannot write more than is absolutely necessary for you to learn what I actually do. So accept these notes as words really directed to you. Now that we have been in the iglu for four hours, it is warm enough to write. It has not yet reached the thawing point, but still I feel quite comfortable. Feelings of comfort and discomfort are really quite relative. At home we would be dreadfully sorry for anyone in circumstances such as ours. But we are merry and of good cheer. Soon it will be Christmas. I hope by that time to be in Anarnitung, a settlement here, and from there go by sled to Kikkerton. And now goodnight, my dear, best-beloved. . . .

December 14, Sednirun In the morning Itu and Tom go back to Kikkerton with all the dogs, excepting two belonging to Jimmy. In leaving we encountered many difficulties in getting down from the icefoot [the narrow fringe of ice formed along the shore by ebbing tides and freezing spray.] The rope tears and I fall up to my knees into water. But I do not get wet at [$-38°$ C]. We first follow the tracks Itu's sled made yesterday and then from Kaivun to Sednirun. Signa builds the iglu in four and a half hours. It is at last finished. The pulling was very hard as we have a heavy load and the snow is very soft. The worst is that everything is wet from sweat and then frozen the next morning. . . .

December 15, near American Harbor It seemed surprisingly warm this morning. It had started snowing. This hinders my observations considerably, but I succeeded in reaching the entrance to American Harbor. Frequently we could scarcely see 100 steps ahead. . . . According to Signa the snow is soft here all year round. . . . Tomorrow we want to start for Operdnivikdjuax, but we shall have to leave some of our things here as they are too heavy to pull over the soft snow. The snow is hindering us a great deal. . . . So you see, that although the plan for such a trip seems very simple, its execution is beset with many difficulties. I feel quite comfortable today, however, since it is comparatively warm and we do not freeze in the iglu. I do not know whether we shall reach our goal tomorrow, but I hope so, because I am really in a hurry. . . . At the rate we are travelling we shall in all probability spend Christmas outdoors. . . .

December 16, north of Pangnirtung   My dear sweetheart. I am writing tonight at the end of a hard day. When we got up at six this morning it looked so dark and threatening that I first thought we would not be able to start out. About [nine inches] of snow had fallen during the night and [it] was very soft. As a result we could proceed only with very great effort and were completely exhausted when we arrived here at noon. We are not three miles from our last iglu and not yet in American Harbor. I had hoped to be there much sooner. . . . I have left a large part of my belongings in the last iglu. We were hardly able to carry what we now have with us, just sleeping bags and something to eat. This morning while we were still in the iglu, Wilhelm and I invented a lamp, that is almost our greatest necessity. To make it we used an old butter tin and cut three holes into the lid. We also made a pot out of an old tin can. Now we have glowing lamps and can quickly brew coffee and our iglu is also warmer. Signa was most discouraged because of the hard work today, and it really is too taxing. I shall stay here tomorrow and survey. . . . Do you know how I pass the time these long evenings? I have a copy of Kant with me, which I am studying, so that I shall not be so completely uneducated when I return. Life here really makes one dull and stupid (only at times however—when I get back to Kikkerton I will be sharp again). I have to blush when I remember that during our meal tonight I thought how good a pudding with plum sauce would taste. But you have no idea what an effect privations and hunger, real hunger, have on a person. Maybe Mr. Kant is a good antidote! The contrast is almost unbelievable when I remember that a year ago I was in society and observed all the rules of good taste, and tonight I sit in this snow hut with Wilhelm and an Eskimo eating a piece of raw, frozen seal meat which had first to be hacked up with an ax, and greedily gulping my coffee. Is that not as great a contradiction as one can think of? . . .

December 18, north of Pangnirtung   . . . The tramping here is very tiring. Yesterday Wilhelm and I went up to American Harbor. It was very difficult because of the soft snow and the piled up coastal ice. Signa had gone south to look for seals in the water holes, but did not see many and got none. He saw a duck which had gotten lost. I really wanted to go to our former iglu today to get a few things, but I turned around because my face might easily have frozen at [− 40° C] and a south wind and it was not absolutely necessary to have the things. Instead, Wilhelm and I climbed a hill behind the iglu and I made some measurements of the height of the sun (it was only forty-five degrees above the horizon) and took observations toward the south and Imigen. Signa stayed home to repair his gun, and in doing so broke it completely. So, if the sled does not come tomorrow, we shall have to go back to Kikkerton as we haven't enough fuel for making fires and since the snow is so soft we are not able to transport our things ourselves. If the sled does not · come we shall have to go to Anarnitung the day after tomorrow—about fifteen miles from here. So you see, everything is most unfavorable for me and I am very cross about it. However, I have not lost courage, what is bad today may be better tomorrow. . . .

December 19, north of Pangnirtung . . . We are still at the third iglu. This morning Signa went to Sednirun, our former iglu, to get tobacco, tea, and carne-pura [a condensed meat beverage]. He has *one* more cartridge for his Mauser, and he is going to try to get a seal with it. Wilhelm and I will go northward to American Harbor. We finally got that far. We left at 7:30 when the temperature was [− 48° C]. We found no trace of the sled and came back. Signa appeared soon after us. He had not been able to use his one cartridge; because of the extreme cold there is lots of fog at the water holes. Since the sled from Kikkerton is not there yet and our oil is used up, I have decided we must go to Anarnitung tomorrow morning. We get everything ready. The valuable things will be packed in the bearskin and pulled by hand [on the furry side, which slid easily on the snow]. We get up at about four o'clock and hope to get to Anarnitung before dark. Isn't that a nice trick of fate, first I have to leave half of my things behind, and then the rest, and now I must be happy that there is an Eskimo settlement near enough to this place that I can get there by evening. I hope I shall have no difficulty getting dogs there, so that I can be in Kikkerton for Christmas. Someday when I shall relate this adventure it will sound terrible and dangerous. Now we are laughing at our bad luck and the surprise of the people in Anarnitung when they see three men arrive from Kikkerton on foot and with two dogs. And we laugh too, imagining what Mr. Mutch will say when his sled arrives here and finds the nest empty! But tomorrow we must crawl into an Eskimo family bed and at last get dry things. I believe that later on when I shall be telling of our trip, incidents like these will be the main subject. We have a long trek ahead, fifteen miles without a path or sign post! At least I shall get as far as I wanted since Anarnitung was the goal of this trip. This evening we stuff ourselves with seal meat, then we shall have to walk as long as our legs will carry us. I wonder what you are doing now, my love. When you think of me you cannot possibly picture me in the situation in which I now find myself.

[The party was indeed in a very serious situation and the trip to Anarnitung proved far more difficult than contemplated. In the "one central dramatic incident around which the diary and his later popular accounts hinge" (Stocking 1968:148), Boas and his companions wandered for hours in fog and darkness, stumbling and crawling over soft snow that covered thick, jutting sheets of ice. When they finally found the coast, Signa, quite disoriented, had no idea where they were. Hungry and cold, they spent the night tramping about a relatively sheltered place until the moon rose. Then, having found sled tracks to and from Anarnitung, they followed them in the wrong direction, north rather than south. Only when they reached the ice holes at the entrance to Issortuxdjuax, the northernmost fjord of the Sound, did they realize where they were. They turned back and, after twenty-six hours of travel, at last reached Anarnitung.]

December 21, Anarnitung   We got up at three o'clock on the twentieth and were ready to leave at five. The most necessary things were packed into the bearskin and we started northward in a nice cold wind. We reached Sarbuxdjuax safely walking over good ice, but here we met with thick fog and were unable to see ahead any distance, so that it was impossible to find our way. The ice was rough and bad. The dogs refused to continue so Signa had to leave them and the bearskin. We continued as rapidly as we could, but were unable to find land before dark. Suddenly we heard a sled, but it led us in the wrong direction. We listened for the least sound. After the moon rose we found the tracks of a sled which we followed. They led us to Sarbuxdjuax. We turned immediately and at 6:30, having wandered twenty-six hours, we at last reached Anarnitung. Wilhelm's toes were frozen. I had frozen fingers and nose, Signa a frozen nose! We went into O[xaitung]'s iglu and went to sleep immediately. . . . [At four o'clock the same evening:] Oxaitung is giving food to the dogs and promises to take me to Kikkerton. Tomorrow I shall send my things to Sarbuxdjuax in his sled and set up my station there for two days. Then I shall either first explore Anarnitung and surroundings or go up the second fjord from Kingawa. At the end of the week I will probably be back in Kikkerton. In the afternoon I go out with Oxaitung who shows me the iglus of Anarnitung, as well as the boats, an old tepik in which a boy died this fall, and the old hut foundations, which all have names. They are the first of their kind I have seen here. Afterwards we go to the island Igdlungajung, near where there are five other tepiks. We visit Metik, the oldest man living at the gulf [cf. Abbes 1884:36; 1890:57]. I had hoped to get information from him about Foxe Channel, but got very little. Metik had been here in the morning and had received a piece of tobacco from me, for which he was very grateful. When he was young the Inuit went from here to Nettilling in the spring before the ice was gone. They took their boats by sled to the Koukdjuax [River]. From there the women went northward across the lake, while the men went down the Koukdjuax in their kayaks and then up two rivers along the salt water where they hunted caribou. He gave me a long list of names for that region, but he cannot draw, perhaps because he has very bad eyes. He looks strong and healthy, but his hair is gray and

according to what I am told must be about 80 years old. He knew Amarox
and Sigeriax and called the country to which they travelled Ignirn which is
a part of Augpalugtijung where many Eskimo live [cf. Boas 1888:432–33]. . . .
The last day was really taxing—to walk without stopping for twenty-six hours
with the thermometer at [− 45° C] so that I could not keep my fingers and
nose from freezing, with nothing to eat and nothing to drink and no assurance that we would ever find our goal. Well, the adventure ended well enough,
but it is strange that what I hoped was the shortest day of my life turned out
to be the longest. I was unable to catch up on my sleep today, but tomorrow
I expect to sleep wonderfully in my new iglu. I am now writing resting on
the sleeping quarters of the iglu on a caribou skin. I am quite comfortable.
Wilhelm is sleeping to my right and to the left the woman of the iglu sits and
dries my clothes. Kanaka (the man from Kikkerton), Signa, and my host
Oxaitung are sitting in the hall in front of me, eating frozen seal. I am thinking of you, my love. I must also eat my supper—frozen raw seal. Then we
shall have tea and bread. It is customary that the guest gives tea and bread
to the "K'odlunarn" (whites) and the host provides seal meat and tends to
everything else. Enough for today, my darling. I am thinking of you always.

December 22, Sarbuxdjuax (Kingawa)   As intended I rode here this
morning with Oxaitung, Signa, and Wilhelm. . . . It was very cold with a
strong north wind, so that one after another our faces became frozen. We all
of us suffer more or less from the frost. I found it impossible here in Nudnirn
(name of the island in Sarbuxdjuax) to walk against the wind, to make observations *and* to write so that I ἑκὼν ἀεκοντὶ δὲ θυμῷ ["willing, but with
unwilling heart" (*Iliad* IV:43)] gave up working. Wilhelm, both of whose big
toes had been frozen, insisted in Anarnitung that he would be able to come
along, but he felt so unwell that I could make no use of him. I immediately
sent him into the iglu which Signa and Oxaitung were building. I went out
alone, but had to turn back after an hour without having accomplished anything. I cannot change compass and pencil. When I returned at about two
o'clock the iglu was finished. We soon had our dinner. . . . What a difference
between this evening and the evening the day before yesterday. Now in the
comfortable iglu, then outdoors half frozen and half starved. Do you know
what we ate for supper? Butter that was so hard that we had to hack it with
our strongest knife—the way one splits wood—and lump sugar. Oxaitung,
who went yesterday to get our bearskin, said that at first we were very near
Anarnitung and then wandered back and forth and finally went towards Kingawa. The annoying thing is that we crossed the path made by sleds twice
without knowing it. I would like best to return to Kikkerton the day after
tomorrow with Oxaitung and our sled. I want to return here with renewed
strength. I only hope Wilhelm will not be sick, the last few days were really
nerve-racking. . . .

December 23, Anarnitung   Now I am again sitting in Oxaitung's iglu and taking part in great festivity. Oxaitung has caught two seals today and every man in the settlement is to receive a piece. Is it not a beautiful custom among these "savages" [*wilden*] that they bear all deprivations in common, and also are at their happiest best—eating and drinking—when some one has brought back booty from the hunt? I often ask myself what advantages our "good society" possesses over that of the "savages" and find, the more I see of their customs, that we have no right to look down upon them. Where amongst our people could you find such hospitality as here? Where are people so willing, without the least complaint, to perform *every* task asked of them? We have no right to blame them for their forms and superstitions which may seem ridiculous to us. We "highly educated people" are much worse, relatively speaking. The fear of traditions and old customs is deeply implanted in mankind, and in the same way as it regulates life here, it halts all progress for us. I believe it is a difficult struggle for every individual and every people to give up traditions and follow the path to truth. The Eskimo are sitting around me, their mouths filled with raw seal liver (the spot of blood on the back of the paper shows you how I joined in). I believe, if this trip has for me (as a thinking person) a valuable influence, it lies in the strengthening of the viewpoint of the relativity of all *cultivation* [*bildung*] and that the evil as well as the value of a person lies in the cultivation of the heart [*herzensbildung*], which I find or do not find here just as much as amongst us, and that all service, therefore, which a man can perform for humanity must serve to promote *truth*. Indeed, if he who promotes truth searches for it and spreads it, it may be said that he has not lived in vain! But now I really must get back to the cold Eskimo land. . . . This morning I went to Kingawa by sled with Oxaitung and Signa, so that I got as far as I had been by boat in the fall. I had hoped to finish my map as far as Nudnirn. For that purpose I had made a very thick handle for my pencil, hoping that I could hold it in spite of the cold, but unfortunately the point had broken and I was unable to resharpen it. I had to return to the iglu without having accomplished my task. . . . Wilhelm's left foot is so badly frozen that I am afraid I shall not be able to take him to Kikkerton. We put him into his sleeping bag which we tied on Nuvukdjua's sled and drove home. Tomorrow morning Oxaitung and I will drive directly to Kikkerton. Signa and Kanaka have to go by way of Pamiujang and Sednirun. I have arranged with Oxaitung to return with him, live with him and be driven about by him in that neighborhood. As payment I shall give him cartridges for his gun, which he received from the German station. I hope that from here I shall be able to reach Kingawa and the two next fjords. . . . The Eskimo are now sitting around me, telling one another old tales. Too bad I cannot understand them. When I return I shall also learn to understand. . . .

December 28, Anarnitung   Now I am back here again. During all these days I have not had the opportunity to write in my journal nor to my Marie. You can imagine that I was very tired when we reached Kikkerton after our twenty-two-hour ride. . . . Of course Mr. Mutch was aroused immediately by the noise and got up to cook something. Indeed, I could make good use of it. I had eaten nothing for twenty-two hours and had not lived well for fourteen days. So I enjoyed the cocoa and caribou roast thoroughly. I went to bed at about four and slept until ten. In the evening I unpacked, took our Christmas presents to the house, a small Christmas tree out of the box, collected several good cans for our dinner and invited Captain Roach's cooper, Rasmussan (he is a Dane), who is alone at the American station. At five o'clock we had a lighted Christmas tree and a pleasant Christmas celebration. We spent the evening drinking punch and wine as though we were at home. Unfortunately Betty, Signa's wife, came over in the evening. She was drunk and caused us a lot of trouble. . . . We started out again this morning and arrived here safely at 3:30. Wilhelm's toe does not seem to be as bad as I feared. The nail and a part of the ball are peeling off. I have bought several [old Eskimo objects].

December 30, Anarnitung   . . . Last night I dreamt very vividly that I was in America and with you. The dream was so vivid that I was most disappointed when I woke up in the morning to find myself in the iglu. You must not imagine that such a snow hut is a cold home. It is completely papered with skins and two lamps are kept burning. These supply light and heat. We all sit on a large platform which is covered with caribou skins. But I think I still prefer a European home! Only two days more, and the year begins which will take me to you. The time passes almost too quickly for the amount of work I have to do here. If I accomplish everything, I still will not have the time to finish the map and the ethnographic work. I shall, however, attain my own purposes very well. I know very accurately about the migration of the Eskimo and the routes they take, how they travel back and forth, and their relationship to neighboring tribes. Yesterday evening I had a long conversation with an old woman, who came here from far in the north, and who has knowledge of happenings as far north as North Greenland! I am gradually learning to make myself understood somewhat by the Eskimo and to understand them. The language is dreadfully difficult. . . .

January 3, 1884, Anarnitung   I must really catch up with my journal which I neglected very much these last days. On December 31 Oxaitung and I went to Kangertlukduax. . . . We got home at about four o'clock, tired and hungry. . . . After supper I gave Oxaitung a bottle of cognac and Wilhelm and I drank a bottle of Swedish punch and talked until twelve. As we ate supper at seven o'clock, we remembered that it was New Year at home and so I sent New Year's greetings to you at twelve o'clock. I know that you thought of me, probably with as great a longing as I thought of you. But the difference! You were among your people, the happy ones who see you daily, hourly, were among those whom you love. Believe me when I say that the thing almost the hardest to bear here is not to have any one with whom to speak a sensible word, no one who is in any way close to you. But in nine and a half months I shall be back! Oh! could I but give wings to time. How I would hurry to your side so that we might both be comforted. I greeted the New Year with three cheers according to the good old custom, and woke up the next morning to begin the New Year with old work. . . . On January 1 I surveyed the south coast. The weather was clear and cold and at about four o'clock we reached the head of the fjord, where an iglu was built. There were two very ancient graves nearby. There is scarcely a spot here where one does not find traces of ancient habitation. The Eskimo, without exception, ascribe these to the Tudnik ["Tornik" in Boas 1885a:89; cf. 1888:634–36], a fabled people who are believed to have lived here. . . . In the evening I promised to give Oxaitung more cartridges if he would recount some old stories well. Since then he is most anxious to tell stories. During the night our iglu, which turned out to be somewhat too large, was very cold, so that I was hardly able to sleep. . . . On the morning of the third I used an astrolabe to be certain about the time. During the day I went with Oxaitung to K'exertaxdjung. I do not know how many times I froze my fingers while taking three photographs! I found out that Iti who has been my poor patient for many weeks is finally dead. . . . In the evening Oxaitung told me a tale, "Unikartua," i.e. old tales of the origin of the white whales, etc. [cf. Boas EEN; 1888: 635–37].

January 21, Tininixdjuax   Here I have made a long pause. I have again kept my journal in my book and did not get a chance to write to you, my beloved. I am in an iglu again and writing in your book at last. . . . First let me tell you what happened. Early on January 4 I went to the before mentioned fjord with Oxaitung. In the meantime it had become windy and started to snow, so that I could do nothing and we returned to Anarnitung. There we had an unpleasant surprise. Oxaitung's wife, who had had a slight sore throat, was very sick, so there was nothing for me to do but to return to Kikkerton on a sled that was going there next day. I took advantage of the warm weather [−17° C] and took Wilhelm back with me. . . . We had arranged that Oxaitung should call for me after his wife improved. The first thing that happened was that I became sick in Kikkerton, presumably good food no longer agrees with me. Friday [January 11] I was well again and began writing up my observations. It was high time that I did so. I have not yet finished, but still I am a little clearer about them. Last Friday, January 18, I wanted to go to Tininixdjuax with Jimmy Mutch. It is important for me to go there because of my contemplated trip to Foxe Channel. On Thursday somebody came from Anarnitung with the news that Oxaitung's wife was apparently worse, not better. He also reported that many Eskimo blamed me for it, as it really seems as though sickness and death follows my footsteps. If I were superstitious, I really would believe that my presence brought misfortune to the Eskimo! Many are supposed to have said they did not wish to see me in their iglu again, nor Mutch. He became frightened because of this so I set out alone today, Monday, the twenty-first. Just as I expected, I was received here just as kindly as before and am now at home in Tininixdjuax.

[In the autumn diphtheria had broken out in Kikkerton. Boas had recorded in his field journal on October 23 that a woman, very ill with fever and inflamed lungs, had asked for him. He provided salve for her chest, medicine to combat the fever, and opium against her cough, but he could do no more. Her death on October 25 was the beginning of an epidemic. "It is terrible how diphtheria and pneumonia are now prevailing among the poor Eskimo," he wrote only days later. "In almost every tent one or another is sick. Since the death of the woman, two children have died and another is sick. . . . They came to the Doctorā'dluk, as I am now known, with such faith, and I can do nothing" (BFP: FB/parents 10/31/83). The disease spread throughout the Sound—the first reported outbreak of diphtheria in the area. Since the *Germania* and the *Catherine* were the only ships to visit the Sound that season, they must have brought the disease, though no cases were detected aboard either. "Deeply shaken by the devastation which the epidemic caused among the children as well as by the quick and deadly course of individual cases," the Inuit resorted to incantation to discover the cause of the illness. "Thus the angakit, the shaman of the Eskimos, came to the unhappy notion that the disease was connected with my presence" and "an extraordinary unpleasant ill-will formed among the Eskimo against me." At Imigen on the west side of the Sound, "it was declared that no one was to have anything to do with me; above all, no one was to allow me into the huts or lend me their dogs." He received the report, as noted, at Kikkerton while preparing for a trip with Mutch, who now preferred, in light of the reigning distrust, to stay at the station. Boas, however, "thought that this kind of hostility should not be allowed to prevail" and set off with Signa for Imigen, overnighting at Tininixdjuax (Boas 1885b:12).]

January 22, Tininixdjuax . . . Yesterday morning we left Kikkerton with Mutch's dogs. Wilhelm has still to remain in the house, as his foot is no better. The right one is well again, but there is a big hole in the left foot. It really is fortunate that this did not happen to me. What would I have done if I had had to lose all this precious time? We had good weather and Signa and I arrived here at about four o'clock. About two hours distant from the settlement we met natives who had gone out to catch seals. They showed us the way and we quickly reached our destination. You have no idea how anxiously one looks for the appearance of the icefoot on the horizon, and then when one is near to land with what joy one greets the sign of an iglu. It is impossible to tell how comfortable and beautiful it seems when one enters into these dirty, narrow spaces, at the appearance of which I at first turned away in horror. . . . This morning I arranged matters with Piera. Next month he will supply nine dogs and circle Nettilling with us. I must see that I get fifteen dogs for this time, then everything will be arranged. I hope to start on about February 3. Tomorrow I shall go to Anarnitung where I expect to get dogs. I shall work there for a while then come back here to buy seals. Then I have to go to Imigen to borrow dogs and seals, and then back to Kikkerton to make preparations for the journey. How far I shall get depends entirely on the weather. Now my Marie, I have at last reached the point where I shall be able to complete what I came here for. I know now that it is only a small, small part of my original plan, but I shall have to be satisfied with it. I have carried out my own plans well and may be satisfied with the results. The cartographic work too has contributed enough new material. . . . I at least have the satisfaction that I have worked to the best of my ability. Only one month more and half my time shall have passed—the longest half, because from now until my return I shall be busy all the time. In February I shall travel to the north-west, March and April to the south-west. In May I shall leave the south and go north. For a time now I shall have my own dog-team, which I have borrowed here. They will take me to Anarnitung tomorrow morning. . . . Will fortune be good to me that I can hope to see our fondest wishes realized speedily? I do *not* want a German professorship because I know I would be restricted to my science and to teaching, for which I have little inclination. I should much prefer to live in America in order to be able to further those ideas for which I live. But how to do this, I do not know. Well, I cannot do anything about it now and I shall have to wait patiently and see how matters develop when I return. . . . What I want to live and die for, is equal rights for all, equal possibilities to learn and work for poor and rich alike! Don't you believe that to have done even the smallest bit for this, is more than all science taken together? I do not think I would be allowed to do this in Germany. Remember you once wrote me about your father, that all his actions, all his work was for his fellowman. It is the best that can happen to a man, to be able to be fully effective in that way. Whether successful or not, is it not the kind of work that gives the greatest satisfaction? And you, dear girl, will always help me. If my strength should weaken, you will give me renewed strength—just as you give me new strength here. . . . But I must return from my dream to harsh reality! The activities of the Eskimo, the howling of the dogs, the screaming of the children, all in this small iglu, call me back. I often wonder while sitting in this company at night, in what sort of company you are. At least you have the advantage of being able to speak with them. I have, however, sometimes found that what one hears in "society" is worth [no more for me than] the conversation of these people here.

January 23, Imigen I started out with thirteen dogs this morning, but they are all such pathetic animals that they can make scarcely any headway. For that reason I have stopped here in Imigen, as I shall have to stop here sometime anyway. I want to order seals here and see whether I can get better dogs. The men have not yet returned from seal-hunting. I wonder how they have reacted to the ultimatum I had transmitted to Tyson, the Eskimo who would not allow me to enter his house. He is taking the same trip that I am taking this summer and I let him know that he would get nothing from me, even if I saw him starving before my eyes, if he did not first come to me and ask me into his iglu. I hope none of my dogs will run away tonight so that I may proceed unhindered. To my great sorrow, I hear here that Oxaitung's wife died last night. Two Eskimo from Anarnitung, Padlukulu and Hannibal Jack, brought the news. It is really terrible what destruction throat sicknesses have caused among the Eskimo this year. I shall probably go up there tomorrow but I do not yet know where I shall stay. I want to give provisions to Oxaitung immediately, because he may not leave the house for three days. I wish I could persuade Oxaitung to take me up to Nettilling. A few days ago a child died in Kikkerton, whose mother had died here in the fall. The day before she died she sent word to the station asking them to make a box as coffin, because she wished to be placed next to her mother. The child also asked for tobacco to take to her mother [cf. Boas 1888:613]. Isn't that touching? I have noticed quite frequently that the Eskimo face death calmly, although, while they are well, they fear the dead as well as death. I have also seen very great and true love between parents and children. . . . I cannot forget Joe, who is also dead, and who told me how miserable he was because of the death of his son last spring. And these are "savages" who are supposed to be of no worth compared to Europeans! I do not believe that among us people could be found who under similar circumstances would be so willing to work or be as happy and satisfied! I must say I am quite well satisfied with the character of the savage Eskimo. . . . [In Imigen Boas acted quickly to deal with the ill-feeling against him. Immediately upon his arrival, he assembled the men and told Tyson [Napekin], "the chief instigator," that "all intercourse between us would cease until he invited me into his hut." Since the man had only a poor gun and little ammunition and, moreover, intended to travel in the summer to Davis Strait where "he would be completely dependent upon me as no whites lived on that coast," the threat carried weight. Boas thought that his resolute action had been both appropriate and effective. A man immediately invited him into his iglu for the night and the Eskimo gave no signs of mistrust. A few weeks later Tyson came to Kikkerton "especially to reconcile me" with gifts of seal pelts and an offer of service. "With this the incident closed and from then on nothing disturbed the friendly relations between the natives and me" (Boas 1885b:12), although the February 19 entry indicates continuing Inuit reticence.]

January 25, Anarnitung When I arrived here last night I was really too tired to write. It took us from seven in the morning until seven in the evening to cover the few miles from Imigen to here (twenty-four miles at the utmost). . . . Toward the end it was so dark that I walked ahead in order not to lose the trail. It led us all the way around Anarnitung and we finally got stuck in the only entrance to the interior, Itidliaxdjung. We left the dogs and sled behind and climbed over the icefoot and went to Charlie's iglu. Charlie, the father of Oxaitung's wife, his son and Oxaitung were mourning in Oxaitung's iglu. I sent bread and coffee and someone to inquire what they needed. Because of this our bread ration has grown very short. . . . [Oxaitung] seems about the same as before, although he is definitely sad about the death of his wife. He offered, if I wished, to take me to K'aggilortung. . . . At last I have found a second person who at least knows the names as far as Igluling [on the Foxe Basin]: Metik, the oldest man on the sound, who has his knowledge from a woman who went over there long, long ago. Gradually I have gotten information from old people, so that I am better informed as to what the oldest people thought. . . . My census of the country is coming along well. As far as I know, I need only two more settlements, Nuvujen and Naujateling, and then I shall be finished [Much of the census material, sometimes iglu by iglu, is in Boas EEN; portions were published in Boas 1888:426]. . . .

[Further surveys from Anarnitung went badly because of rough ice, soft snow, and fog, and on January 29 Boas left for Kikkerton with Oxaitung and Signa. At this time two Kikkerton families decided to cross the Cumberland Peninsula to visit friends in the Padli area of Davis Strait, a region strangely free of the dog disease. Boas, still lacking dogs, joined them, but the snow was so thin, the ice so rough and rocky, that it soon seemed useless to proceed. Although two continued, with instructions from Boas that he wanted as many as eighteen dogs, his western trip to Lake Nettilling and beyond was now almost hopeless: if the Padli dogs came at all, they could not arrive before the end of March, too late for a proper trip to the west coast. But he persisted in the hope that he could yet get as far as Igluling and even Admiralty Inlet. "It was a mistake," he later realized, "not to have immediately foresworn the trip and turned myself to research on the west coast of Cumberland Sound for the rest of the winter. It was so very hard, however, for me completely to abandon a plan which I had long nurtured and cherished and worked for; so, as long as a spark of hope remained, I staked everything on reaching the longed-for Foxe Basin" (Boas 1885b:14). Still hoping that he might get a team from Padli, Boas went to Anarnitung to collect seal meat for them. The hunting was unsuccessful, partly due to an unusual paucity of seals at the water holes and partly to the terrible weather.]

February 14, Anarnitung   Today I went hunting, but not with exactly splendid success. The only thing I shot was pulled under the ice by the current. There I sat, like an Eskimo, behind my ice hole at the water's edge and patiently waiting for a head to appear. You cannot imagine what an impression it makes in this cold season to sit so near the edge of the water and to hear the roaring and foaming. Thick fog from the cold water envelops me. At my feet the water foams and hisses. Only a strong current keeps the water from freezing here. My resting place shakes and trembles as the pieces of ice strike it. These are finally pulled under by the force of the current and I can feel them drifting about under my feet. Suddenly another large piece breaks off and I must retreat quickly in order not to be too close to the water. In a few minutes there is wild chaos where I stood. . . . I shall try my luck again tomorrow. I want to bring back one seal. . . .

February 15, Anarnitung   Today I again went hunting seals at Sarbuxdjuax, but with no better luck. The only seal I saw tore himself from my spear and disappeared under the ice. Today I hunted just as an Eskimo, with a spear and all that goes with it. I sat beside the water just as patiently as they do. . . . Oxaitung was the only one who caught anything, two seals, which I immediately acquired. Metik was here this evening and told an endlessly long story. . . . This morning my young friend Tokā'ving brought me seal for which he wanted tobacco which I gave him. . . . As you see Marie, I am now a true Eskimo. I live as they do, hunt with them and belong to the men of Anarnitung. I have hardly any European food left, eat only seal and drink coffee. I hope in this way soon to have acquired a sufficient number of seal so that I can soon start on my journey to Nettilling. Although seal hunting bores me dreadfully, I do it as it is the only way of obtaining what I need. I must get away this month. Perhaps I shall still get dogs from Padli. That would be a piece of good luck—to be finally rid of the dog problem.

February 16, Anarnitung   A strong N.W. gale has been blowing since last night. However, the sleds set out for Sarbuxdjuax this morning. Through a misunderstanding the sled on which I intended to travel had left. I tried in vain to catch up with it. I had to turn back and remain indoors the rest of the day. Actually I lost nothing because of this. The Eskimo brought back nothing, so I certainly would not have caught a thing. They said "*Sarbukdŭak komáiliadlu udlums*" which means "Sarbuxdjuax today difficult" and I imagine that the wind which became stronger during the day was very trying for the hunters. . . . I listened to stories and wrote down words. My glossary is really growing, but it is about time I started it. I wish I could draw well so as to draw you a picture of our iglu. You can see what the outside looks like from photographs, but not what the inside is like. Picture to yourself a room about

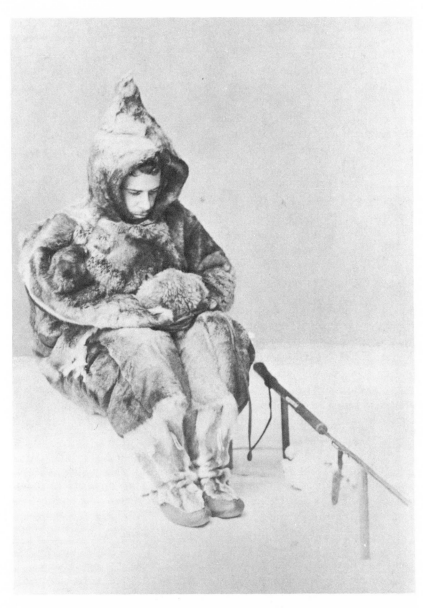

"Eskimo awaiting return of seal to blowhole," reads the caption of the *Central Eskimo* engraving (fig. 399) based on this studio photograph of Boas in his caribou suit. Photograph by J. Hulsenbeck, Minden, 1885 (?). Courtesy American Philosophical Society.

twelve feet in diameter. Vaulted ceiling lined with sealskin—in the back of the house there is a bank of snow about three feet high with a smooth surface for living—in the back also a big pile of all kinds of things, skins clothing etc. and all the dear Inuit!—two other equally high snow banks on which the lamps stand. The kettles hang over the lamps—above this for drying a network of skins, which is full of clothes, day and night . . . on one side the provisions, on the other the garbage—it is difficult to accustom oneself to this sight. In the space that remains, about six feet in length and four in width, there is a large block of snow which is used to close the door at night—usually by two or three people, but I have seen six or seven. . . . There are one or two small iglus which serve to keep the cold away and are also used for storage. And then you should see these long-haired fellows sitting here. Their hands are usually folded over their bellies, their heads usually bent sideways, they talk, laugh, and sing. Once in a while someone seizes a knife and cuts off a large piece of seal meat which he devours. If it is frozen it is chopped up and eaten by all, including myself, with the greatest enjoyment. Strangely enough, while eating and talking they almost always look at the wall and not at one another. There is one old man named Metik (duck) whom I especially enjoy. As soon as he sees me coming he calls out "*asshoyoutioli!*," which means "how are you," and follows, in the most beautiful pidgin English used by the Eskimo who know English words, with all kinds of stories. Thus I live day after day. No wonder I long for sensible conversation and for someone who really understands me! Unfortunately this time I did not bring a book to read, so I cannot help myself. I read all the advertisement and everything else on one page of the *Kölnische Zeitung*. In four days I shall have been away eight months. I have heard from none of you for four and a half months. . . .

February 17, Anarnitung   A bad day was followed by a worse one. There is a storm from the northwest and one cannot see ahead ten steps. And it is unpleasantly cold. So the Eskimo stayed home and are lazing about all day. Do you think it is possible for me to write under these circumstances? As soon as I start, I throw the book to the ground impatiently. Everything appears so unpleasant. Everything I start turns out badly and it will not take much to make me feel very depressed. If I only can get home this year and find you, my Marie. My heart yearns for you, my dearest possession.

February 18, Anarnitung   Another day lost. In spite of the fact that it is still blowing badly, we went to the water hole. The Eskimo have to go because they have been half-starved as a result of the poor hunting season. You should see how greedily they devour the last of my dry bread, which I have given them. But I cannot feed the forty-three people of this settlement during the days of hunger. [After having come to Anarnitung to secure seals for the anticipated dog-team, Boas "instead of being able to complete my

provisions, . . . had to furnish supplies to the starving people" (Boas 1885b:14).]
I give two sick children and Oxaitung's family everything they need. Oxaitung has taken another wife, but she does not live in his iglu. This morning
we went to the water hole. When we got there it was still high tide and we
had to wait until it went down. As it was not getting to be low tide, the
current was weak, and new ice was forming. So it took until one o'clock
before the ice was so that we could get to the water. And so we sat there and
all that we accomplished was that all of us combined saw one seal. Some
Eskimo who had been at another water hole brought home three small seals.
Since it gets worse every day I shall go to Nexemiarbing tomorrow to talk to
Piera again and then go back to Kikkerton.

February 19, Nexemiarbing Last night I finally collected a team of dogs.
I left this morning at about nine o'clock. I have to suffer a great deal because
of the sickness that is prevalent here. I know that many Eskimo are unwilling
to deal with me although they do not dare to show it openly. None of them
wanted to lend me dogs, but when I asked them they did not dare refuse. It
was a horrible day, storm from the north in the morning, a little better in the
afternoon. We arrived here before sunset. As the men returned from seal
hunting, I again had a most unpleasant surprise. The dog sickness has again
broken out and Piera, on whom I depended most, has only seven dogs! I
really do not know what is going to happen! . . .

[Returning again to Kikkerton on February 20, Boas found that Weike's
foot was better, collected some more stories and "learned something about
Turgnaing, the spirit of the Eskimos" (BFP: Field Journal 2/21/84). From
Kikkerton he made an overnight trip with Mutch to Warham Island to survey
the south coast. . . . A few days later he travelled to Naujateling to visit
Roach on his ship wintered there. He found the poor man's feet badly frozen
from a night spent on the ice, and returned to Kikkerton greatly depressed.
All his exploratory plans had been frustrated by the poor seal catch, by bad
weather, but most of all by the devastating dog disease. He had finally given
up even the smallest hope for a great western trip to the shores of Foxe
Basin.]. . .

March 7, Kikkerton I have not been able to write for days, my Marie.
I was not able to find a place on the boat to which I could retire and speak
to you. I must find comfort in you from the troubles and cares that worry me
day and night. It's easy to say that one should keep one's head up, but that's
really very hard with this wretched dog disease that endangers even my trip
back from Padli. Oh! Marie I could not bear not to return this summer. You
are waiting for me and I long for you day and night. I must see you and rest
in your arms from all these cares and fears. The sickness has reigned here
unceasingly for a month and Piera, with whom I was to travel west, has lost
seven of his ten dogs so that I have given up all hope. . . . It will be impos-

sible for me to leave here for Padli without help. You can imagine how un-
bearable it would be to sit around here all summer doing nothing and with
no prospect of leaving here in the fall. For days now I feel so depressed and
hopeless that I must come to you for courage. I simply cannot stay here,
Marie. You draw me with such a force. I must press you to my heart. Oh, I
hardly know myself what I am writing. Now you see what has become of my
much boasted of courage. . . . You see what a weakling your Franz is! I scold
myself a thousand times but cannot rid myself of the weight that rests on my
heart. . . . Will you think less of me, Marie, because of it? You must know I
am distressed by the thought that I might have to be without you for another
whole year. . . . You cannot imagine how difficult it is to live, without speaking to a sensible person for so long a time. The few moments I have allotted
to myself you may judge from my words to you. I am very often unable to add
a word to you in my dry daily reports. I might do it more often, but when I
have to listen to the conversation between Jimmy Mutch and his wife, such
insipid and often vulgar talk, the pencil drops from my hand. How can I
visualize your pure image in these surroundings? I am often revolted by everything I see and hear about me. Nevertheless Mutch is a comparatively decent
man. I must do him justice. In seventeen years of almost uninterrupted living
in this country, he has learned much. He is honest and open and does not
try to hide his weaknesses. But the people on the American ship! It revolts
me to have anything to do with them, but I am more than glad that I am not
condemned to spend the entire winter with them. Only the second helmsman, a German-American, is a good and acceptable person. I am really sorry
for him that he has to live and work a whole year in such company. . . . I
realize more surely from day to day that I am not meant to live in loneliness.
I need people very much, people who really have a right to the name. I feel
much better now that I have poured out my heart. It seems to me as though
the weight on my heart had become lighter. . . .

[From the depth of his despair, new hopes arose. Two men arrived from
Saumia, the area at the tip of Cumberland Peninsula, and reported an abun-
dance of dogs in their settlements, which, like Padli on Davis Strait, was
untouched by the devastating epidemic. A journey there promised also to be
of interest because the southern part of Cumberland Sound was completely
unknown. With the grand plan for exploration of Foxe Basin's Baffin shore
finally abandoned, he could turn to possibilities closer to hand. "Now the
most unhappy time of my stay in the Sound was past; from now on my luck
turned favorable again" (Boas 1885b:14–15). He left on March 12, climbing
the pass at the head of Anartuajuin Fjord and descending to K'airoliktung
Fjord on Davis Strait.]

March 19, Ukiadliving I have never yet written from so far away from
home as I now am. I am in Ukiadliving, on the coast of the Davis Strait,

where I went to buy dogs. It was a difficult trip, five nights in a cold iglu, until I at last arrived here. You cannot picture to yourself what cries and astonishment greeted me here. I am the first European to have visited this corner [cf. Boas 1885b:16]. Fortunately my business went off better than I had expected. I now own ten dogs and therewith the means to leave Cumberland Sound. I hope I can get a few more so that I shall have a good team.

March 20, Ukiadliving   I went out yesterday morning in order to explore a little of the coast to the north and at the same time to try out my dogs and perhaps return or exchange some of them. . . . I had expected to find this side of the Davis Strait rather accurate on the map, but I cannot discover from it where I am. I really think, Marie, I have never experienced a spring that has made such a springlike impression on me. . . . Everything still appears wintery, but. . . . you should see how wonderfully the sun shines on everything; how pleasing it is to feel the warm rays! We have, of course, seen the sun all winter long, but now we feel its warmth and it gives me the impression that any day now the ice will begin to melt. Nine months ago I left Hamburg and seven more and I shall be with you. . . . You once asked me how I would be when I returned. I know now that I will be the same as when I left. What I have seen and experienced here has not changed me, perhaps made me a little more sensitive to all the beauty and goodness that is to be found at *home,* and also I take greater pleasure in associating with others than formerly. . . . In another month my wanderings start. At that time I wish to go up Kingnait Fjord so that at the beginning of May I will be in Padli. Then I shall hang up your picture in my iglu, where I shall remain for some time. It is going to be hard work to take all my things over land to Padli!

March 29, Nexemiarbing   [Catching up on a gap in the diary, Boas tells that he drove his team as far north as Sakiak Fjord, then made a relatively easy trip back to Kikkerton. There he found a pleasant surprise: some Padli Inuit had come to the Gulf, and Mutch had bought five dogs from them. Equally pleasant was the news that two American ships had visited Padli the previous summer.]   . . . I felt my blood stream to my heart as I again was able to hope to go to you! O, Marie, how happy I shall be if my good luck leads me to an American vessel. It does not sail to New London but to St. John's in Newfoundland, but that would not bother me. St. John's is not outside the world as this country here is and a few days would take me to you. I have made a heavy line under the first of November in all my journals and calendars. That is the day I will be in New York or in Minden. Six months more in this country. On the twenty-seventh I began to pack my things. I underlined that day in red on my calendar, the day on which I began to prepare for my journey home. . . .

[On March 28 Boas left Kikkerton with Signa on an abbreviated version of his original western exploration. "I wanted at least to see the longed-for Lake Nettilling and to catch a glimpse of the form of the land west of the Gulf" (Boas 1885b:16–17). Reaching the lake on April 1, Boas, always very conscious of anniversaries, made the most of the coincidence with his visit a year previous to Stuttgart.]

April 1, Kangia How could I let this day go by without writing you at least a few words. Our thoughts today are centered on the same event, the day on which we last saw one another. . . . Doesn't it strike you as remarkable that today, without any intention on my part, I am to reach the so-longed-for Lake Kennedy? And it seems as though it again will be a beautiful day. Yes, even here, in the midst of snow and ice, it is spring. The sun shines so warm and I feel spring in my heart. . . . Today I am writing from the upper end of the long fjord which forms the way to the interior and today I should see the lake. . . .

April 1, evening, Nettilling . . . At last! But here at my goal, I turn around again, right where I had thought I would really begin. Is it not strange, Marie, to arrive here today and that I must turn back, without accomplishing that which I had wanted? But last year I made up for what I missed while this year I am saying goodbye to this country forever. Off and away. You, beloved, need not wait because of the stupid Lake Kennedy which will still be here for someone else to visit. . . . This morning we drove up from Kangia past a chain of lakes, separated from one another by narrow strips of land. Low granite hills and steep cliffs surround these basins of water. Before we started every strap of walrus skin on the sleds was carefully put away. The Eskimo are not allowed to take walrus skin into the land of the caribou.

April 3, Kangia Since there are reports of other kinds of rock in this neighborbood, I proceeded for another hour but found only a red variety of granite. We turned back, the weather was beautiful and before eight in the evening we reached Kangia. Three times during the day we were delayed because we hunted caribou. . . . We were so near the first herd that I hoped we would be able to shoot, but then the dogs broke loose from the sled and the caribou fled. Fortunately Signa could hold on to the sled, but the dogs could not be held. The last dog broke loose, but fortunately returned in a quarter of an hour. Last night when Signa wanted to cut seal meat for the dogs, the ax handle broke so that I could not feed them until this morning. . . . You should see me now—dirty. Since I left Kikkerton, no water has touched my face or hand—it is too precious—and I have been burned black by the sun, so that I scarcely recognize myself. . . . [Arriving in Kikkerton on April 7, Boas moved some provisions up Kingnait Fjord in anticipation of his trip to Davis Strait, attempted some more surveys of the west coast of the Sound, and made another trip to Imigen to secure seals.]

April 22, Imigen . . . The dog sickness has again appeared in Kikkerton, but my team has been spared. I hope this worrying time will soon be
over and then I shall go onwards to you in good spirits! . . . Time is now
fleeing too rapidly—on account of bad luck, lack of dogs and bad weather, I
have not finished my work here, but at least I know that I have done what I
could. During the last two months I have slept in a bed only about seven
days, the rest of the time I never took off my clothes! . . . It would be terrible
if I had to stay here another year. I have plenty of food but I could not travel
because my trade goods would be used up.

April 23, Kikkerton   With hard snow we proceeded quite rapidly and I
am entering Kikkerton for the last time. You have no idea how boring it is
to cross the Sound when there is nothing to see but snow and ice, no land,
no variety on the whole long route. Only the blinding white of the snow
which hurts the eyes so much that one does not keep them open. So far I
have luckily escaped snow blindness. I am very careful but every day I am
afraid that it might happen to me. My eyes hurt me most of the time but that
is not worth mentioning. . . . [Although utterly sick of travelling on the
Sound, he made one last trip, to Nuvujen, to complete his census and map.
After intense preparation and packing, Boas then left Kikkerton on May 6
for Davis Strait, where he planned to board a ship. "Cordially I said goodbye
to the whalers whose friendly support had been so valuable all winter. From
now on . . . I would have to depend on what little I could carry on my sled
and what I could secure from hunting" (Boas 1885b:17–18). Signa would
accompany them to the strait and then return to Kikkerton, leaving Boas
and Weike (travelling for the first time since his frostbite) dependent on the
Davis Strait natives for whatever guidance and assistance they needed.]

May 8, Niutang . . . Up to this time we have had the most glorious
weather, the sky is blue, the sun warm and one hears the water trickling
down the rocks. Even the snow on top of the ice is beginning to melt under
the rays of the sun or at least to soften. I drove the sled all day long without
wearing my sealskin jacket. A woolen shirt sufficed to keep me completely
warm. . . . We are now near the end of Kingnait. Here is a deep valley where
there used to be a large settlement. One can still see the remains of the huts
where, a long time ago, according to folklore, Tudniks and Eskimo had lived
together until the first were driven out. Many tales and traditions derive from
this place . . . of the quarrels of the Eskimo of the west coast of the sound
and their battles with one another.

[The journey was very arduous. The ice on Kingnait Fjord, pressed together into great blocks, made travel difficult, and the overland portion required heavy hauling over a series of steep terraces. "The labor required to
ascend these heights was so unspeakably difficult that I was forced to leave

the bulk of my provisions and possessions at Tornateling canyon. If my provisions had already been trifling, the little I now took with me could only be regarded as emergency supplies to supplement poor hunting" (Boas 1885b:19). On May 18, after eleven days of heavy packing, they reached the head of Padli Fjord and, on May 22, Padloping, the settlement at its mouth.]

May 25, Padloping   My dear Marie: If I have not written for many days, there are good reasons. I was at first too tired out, when I was on land, to write much,. and now for days I have been snowblind. Even today it is difficult to write because of my eyes, but at least I can make the attempt. I am now at the mouth of Padli Fjord. Tomorrow I shall go further north. Thank goodness the most difficult part of this journey has been conquered and in a few days I can reach the place to which ships come. I would rather embark and sail home tomorrow. The Eskimo here tell me that the "Wolf," the only American ship that comes here, is always the first to arrive. How happy I shall be to see the smoke from her funnel! . . . The ice *may* still upset my plans. . . . It would be too great a stroke of bad luck if, just this year, ships could not get through! . . .

May 28, Padloping   . . . How many disappointments this year has brought me, but you, my only beloved, have helped me to bear them all and now my troubles here seem so insignificant, since I know that you are mine. Sometimes I look back on what I have accomplished through the eyes of my colleagues who sit at home and criticize and I find, without overestimating myself, that it is quite a considerable accomplishment that deserves to be recognized. I have told you often enough what I think of it, that I consider the fame awarded to an explorer of strange lands of little worth, one is nothing more than a handyman! But I can recognize a field worthy of a man's labors and when I strive for my ideals, with or without success, you, my Marie, help me. . . . My work now is mere child's play in comparison to that of the winter. As soon as the sun shines it will be as warm as at home. I have only three more fjords to observe before I reach the harbor into which the ships come.

June 5, K'exertuxdjuax   I hope you are not angry with me, my Marie, that I write so infrequently. I really cannot help it for I am either snowblind or dead tired from travelling. I always drive my own dogs now and after I have been travelling ten hours over the soft snow, I am glad to sleep after I have organized my notes. . . . Shall I tell you about the last few days? One is like the other. Snowblindness, bad weather, and deep snow bother me endlessly. . . . It really is wretched how my big travel plans have shrunk. But I *must* be satisfied. Oh! Marie, when I shall think back on this time, with all its sufferings and cares and joys, it will probably seem like a long dream. And I think it will seem that way to you too, becaue you had to think of me so far from home.

[With Sanguja, a Padli Inuit who was his almost constant companion and guide on Davis Strait, Boas and Weike moved northwest along the strait. Travel conditions were terrible in the thawing snow and at times they resorted to travelling at night when there was a firm surface. On June 16 they arrived at Idjuniving, a settlement on a harbor frequented by trading vessels. Boas was overjoyed at seeing the Eskimo busy preparing oil and pelts for the traders. "Everything is aimed at the arrival of the ships and I cannot believe they will disappoint us this year." There was still work to do, however, because he wanted to survey the coast as far as Cape Henry Kater. The next month, to and from Siorartijung, his most northerly point, was an extremely difficult time. Heavy fog, spring snowstorms, a face-swelling toothache, snowblindness and days without food for men and dogs plagued the journey. "I do not think I shall ever in my life forget horrible Home Bay!" he wrote on July 1. It was the worst time of his entire year. Partial compensation came on July 4 when he found a man at Niaxonaujang, "probably the last new Eskimo I shall meet," who came from Igluling "and has often travelled along the coast of Foxe Channel all the way to Nettilling." This was a welcome confirmation of his travel route thesis.

The impending end of his travels gave him comfort. "You cannot imagine how happy I will be no longer to have to sit on a sled." In mid-July he settled down at Idjuniving to work on his ethnographic material while anxiously awaiting the coming of a ship. Finally, on August 19 a Dundee whaler was seen, then lost in the fog before it could be reached. "This was a bitter disappointment, yet its presence gave a comforting certainty that the whaling fleet had reached the coast" (Boas 1885b:21). On August 26 two ships were reported anchored at the edge of the ice. The dogs were quickly harnessed and, after several hours' travel over the difficult ice, they reached the ships, two Dundee vessels. Both captains welcomed them and offered return passage. The next day the *Wolf*, under Captain John Burnett, arrived. Since she was sailing to St. John's almost immediately, Boas unhesitatingly chose her. He reached the Newfoundland port on September 7. His trip from there to New York was frustratingly slow, but he arrived on the twenty-first and was reunited with Marie Krackowizer at Lake George two days later.]

Judged in terms of Boas' original intentions, the expedition was a failure. "Fortune has favored me but little," he wrote as he left Cumberland Sound, "none of the hopes I had when I arrived here have been fulfilled" (BFP: FB/parents 4/30/84). His late arrival was an initial, if not entirely unexpected, setback; both weather and hunting were exceptionally bad all winter; above all, the death of so many dogs denied him access to the only means of Arctic transportation. But despite these reversals, he could be satisfied with his results. He had made an accurate survey of most of Cumberland Sound and much of Davis Strait, all previously inaccurately rendered. Able to survey Lake Nettilling only sketchily and the rest of the interior not at all, he nevertheless secured sufficient information to draw a close approximation of the actual outline of the interior lakes and the entire coast and to conclude that Foxe Channel was a basin. When his geographical monograph, *Baffin-Land*, was published in 1885, Georg Gerland described it as among "the best of Arctic researches that we possess," and among "the most distinguished geographical works of recent years" (Gerland 1888:600–602).

His ethnographic results, though completed by April 1886, were not published as *The Central Eskimo* until 1888. The monograph reflected fairly his ethnological data-gathering in its emphasis upon human geography (anthropogeography), the description of subsistence activities and material culture, and the recording of traditions and songs. He gave almost no attention to social structure and only a little to ceremonial and religious life. His work in linguistics was not published until 1894, and was by his own account "defective and incomplete": having assumed that missionaries had already given a sufficient picture of the language, he was "not clearly conscious of the importance of linguistic studies during the entire trip" (Boas 1894:97). Nevertheless, within its scope and context, his ethnography was sophisticated and sagacious.

Retrospectively, of course, the most significant aspect of Boas' experience in Baffin Island was his ethnographic immersion among the Inuit. His life and reputation were to be made in anthropology, and this was his initiation. A shift of interest was already evident by the end of the Cumberland Sound trip: "My work among the Eskimo satisfies me more than my travels" (BFP:FB/ parents 4/30/84). Participation in the life of the Inuit also sharpened his social sense and his belief in the equality of virtue among peoples. The kindness and sensitivity of the Eskimo, the sympathetic tact that they demonstrated in their personal relationships, gave proof that inner character, their *herzensbildung*, was far more significant than the gloss of civilization and learning.

All the more regrettable, then, was the inevitability of the destruction of the Cumberland Sound Inuit. Already they had shrunken in number from thousands to hundreds. It was important "to save what can yet be saved" of their tales and customs (Boas 1885b). While Boas did not cease being a geographer, he began to see the tasks of ethnography as "more pressing" (RBP: FB/Bell 3/19/86). The shift of his priorities from geography to anthropology was coincident with a movement of his ethnographic interests from the Eskimo to their southern and western neighbors. Although he continued to publish and even to direct research on the Eskimo for years, it was not long after his return to Germany that he interrupted, almost happily, his work on "the eternal Eskimo" (BFP: FB/parents 1/25/86) for a quick study of a Bella Coola touring troupe. This and other influences turned his attention to the Northwest Coast of America (Cole n.d.; cf. Stocking 1974:87–88), and in the fall of 1886, he took leave of his announced courses at the University of Berlin to return to America for his second field trip, this time to British Columbia (cf. Rohner 1969). Marrying Marie Krackowizer on March 10, 1887, he was thenceforth to reside in the United States.

REFERENCES CITED

Abbes, H. 1884. Die deutsche Nordpolar-Expedition nach dem Cumberland-Sunde. *Globus* 46:294–96, 312–15, 320–22, 343–45, 365–68.

———. 1890. Die Eskimos des Cumberlandgolfes. In *Die internationale Polarforschung, 1882–1883: Die deutsche Expeditionen und ihre Ergebnisse*, ed. G. Neumayer. Vol. 2: *Beschreibende Naturwissenschaft*, 1–61. Berlin.

BFP. See under Manuscript Sources.

Boas, F. 1883a. Über die Wohnsitze der Neitchillik-Eskimos. *Zeitschrift der Gesellschaft für Erdkunde zu Berlin*. Ser. 3, 18:222–33.

———. 1883b. Im Eise des Nordens. *Berliner Tageblatt*, Nov. 4.

———. 1883c. Aus dem Eise des Nordens. *Berliner Tageblatt*, Nov. 25.

———. 1884a. A journey in Cumberland Sound and on the West Shore of Davis Strait in 1883 and 1884. *Am. Geog. Soc. N.Y., Bul.* 16:242–72.

———. 1884b. Die Eskimos des Cumberland-Sundes und der Davisstrasse. *Berliner Tageblatt*, Nov. 2.

———. 1884c. Reise nach Paguistu. *Berliner Tageblatt*, Nov. 9.

———. 1885a. *Baffin-Land: Geographische Ergebnisse einer in den Jahren 1883 und 1884 ausgeführten Forschungsreise* (Ergänzungsheft No. 80 zu *Petermanns Mitteilungen*). Gotha.

———. 1885b. Unter dem Polarkreise. *New-Yorker Staats-Zeitung*, Feb. 1.

———. 1888. *The Central Eskimo*. 6th Ann. Rept. Bur. Ethn. Washington.

———. 1889. On alternating sounds. In Stocking 1974:72–76.

———. 1894. Der Eskimo-Dialekt des Cumberland-Sundes. *Mitteilungen der Anthropologischen Gesellschaft in Wien* 24:97–114.

BPP. See under Manuscript Sources.

Cole, D. N.d. Franz Boas and the Bella Coola in Berlin. *Northwest Anth. Res. Notes*. In press.

EEN. See under Manuscript Sources.

Freeman, J. F. 1966. *A guide to manuscripts relating to the American Indian in the library of the American Philosophical Society*. Philadelphia.

Gerland, G. 1888. Review of *Baffin-Land*, by Franz Boas. *Deutsche Litteraturzeitung* (April 21):600–602.

Kluckhohn, C. & O. Prufer. 1959. Influences during the formative years. In *The anthropology of Franz Boas: Essays on the centennial of his birth*, ed. W. Goldschmidt, 4–28. San Francisco.

Neumayer, G. 1891. *Die internationale Polarforschung, 1882–1883: Die deutsche Expeditionen und ihre Ergebnisse*. Vol. 1: *Geschichlicher Theil*. Berlin.

RBP. See under Manuscript Sources.

Rohner, R. P., ed. 1969. *The ethnography of Franz Boas: Letters and diaries of Franz Boas written on the Northwest Coast from 1886 to 1931*. Trans. H. Parker. Chicago.

Stocking, G. W., Jr. 1968. From physics to ethnology. In *Race, culture, and evolution: Essays in the history of anthropology*, 133–60. New York.

———. 1974. *The shaping of American anthropology, 1883–1911: A Franz Boas reader*. New York.

MANUSCRIPT SOURCES

The letter-diary to Marie Krackowizer [Boas] is contained in the Boas Family Papers (cited herein as BFP) in the Franz Boas Collection at the American Philosophical Society, Philadelphia. The BFP also contain a shorter letter-diary from Boas to his parents, his Baffinland field journal, and a letter-diary kept by Marie. Additional relevant materials are included in the Boas Professional Papers (cited as BPP), and the Franz Boas Collection of American Indian Linguistics (Freeman 1966:20, 161) includes his "Eskimo Ethnographic Notes from Baffinland" (cited as EEN). In addition to the American Philosophical Society sources, I have cited material from volume four of the Robert Bell Papers (RBP) in the Public Archives of Canada. I would like to thank Franziska Boas and the American Philosophical Society (the holders of the literary property rights of the Boas manuscripts) for graciously permitting the publication of the letter-diary and the accompanying photographs, as well as the manuscript librarians at the Society, Stephen Catlett and Beth Carroll, for their assistance in the project.

ETHNOGRAPHIC CHARISMA AND SCIENTIFIC ROUTINE

Cushing and Fewkes in the American Southwest, 1879–1893

CURTIS HINSLEY

In one of the swift closing scenes of *The Last of the Mohicans*, Uncas stands before his Huron captors, anticipating death yet stolidly disdaining their taunts and tortures. As James Fenimore Cooper presents the picture, "in the very center of the lodge, immediately under an opening that admitted the twinkling light of one or two stars, stood Uncas, calm, elevated, and collected. . . . Marble could not be colder, calmer, or steadier than [his] countenance. . . ." (1826:288, 293). Uncas would soon die at the hands of the treacherous Magua, and thus the noble Red race of America would be symbolically extinguished, not by White civilization but by its own dark side of undisciplined bloodlust. As Cooper's phrases indicate, for White Americans the marbling and bronzing of the American Indian began at an early date; the transformation of the aborigine from historical actor to aesthetic object, as unfeeling as stone, was a significant cultural exercise that lasted well into the twentieth century. From the cigar store to the United States Mint, from statuary to small change, the artistic abstraction of the Native American served to deflect a painful history of violence and injustice.

Given public preference for sentiment and stereotype, it is hardly surpris-

Curtis M. Hinsley teaches American history and history of science at Colgate University. He is currently writing a book on the history of anthropology in Boston, 1860–1920, centering on the Peabody Museum of Archaeology and Ethnology. With Lea S. McChesney he is also co-authoring a narrative history of the Hemenway Southwestern Archaeological Expedition under Frank Hamilton Cushing (1886–1889). He is the author of *Savages and Scientists: The Smithsonian Institution and the Development of American Anthropology, 1846–1910*.

ing that anthropological fieldwork emphasizing attention to the historical and ethnographic integrity of specific peoples did not find fertile conditions for growth in nineteenth-century America. Some serious efforts occurred: the observations of Lewis Cass and Henry Rowe Schoolcraft in the upper Michigan peninsula of the 1830s; Albert Gallatin's promotion, through the first American Ethnological Society, of historical and linguistic inquiries; the early work of Lewis Henry Morgan; the paintings of George Catlin and Charles Bird King; and the less-heralded labors of missionaries such as Stephen Riggs and Cyrus Byington. Still, not until the last quarter of the previous century did individuals begin to undertake fieldwork in North America in a conscious, sustained effort to record, study, and understand the remaining Native American peoples. The organizational center of this development was the Bureau of American Ethnology (BAE), the most important regional focus became the Southwest, and the leading though certainly not sole figure was Frank Hamilton Cushing. It was among the anthropologists working in the Southwest, led by Cushing in the 1880s, that the patterns and styles of North American fieldwork first began clearly to emerge.

"Their history is, to some extent, our history," Schoolcraft wrote of the Iroquois in 1846 as he urged study of Native American peoples. For its handful of nineteenth-century enthusiasts, anthropology in the United States always possessed psychological and political bearing on the national purpose. In defending their enthusiasm, they commonly cited two goals, one practical and the other scientific: more efficient and humane government policy, and better knowledge of civilization through study of its antecedent forms. John Wesley Powell used precisely this dual argument in his successful lobbying to establish the Bureau of Ethnology in 1879; variations on the theme were common. Beneath the practical and scientific justifications, though, lay a deeper stratum of purpose, best expressed by Schoolcraft, that lent a unique style to American fieldwork in these years. The distinguishing element was a sense of identity based on shared historical mission and common stewardship of the continent. "It has been given to us, to carry out scenes of improvement, and of morals and intellectual progress, which providence in its profound workings, has deemed it best for the prosperity of man, that *we*, not *they*, should be entrusted with. We have succeeded to their inheritance" (Schoolcraft 1846:28–29). Understanding our predecessors in this teleological history became an integral part of the burden of American progress.

This conviction placed Native Americans within the national experience by definition, and it determined that, however ignorant or cruel popular attitudes or public policy toward the Indian might become, the dominant culture could never achieve complete separation of identity. By the same token, early North American anthropologists often carried into the field more than a sense of studying "savagery" or "mankind"; some took as well a spirit

of exchange, which *in extremis* could shade into confusion of personal identity, but which commonly encouraged liberality of judgment: "I mean to say
that by thoroughly studying and revealing the life and traits of the Indian,
we cannot fail, if happy in our mission, of exciting interest in him where
none existed before; cannot fail of showing him to be more human than we
had supposed him, more capable of being made usefuler [sic] and better than
it has been supposed possible—. . . " (HCP: FHC/Miss Cushing 2/16/84).

While life in the field is an individual experience, it is institutionally
filtered, and it is extremely important to consider the roles of sponsoring
institutions in differing historical contexts in accounting for the nature of
fieldwork, as experienced and as reported. For example, prior to Cushing's
famous sojourn (1879–84) at Zuni pueblo, ethnographic data based on extended exposure had often come from missionaries, but their purposes and
roles usually inhibited intimate or sympathetic observation. When the Dutch
anthropologist Herman F. C. Ten Kate visited Zuni in 1883, he noted that
whereas the Cushing household occupied the lower level of the governor's
house, and the local trader, Douglas D. Graham, had his trading post in a
small street in the pueblo, the local missionary lived outside the pueblo.
Edmund Wilson, arriving sixty years later, recorded that "the present Catholic priest in the pueblo is said to feel that he has made some progress, now
that the Zuñis, after a quarter of a century, when they meet him out of doors,
do not spit at him" (Wilson 1956:13). True, Zuni has always been a notably
resistant community (Pandey 1972), but such instances suggest inherent ethnographic limits to the missionary endeavor. Conversely, maverick individuals, such as Thomas Keam and Alexander Stephen among the Hopis, or
James G. Swan on the Northwest Coast, who settled down to trade, live,
and intermarry with Native Americans, lacked the institutional means to
communicate their valuable knowledge to public or professional audiences.

Again, the patterns of nineteenth-century exploration and settlement of
the trans-Mississippi West encouraged sweeping accounts of the country for
politicians and public, and postponement of narrower studies, whether of
geological or cultural configurations. The survey, too, was an institutional
form, and the chief preoccupation of the territorial survey years (1865 to
1879) was to determine the boundaries and resources of the usable continent.
The free-wheeling, competing post–Civil War surveys of Powell, Wheeler,
King, and Hayden lasted little more than a decade, giving way in 1879 to a
consolidated U.S. Geological Survey that soon became regionally and
professionally fragmented. Similarly the new Bureau of Ethnology, established with the Geological Survey and placed in the Smithsonian Institution,
carried within it the surveying and mapping tradition—but also the rudi-
ments of particularistic ethnography. In this and other ways the organizations
directed by John Wesley Powell were important transitional mediums (Hins-

ley 1981:151–55), demonstrating that while institutions reflect intentions, they also may develop new purposes along the way.

Cushing had few models for his fieldwork, but many visions and ambitions. Comparing himself to a bee indiscriminately in search of honey, he wrote to his cousin in 1884: "I have to have knowledge of savage life, and it matters less to me where I find it, than it does in what measure I find it. Zuñi, therefore, while I confess it to be a patch of thorns in the side of a civilized being, is attractive to me because of the satisfaction it gives to my craving after knowledge of savage lore and life" (HCP: FHC/Miss Cushing 3/16/84). On a subsequent occasion Cushing explained his obsession with the Southwest by recalling a recurrent dream he had had while living in a tower of the Smithsonian Building in 1876. Dangling from the edge of a mountain, he sees a "pagan altar" below and a Kachina doll at his feet, and feels "awed, beyond measure, yet happy to the verge of ecstasy":

> It may be that the chill of a windy winter night caused me to dream of wild desolate lands, the height of my tower home, of mountains . . . and my studies among the relics and idols of primitive man gathered the world over of an idol stranger than any I had studied. . . . Be all this as it may, my eyes were first turned toward Zuñi by a vision of the night . . .
>
> (HCP: FHC/Lecture notes c. 1890)

Typically, Cushing here personalized history. In actuality it was Spencer Baird, director of the National Museum, who first turned Cushing toward Zuni. Between 1876 and 1879, Cushing catalogued collections for Baird in the National Museum, awaiting an appropriate field opportunity and lamenting the "socially dead, morally dead, intellectually dead" atmosphere of Washington (HCP: FHC/Mr. Leech c. 1878). Finally Baird assigned him as the Museum's representative on the BAE's first southwestern expedition, under James Stevenson. The instructions to Stevenson were broadly ethnological and archeological, the approach was that of a survey, and the expedition model was quasi-military—an "ethnological campaign," Baird called it (MCSP: SB/JS 7/10/83). Baird sought material collections for the Museum, while Powell, following Lewis H. Morgan's most recent theories, wanted the expedition to study pueblo architecture and domestic arrangements.

Unexpectedly, Cushing chose to stay at Zuni when the rest of the Stevenson party moved on to other sites. The stories of Cushing's physical sufferings and gradual acceptance among some groups in the pueblo, his initiation into the Priesthood of the Bow, and the bestowing of his Zuni name, Medicine Flower, have become part of the folklore of American anthropology, and have justified the claim that he pioneered the method of participant-observation in North America (Brandes 1965; cf. Mark 1976 and Green 1979). The initial weeks in the home of the Zuni governor, Palowáihtiwa, were extremely difficult for Cushing, due to lack of communication, physical discomfort, and barely palatable food. Cushing immediately realized that without the language Zuni culture and history would remain closed to him; indeed the corpus of his published work reflects everywhere Cushing's heavy reliance on analysis of etymology and sound as keys to mental structures and cultural connections. His attention to recording folktales and mythology illustrated his conviction, shared by Franz Boas, that "the ethnologist's function supplements the historian's; [the ethnologist] is able to restore thousands of his missing pages" (HCP: FHC/Miss Cushing 3/16/84). But all this, he saw, was impossible without the language:

> I conversed at first in broken Spanish, which after the end of two months proving insufficient for my needs I began earnestly to study the native speech. Whatever other accessories to my success I may have neglected I have never neglected this. Too ill at times to write my full notes I have nevertheless set down my little daily acquisitions in this direction and thus, word by word, I increased my store until I [could] carry on a broken, strange mixture of Zuñi and Mexican conversation, gradually dropping the latter. . . . This as the very first of all I have labored at incessantly, and my reward is that today at the close of eight months' study I speak a strangely complicated tongue, not perfectly but fluently and easily . . .
>   (HCP: FHC/Report on the Zuni Language c. 1880)

Within a year Cushing not only had come to realize that Zuni culture was immensely rich in social complexity, art, knowledge, and history, but he also was convinced that behind daily appearances of pueblo life stood a coherent system of belief. He was certain that the keys to this religious system would unlock the riches of Zuni life and knowledge. He believed that the songs, dances, and ritual language of the Zuni priesthood had probably retained these keys to understanding in the most distilled and conservative form, but that clues could be discovered in even mundane activities, such as cooking. It is, in fact, the discovery of the importance of the mundane, in artifacts or activities, and their complex connection to the sacred, that was a hallmark of Cushing's ethnography. In other words, Cushing came to the vital insight—at direct variance with prevalent American attitudes at the time—that, far from being lost, Zuni history and beliefs lived on in the daily life of the pueblo. This is what he meant when he insisted that Native Americans were deeply "religious" peoples:

> Of all the people on this continent, not excluding ourselves, the most profoundly religious—if by religion is meant fidelity to teachings and observations that are regarded as sacred—are the American Indians. . . . For with them,

sociologic organization and government and the philosophy and daily usages
are still so closely united with religion, that all their customs, which we consider as absurd and useless, grow from it as naturally and directly as plants from
the soil.

(Cushing 1897:12)

Understanding such deeply rooted patterns, he saw, required time, patience,
and sympathy. After two years at the pueblo Cushing found himself just at
the threshold of understanding:

As a consequence of my initiation I have had a world of facts opened up to
me, which I had despaired of ever reaching. I had from my former standpoint
exhausted the subject with the exception of a few details, and was preparing
to come home permanently during early January of 1882 . . . but from the
present I see nothing but the most constant work, with the best of facilities for
at least four years to make my work *exhaustive*. . . . Indeed, my disappointment
would be almost irreparable, were I unable to study for a period almost as great,
from the *inside*, the life of the Zuñis, as I have from the outside. After having
secured the two necessities, the absolute confidence and language of the Indian, I feel it my duty to use these necessities, or advantages, to the fullest
extent of their value, toward the end which I acquired them for.

(FHCP: FHC/S. Baird 10/12/81)

The recognition of a living history at Zuni inspired in Cushing the spirit
of mutual exchange that marked his anthropology. In 1882 he travelled eastward with prominent Zuni men, not to impress upon them the power of
American civilization, but to share his life with them as they had done with
him. "I owe a lasting debt of gratitude to the people of Zuñi," he explained:

They have been forging for me, during the past two years of doubt as to my
genuineness, the keys which enable me to open their vast and ancient treasure-
house of Ethnologic information, have treated me with strange goodness and
distinction; and in my gratitude, I . . . wish to do all I can toward the amelio-
ration of their condition, and toward convincing them that I *am* what I have
always claimed to be, their *friend*.

(FHCP: FHC/J. C. Pilling 1/15/82)

The eastern tour of 1882 marked the end of Cushing's first Zuni phase and
his emergence as a figure of public notoriety and growing ambition. Appearing with the Zunis in Chicago, Boston, and Washington, he sought to promote cross-cultural understanding and at the same time to prepare alternative
institutional foundations for his anthropology. On returning to Zuni with his
White bride, Emily Magill, her sister Margaret, and a Black male cook, Cushing
did not readopt the austere lifestyle of his early months at the pueblo. Now
occupying the entire ground floor of Palowáihtiwa's adobe, the Cushing

Cushing performing for a hometown audience, Albion, New York, c. 1890. Courtesy Swan Library, Albion, N.Y.

household became a scene of domesticated ruggedness and cultural commingling for visiting anthropologists:

> The small, dimly lit apartments present a strange jumble of Indian and Japanese artwork and Oscar Wilde's "aesthetics." The floor is covered and the walls are hung with colorful Navaho rugs, and bear and puma skins, while above an Oriental divan Cushing's costume as a priest of the Order of the Bow is hang-

ing. It's a pretty outfit, that colorful round shield bedecked with feathers and the graceful bow and quiver of puma hide. Here your eye falls upon rifles and revolvers, there on a bookshelf; here on a chest with fine porcelain and Zuñi pottery, over there on Japanese fans, peacock's feathers, sunflowers and multi-colored Hopi baskets, which here and there decorate the walls. A soft light shines through the small rectangular windows and bathes the picturesque interior in shimmering halftones of richness and strength.

(Ten Kate 1885:275)

Already Cushing had grown restive in the confines of BAE anthropology, which was not sufficiently flexible to permit in official publications the poetic form, imaginative digressions, and hyperbole that were becoming the Cushing style in thought and writing. Not surprisingly, then, as he now made a home at Zuni Cushing also began searching for independent, permanent support for what he would call his "internal" method of ethnography—a combination of linguistics, daily observation, and intuition. Cushing was struggling with the dilemma of communicating knowledge about one culture in the "scientific" categories of another without distorting Zuni reality. Furthermore, he recognized that it was an institutional as well as an intellectual challenge.

He attacked the problem of institutional support by addressing various audiences at once. Working partly through a Boston journalist, Sylvester Baxter, he popularized his Zuni life in Century magazine, and in Boston periodicals and newspapers, while writing professionally oriented pieces as well. In this way Cushing developed a network of support, centered in Boston, that included such luminaries as John Fiske and Edward Everett Hale. In 1886 the efforts bore fruit. Cushing had long since been convinced through his studies of Zuni mythology and language that the pre-Columbian history of the Southwest, and its relationship to Central and South American cultures, could be traced. Specifically, he hypothesized that ancestors of the Zunis had built and occupied the famed Seven Cities of Cibola referred to by Spanish conquistadors. He decided to organize a major expedition to investigate the history of the Southwest from four directions simultaneously: ethnography, historical documentation, archeology, and physical anthropology. In late 1886 the Hemenway Southwestern Archaeological Expedition, financed by Mary Hemenway of Boston with $25,000 a year, left for Arizona under Cushing's direction. For two years the party—Cushing, his wife and sister-in-law, Frederick W. Hodge, and several assistants—excavated ruins between Tempe and Phoenix, and briefly in the vicinity of Zuni. To supplement these activities Cushing took on Adolph F. Bandelier as historian. Bandelier assiduously copied Spanish documents in Sante Fe and Mexico City in order to reconstruct regional history through Spanish eyes. Cushing also hired two physical anthropologists, H. F. C. Ten Kate and Jacob Wortman, to take measurements of neighboring tribes (Maricopa, Yuma, Pima) and to study the skeletal remains from the excavations.

Mrs. Hemenway and Cushing envisioned a Pueblo museum in Salem, Massachusetts, to serve as a permanent locus of study of the Southwest under Cushing's direction. More important, though, the patron and the anthropologist shared a strong affinity for the poetic knowledge of the Zunis and other Native Americans. During the summer of 1886 Mrs. Hemenway, a widowed philanthropist who controlled an estimated $15 million, had listened attentively to Cushing's renditions of Zuni folk tales in her mansion at Manchester-by-the-Sea, Massachusetts. While she has remained an enigmatic figure, it is apparent that Mary Hemenway endorsed Cushing's "insider's view" of Zuni thought, possibly because she sensed, with him, piety and strength in deep traditions that seemed to be lacking in the industrial civilization of America. It was the search for the coherence of Indian life, vested in long, living history, that was the spiritual center of the Hemenway Expedition under Cushing.

By most measures the Expedition of 1886–88 was a failure: Cushing's imagination wandered; he kept poor field notes; he fell miserably ill; he published very little. The sympathy and intuition that had served him so well as a linguistic ethnographer at Zuni proved less helpful in archeology, and the expedition structure, which required attention to mundane daily affairs of finances and supplies, taxed his limited energies. Cushing found it particularly difficult to work in association with the advisory board in Boston, and his expedition eventually dissolved in a flurry of accusation and recrimination. In early 1889, when he was desperately sick, Cushing even consulted a seer whose analysis and prophecy of the expedition undoubtedly pleased him:

> Mr. Cushing will assert himself more than he has done before. In his anxiety to be perfectly just to each man, he has given up too much to them, individually, & allowed them to contend too much with him, thus wasting his force. . . . There has been too much conceit and vanity, as to their own abilities. Too many scientists so-called. He can furnish the scientific part. . . . When he trusts to and uses his intuitional powers more, along with his practical opportunities for observation, he will attain greater results more quickly . . .
> (HCP: Julia H. Coffin, "Experiments in Psychometry," 4/9/89)

Coffin's prognostications proved to be grossly inaccurate. As Cushing's health and his enterprise collapsed, Mrs. Hemenway's son, Augustus, turned to a former Harvard classmate, Jesse Walter Fewkes, to head the Expedition. Fewkes served until the Expedition closed when Mrs. Hemenway died in 1894, and brought a new style to southwestern fieldwork. The contrast with Cushing could not have been sharper. Fewkes had been trained in natural science at Harvard, specializing in marine biology, and in the mid-eighties

Jesse Fewkes at the beginning of his anthropological career, 1889. Courtesy Museum of Comparative Zoology, Harvard University.

had served as an instructor and curator at the Museum of Comparative Zoology. By 1889, however, Alexander Agassiz, the Museum's director, had become dissatisfied with Fewkes' work and denied him reappointment. The Hemenway opportunity thus came to Fewkes at a critical juncture; despite lack of experience in anthropology, he accepted readily.

Fewkes spent his first field season, 1890, at Zuni; the following year he moved to Arizona for the first of many seasons at the Hopi mesas. Although Fewkes did not leave first-hand accounts of his experiences, his assistant in the field, John G. Owens, has provided a portrait of Fewkes in pueblo country. Fewkes arrived at Zuni in June, 1890, with no knowledge of the language and, it is apparent, a strong sense of insecurity as the successor to the famous Cushing. The Cushing model was ever-present; on the railroad trip westward, following Fewkes' advice, Owens was hurriedly reading Cushing's *Century* accounts of life at Zuni. Recently widowed, Fewkes approached the Southwest stolidly and humorlessly, determined to survive and produce. He and Owens took up residence in a house built by Cushing with Hemenway money; for food they avoided native fare, depending mainly on canned provisions purchased by Mrs. Hemenway from "the finest grocery in Boston."

Fewkes was not an adventurous field man; after being thrown from a pony in his first month, he steadfastly refused to get on another animal, often walking many dusty miles as a result. While he and Owens gained access to rituals and recorded the sights and sounds of the Zuni Corn Dance and other celebrations of the summer months, their obvious inability to communicate and lack of familiarity created tangible distance. Like others of his generation who came to anthropology from the natural sciences, which were still highly taxonomic and descriptive, Fewkes was a good visual observer and sketch artist. But visual observation alone can actually distance the investigator, and mere description is not understanding. For all his effort Fewkes remained an outsider. Where Cushing patiently wrote down and translated Zuni folktales, Fewkes pioneered with the gramophone—an advance in technology, but possibly a retreat from understanding.

There were memorable moments: Owens records at one point that Fewkes has eighteen squaws and little girls in his room, "smoking his pipe and entertaining them with his limited vocabulary." But Fewkes depended heavily on others for entree and information. At Zuni this function was performed by trader Graham; among the Hopis, where Fewkes spent much time in the nineties, he relied on Alexander Stephen, Thomas Keam, and Keam's "right-hand Indian" (as Owens called him), Tom Pa-láe-a. Washington Matthews, student of the Navahos and friend of Cushing, reported with disgust to Cushing that "Our Boston friend, while in Zuñi never spoke a word of Zuñi and didn't know a word of Spanish . . . yet he learned all about them in two months. What a pity it is we have not a few more such brilliant lights in

Ethnography!" (HCP: WM/FHC 1/7/91). Alexander Stephen, who sat with Fewkes through days and nights of Hopi dancing, imparted his own knowledge, gained over a decade, with little recognition in print. While Fewkes appropriated his insights, Stephen viewed Fewkes as his sole means of communicating his knowledge to the larger world. He appealed to Fewkes to recognize his position: "My dear boy—pity the hermit. You never have led the life—but your desert experiences tell you what it is. They tell you all the external conditions—but there are vivid strokes of hell in it that can not be observed—they must be felt" (Wade & McChesney 1980:8).

Cushing had not produced as expected because, it was generally thought, he had become too enmeshed in the web of Indian life, had let his "personal equation" run away with him, and had not kept good records (Hinsley 1981:201). Fewkes intended to display a new professionalism. He would produce regular, short, focussed studies, turning out three or four for each season's work. The resulting pressure became intense. Owens came to see Fewkes as an impatient, ambitious, proprietary, and jealous man, willing to appropriate the ideas and observations of others. The full revelation, recorded by Owens in the summer of 1891, is worth relating at length:

> Last year when we went to Zuñi I rather understood that Dr. F. was going to write up everything and while I took all the notes I could get, I published very little. Indeed it was only toward the end of our stay there that I got that paper on Games. Among the people at Zuñi he—the Dr.—made the reputation of being very selfish. In that, I most decidedly agree with them. I submitted to a good many things only because I had to. When we came out this year he "rounded me up" very thoroughly on the [railroad] cars, chided me for not getting more last year and hoped I might get "something good" this summer. His manner of putting it made me quite angry, but I smothered it. However I made up my mind *that I would get something*. Two investigators on kindred subjects had better be as far apart as possible, so I wanted him to let me work on some cliff ruins near Flagstaff. He said, yes, but when we got near Flagstaff, he said, I guess you had better go up with me [to the Hopi mesas]. That settled that. Before we got here, one day at Mr. Keam's, I asked him a simple question & he replied: "We must each work it out independently." You count on it, I made up my mind we would do it, and when we got here he took his subject, "The Dances" & I mine, the "Agriculture & Foods of the Moquis." Of course they overlap in a couple of places; they must under conditions such as we have here. Whether it is luck or not, I have made several good discoveries since we came. . . . Now the fact is he has gotten very jealous. I suppose that is rather presumptuous for a subordinate to write about his superior, but I believe it is true; for "actions speak louder than words" & they (words) spoke loud enough today. We are nearing the solstice and today the priests made bahos to plant tomorrow for rain. I thought it belonged to my subject & when I found them at it this morning, I did not send for the Dr. It proved to be a very fine thing

and about 3 o'clock he came along & was *white with rage*. I think I did what was perfectly honorable, but he says not and the fact is I came nearly having to take my valise & go tonight. He got the last part of the thing, but I got it all. I am convinced it is nothing but jealousy. That sounds like self-praise, but this year has at least made me confident that if other people can get these things out I can. At least I don't believe I am behind in this race. . . . Tonight I wish the summer was over and everything all right. Money is the only thing that holds me tonight. If I were only a little better off, I would certainly say: "To Halifax with your Expedition," then pull up my stakes & move on to this very mesa and we would see who would have the best paper at the end of the summer. An ordinary fellow, such as I am, dont mind getting kicked around one summer, but when it comes to the second, he rather tires of it.

(JGOP: JGO/D. Stratton 6/18/91)

Fewkes' new professionalism in ethnography involved turning out the very sort of fragmentary, descriptive pieces that Cushing had refused to produce. The picture of Indian life Fewkes drew was piecemeal, from the outside in-ward—not, as Cushing prescribed, from a central core of understanding out-ward. Each summer he and Owens arduously gathered their "points" of eth-nography, then compiled enough of them to construct articles on ritual, songs, games, etc., to be published in the Expedition's *Journal of American Archae-ology and Ethnology*. Fewkes saw himself as a disciplined scholar in constant communication with a scientific audience; in contrast to Cushing, he would be a reliable producer. But his ambition had a nasty side, causing Owens to have second thoughts about a career in anthropology:

During this last year I have come in contact with many of what we call "inves-tigators." They are men of eminence, men we all respect, indeed the men who give us the books we quote as "authority" on the different subjects. But, as I get a glimpse into this class of original investigators, *when they are not on dress parade*, I see stamped on the countenance of almost every one the rankest jealousy. Almost every one seems to look upon the work of every other one as so much "rot."

(JGOP: JGO/D. Stratton 4/24/91)

If Owens deplored the pettiness of competitive work in the Southwest, Cushing berated Fewkes for his basic failure to grasp ethnographic method and purpose. Cushing reached new degrees of abuse when writing of Fewkes, revealing a wide chasm between their conceptions of their work:

To say nothing of the man's past relations to me, I think the proposal to submit my manuscript to such an utterly incompetent judge of ethnological data, as that stupidly indiscriminating and perspiringly painstaking recorder of mean-ingless, disjointed, random half-observations of mere tribal externalities, al-ways misnamed (and yet, invariably set forth as accurate scientific material for future use!)—is the most presumptuously insulting proposition on the part of those who once so heartily endorsed my interpretive methods, that could be offered.

(ESMP: FHC/ESM 3/6/93)

Through Cushing's splenetic phrases emerges the trauma of adjustment between field experience and institutional developments, which was probably the central issue for his anthropological generation. A community of scientific anthropology on the model of other sciences required a common language of discourse, channels of regular communication, and at least minimal consensus on judging method. These goals all entailed imposing a degree of discipline on the imagination of the individual worker in the field. Trained through the graduate level under Louis Agassiz at Harvard, Jesse Fewkes was "disciplined," and he undoubtedly knew well the formalities of professional discourse. Cushing was brilliant but undisciplined; he insisted that institutions mold themselves to his method and fancy. This proved impossible. As Adolph Bandelier perceived in his important critique of anthropology in 1885: "Our age is above all a *critical* age. It does not merely examine. In the interest of truth it *dissects* and *compares*" (Bandelier 1885:6). Cushing's "internal," poetic mode of understanding raised problems of verification and accountability that to a generation enamored of analytical reasoning seemed insurmountable.

Over the past century every generation of American anthropologists seems to have discovered the Southwest, and especially the Zuni Indians, anew; indeed, the list of visiting anthropologists at Zuni has become so long that they have themselves become a controversial part of Zuni folk memory and a subject of study (Pandey 1972). In various odd ways, moreover, the Zunis and the students of Zuni culture have assumed a place in the more general Anglo-American literary tradition. Edmund Wilson visited the reservation in 1947 and popularized his impressions (including a section on the anthropologists) in his famous cross-cultural study, *Red, Black, Blond and Olive* (1956). Wilson had been preceded in this century, of course, by Ruth Benedict's *Patterns of Culture* (1934) and by the thorough, less popular studies of Ruth Bunzel in the thirties. Most interestingly, though, in 1932 Aldous Huxley produced his brilliant dystopian novel, *Brave New World*, in which he drew sharp contrasts between a sterile, regimented, drugged civilization of the future and the organic, free, sensual cultures of the aboriginal Southwest. Generally unnoticed has been the fact that Huxley's doomed protagonist, John the Savage, the White Indian, was clearly inspired by the Cushing legend. Indeed, two of the Zuni names which Huxley employs—Palowáihtiwa and Waihusiwa—belonged to Cushing's close friends (Huxley 1932:136, 143).

There is a certain justice that Cushing should have lived on in literature as well as in science, for he was a man of primarily metaphorical insights. It should not be surprising, then, to learn that his final effort from the Hemenway Expedition was not an attempt at "working up" his fieldnotes, but a series of reflections appended to *The Song of the Ancient People,* an epic poem of the Southwest by Boston poetess Edna Dean Proctor. Cushing called his contribution "Commentary of a Zuñi Familiar" (Proctor 1893:27–49). Dictating it while he was feverishly ill in 1892, he considered it his finest product of the Hemenway years, and in its title he came closest to describing his own anthropological role as intimate translator and mediator between cultures.

In April 1900, Cushing choked on a fishbone at dinner in his Washington home and died. He was forty-two years old. Fewkes enjoyed a much longer career, joining the Bureau of American Ethnology in the mid-nineties and eventually, in the 1920s, taking charge of the institution founded by Powell. He remained there until his death in 1930. In their disparate fates, as in their distinct field practices in the Southwest, lay revealing indications of the alternatives and tensions within the American anthropological tradition. Whether one looks at purpose, method, or institutional structure—all of which are closely related—Cushing and Fewkes operated at polar points. In the best tradition of the holistic, empathic humanities, Cushing sought to convey the complex historical richness of one culture to another (and vice versa), looking first to the deepest internal mental and social configurations. He saw little sense in anything less. This purpose prescribed for him a method of observation and intuitive connections that in turn required the faith of a patron rather than the routine of a bureaucracy. Cushing was extremely fortunate, in fact, in having enjoyed the support of a series of individuals— Powell, Hemenway, Phoebe Hearst—who attached few strings to their faith and funds. On an institutional continuum, then, Cushing occupied a position of extreme individualism.

Although he was repeatedly accused of violating the canons of scholarship, Jesse Fewkes belonged by training and temperament entirely to the established institutional world of American natural science. A forerunner of the trait list school, Fewkes believed that persistent observation would eventually yield sufficient data to assemble a coherent picture of the external forms of other cultures. That he believed in the possibility of any deeper understanding is, I think, doubtful. But for his purposes Fewkes required the steady, long-term support, the regularity and the focus best represented by government bureaucratic structure.

The point at issue here is not the gains and losses in the institutionalization or professionalization of American anthropology so much as the varieties of institutional forms and their intimate relationships to the investigator's purpose and method. Cushing and Fewkes embodied the struggle, as their generation experienced it, between intuitive understanding and disciplined knowledge, and the contest continued within Boasian anthropology. Franz Boas knew both the humanist tradition of Cushing and the natural science of Fewkes; because he embraced both, Boasian anthropology as it developed in the first decades of the twentieth century contained the tensions and ambiguities—and possibilities—of an intermediary, embracive position between individualism and bureaucracy, holistic and elemental knowledge, imagination and discipline (cf. Stocking 1974). Boas sowed the seeds of the trait list, emphasizing the importance of gathering materials for systematic comparison; but he also from the very beginning recognized the critical value of recording texts as windows into internal mental life (Stocking 1977). Similarly, as an institutional form, the university department of anthropology, according to Boas' vision, was intended to retain the virtues of both patron and bureaucracy, permitting the imaginative genius to flower in a disciplined environment of reliable financial and moral support.

ACKNOWLEDGMENTS

I wish to thank Lea S. McChesney, of the Keam-Hemenway Project at Peabody Museum of Archaeology and Ethnology at Harvard, for valuable assistance in locating materials, and for good discussions.

REFERENCES CITED

Bandelier, A. F. 1885. The romantic school in American archaeology. New York.
Brandes, R. S. 1965. Frank Hamilton Cushing: Pioneer Americanist. Unpublished doctoral dissertation, University of Arizona.
Cooper, J. F. 1826. The last of the Mohicans. Boston (1896).
Cushing, F. H. 1897. The need of studying the Indian in order to teach him. Albion, N.Y.
ESMP. See under Manuscript Sources.
Fewkes, J. W., ed. 1891–1908. J. Am. Arch. & Ethn. 1–5.
FHCP. See under Manuscript Sources.
Green, J., ed. 1979. Zuñi: Selected writings of Frank Hamilton Cushing. Lincoln, Neb.
HCP. See under Manuscript Sources.
Hinsley, C. M. 1981. Savages and scientists: The Smithsonian Institution and the development of American anthropology, 1846–1910. Washington.
Huxley, A. 1932. Brave new world. New York (1946).
JGOP. See under Manuscript Sources.

Mark, J. 1976. Frank Hamilton Cushing and an American science of anthropology. *Persp. Am. Hist.* 10:449–86.

MCSP. See under Manuscript Sources.

Pandey, T. N. 1972. Anthropologists at Zuni. *Procs. Am. Phil. Soc.* 116:321–37.

Proctor, E. D. 1893. *The song of the ancient people.* Boston.

Schoolcraft, H. R. 1846. *An address, delivered before the Was-Ah-Ho-De-No-Son-Ne, or new confederacy of the Iroquois, at its third annual council, August 14, 1846.* Rochester, N.Y.

Stocking, G. W. 1974. The basic assumptions of Boasian anthropology. In his *The shaping of American anthropology, 1883–1911: A Franz Boas reader,* 1–20. New York.

————. 1977. The aims of Boasian ethnography: Creating the materials for traditional humanistic scholarship. *Hist. Anth. Newsl.* 4(2):4–5.

Ten Kate, H. F. C. 1885. *Reizen en onderzoekingen en Noord-Amerika.* Leiden.

Wade, E. L., & L. S. McChesney. 1980. *America's great lost expedition: The Thomas Keam collection of Hopi pottery from the second Hemenway Expedition, 1890–1894.* Phoenix.

Wilson, E. 1956. *Red, black, blond and olive: Studies in four civilizations: Zuñi, Haiti, Soviet Russia, Israel.* New York.

MANUSCRIPT SOURCES

In writing this paper I have drawn on research materials collected from the following manuscript sources, cited as abbreviated:

ESMP   E. S. Morse Papers, Phillips Library, Peabody Museum, Salem, Mass.

FHCP   Frank Hamilton Cushing Papers, National Anthropological Archives, Smithsonian Institution, Washington.

HCP   F. W. Hodge/F. H. Cushing Papers, Southwest Museum, Los Angeles.

JGOP   John G. Owens Papers, Peabody Museum Archives, Harvard University, Cambridge, Mass.

MCSP   Matilda C. Stevenson Papers, National Anthropological Archives, Smithsonian Institution, Washington.

I would like to thank all the repositories and archivists for their helpful assistance.

THE ETHNOGRAPHER'S MAGIC

Fieldwork in British Anthropology from Tylor to Malinowski

GEORGE W. STOCKING, JR.

In the informal give-and-take of everyday disciplinary life, anthropologists occasionally speak of themselves in terms traditionally applied to tribal groups or folk societies. Since the latter are entities a more rigorously professional discourse has come to regard as problematic, one hesitates to suggest that an investigative community has taken on some of the characteristics of its subject matter. But there are similarities nonetheless, especially in relation to what has come to be regarded as the constitutive experience of social/cultural anthropology—and this in a multiple sense, since it at once distinguishes the discipline, qualifies its investigators, and creates the primary body of its empirical data. Even in an age when it is becoming increasingly difficult to carry on in traditional terms, fieldwork by participant-observation, preferably in a face-to-face social group quite different from that of the investigator, is the hallmark of social/cultural anthropology (Epstein 1967; Jarvie 1966; GS 1982).

As the central ritual of the tribe, fieldwork is the subject of a considerable mythic elaboration. Although there are variant versions of the charter myth in different national anthropological traditions (Urry n.d.), there is one so widely known as to require no recounting, even among non-anthropologists. Its hero is of course the Polish-born scientist Bronislaw Malinowski, who,

George W. Stocking, Jr., is Professor of Anthropology and Director of the Morris Fishbein Center for the Study of the History of Science and Medicine at the University of Chicago. Author and editor of numerous books and articles on the history of anthropology, he has for some time been engaged in research on various aspects of the history of anthropology in Britain.

while interned as an enemy alien in Australia during World War I, spent two years living in a tent among the Trobriand Islanders, and brought back to Britain the secret of successful social anthropological research (Kabery 1957; Leach 1965; Powdermaker 1970). Although Malinowski had by the 1960s lost his status as shaper of anthropological theory (Firth ed. 1957; Firth 1981; Gluckman 1963), his place as mythic culture hero of anthropological method was at once confirmed and irrevocably compromised by the publication of his field diaries (BM 1967), which revealed to a far-flung progeny of horrified Marlows that their Mistah Kurtz had secretly harbored passionately aggressive feelings towards the "niggers" among whom he lived and labored—when he was not withdrawing from the heart of darkness to share the white-skinned civilized brotherhood of local pearlfishers and traders (e.g., Geertz 1967; cf. Conrad 1902).

Disillusion has elicited a small body of literature either further scrabbling at the hero's feet of clay (Hsu 1979) or attempting to refurbish his image (including some strained attempts to suggest he may never have actually said the damning word [Leach 1980]). But it has so far led no one to probe historically the mythic origins of the Malinowskian fieldwork tradition. Seeking neither to debunk nor to defend, the present essay (cf. GS 1968a, 1980a) attempts to place Malinowski's Trobriand adventure in the context of earlier British fieldwork, and to show how his achievement—and its self-mythicization—helped to establish the special cognitive authority claimed by the modern ethnographic tradition (cf. Clifford 1983).

FROM THE ARMCHAIR TO THE FIELD
IN THE BRITISH ASSOCIATION

Let us begin with the state of anthropological method before the culture hero came upon the scene—for this, too, is part of the myth we seek to historicize. A good place to start is the year before Malinowski's birth, a moment which in mythic time is still part of the pre-promethian period when evolutionary titans, seated in their armchairs, culled ethnographic data from travel accounts to document their vision of the stages of creation of human cultural forms. While the major early statements of evolutionary anthropology (e.g., McLennan 1865; Tylor 1871) were based on essentially this sort of information, it is also the case that the evolutionary anthropologists were very seriously concerned with improving the quantity and quality of their empirical data. Their initial approach to the problem in the early 1870s had been through the preparation of Notes and Queries "to promote accurate anthropological observation on the part of travellers, and to enable those who are not anthropologists themselves to supply the information which is wanted for the scientific study of anthropology at home" (BAAS 1874:iv). In assuming that empirical data collected by gentleman amateurs abroad could provide the basis for the more systematic inquiries of metropolitan scholar-scientists, anthropologists were in fact following in the footsteps of other mid-Victorian scientists (cf. Urry 1972). But by 1883, events were already in process that were to draw more closely together the empirical and the theoretical components of anthropological inquiry.

By this time, E. B. Tylor, who had just come to Oxford as Keeper of the University Museum and Reader in Anthropology, was in regular correspondence with people overseas who were in a position to collect first-hand ethnographic data—notably the missionary ethnographer Lorimer Fison (EBTP: LF/EBT 1879–96). And while Tylor's position did not involve regular graduate training of students as fieldworkers in anthropology, his lectures were attended by several whose careers in the colonies were to provide significant ethnographic data, including the Melanesian missionary Robert Henry Codrington and the explorer of Guiana (and later colonial official) Everard Im Thurn (EBTP: lecture registers; Codrington 1891; Im Thurn 1883). Furthermore, when anthropology achieved full section status in the British Association in 1884, Tylor was instrumental in establishing a Committee "for the purpose of investigating and publishing reports on the physical characters, languages, and industrial and social condition of the North-western Tribes of the Dominion of Canada" (BAAS 1884:lxxii; cf. Tylor 1884). Founded with an eye towards the United States Bureau of Ethnology, which was already "sending out qualified agents to reside among the western tribes for purposes of philological and anthropological study," the Committee began by preparing a "Circular of Inquiry" for the use of government officers, missionaries, travellers, and others "likely to possess or obtain trustworthy information." The data thus obtained were to be edited and synthesized by Horatio Hale, whose "experience and skill in such research" were attested by his role in the U.S. Exploring Expedition some fifty years before (BAAS 1887:173–74).

Occasioned by the earlier British Association questionnaire having gone out of print, the Committee's new Circular was largely stripped of theoretical orienting remarks—with which Tylor, especially, had embellished his sections of *Notes and Queries* (BAAS 1874:50, 64, 66). Although Tylor (apparently the principal author) still directed the inquirer toward many of its presumed empirical manifestations, the Circular contains no explicit mention of "animism." More strikingly, in trying to reach "the theological stratum in the savage mind" inquirers were cautioned against asking "un-called for questions," but urged rather to watch "religious rites actually performed, and then to ascertain what they mean." Similarly, the collection of myth-texts "written down in the native languages," "translated by a skilled interpreter," and explicated along the way was "the most natural way" to get at "ideas and beliefs which no inquisitorial cross-questioning" would induce the Indian story-teller to disclose (BAAS 1887:181–82). Tylor was throughout his career concerned with issues of method, and one assumes that a decade of further reflection in the context of his correspondence with such observers-on-the-spot as Lorimer Fison had contributed to a heightened ethnographic sophistication. By this time, he was no longer willing to rest satisfied with research by questionnaire. From the beginning of the Northwest Coast project, it was assumed that, based on the results of such inquiry, some of the "more promising districts" would be the subjects of "personal survey" by Hale, or (when it became evident that his age would make this impossible) by an agent who "would act under his directions" (BAAS 1887:174; cf. Gruber 1967).

FROM MISSIONARIES TO ACADEMIC NATURAL SCIENTISTS

The Committee on the North-western Tribes of Canada was only one of a number established by the British Association in the 1880s and 1890s for empirical anthropological research both in the colonial empire and within the United Kingdom.[1] In the present context, however, it is particularly noteworthy for the personnel who were to serve as Hale's agents in the field. The first man chosen was a missionary who had worked for nineteen years among the Ojibwa and who travelled summers farther west to recruit Indian children for his mission school (Wilson 1887:183–84). Reverend E. F. Wilson, however, was soon to be replaced by a young man better known in the history of ethnographic methodology: the German-born physicist-turned-ethnologist Franz Boas, whose work on Vancouver Island in the fall of 1886 brought him to the attention of Hale and the Committee. Although the

1. Aside from several committees specifically concerned with physical anthropological or archeological data, BAAS committees with ethnographic concern included: one on "the tribes of Asia Minor" (BAAS 1888:lxxxiii); one on "the natives of India" (BAAS 1889:lxxxi); one on "the transformation of native tribes in Mashonaland" (BAAS 1891:lxxx); one for an "ethnographical survey of the United Kingdom" (BAAS 1892:lxxxix); one for an "ethnological survey of Canada" (BAAS 1896:xciii). There were also several committees appointed to support or supervise expeditions initiated outside the Association: one for Haddon's Torres Straits Expedition (BAAS 1897:xcix); one for W. W. Skeat's Cambridge Expedition to Malaya (BAAS 1898:xcix); one for W. H. R. Rivers' work among the Todas (BAAS 1902:xcii).

details of Boas' decade-long relationship with the British Association Committee are for the most part beyond the scope of the present inquiry (Rohner 1969; GS 1974:83–107), it is worth noting that his employment marks the beginning of an important phase in the development of British ethnographic method: the collection of data by academically trained natural scientists defining themselves as anthropologists, and involved also in the formulation and evaluation of anthropological theory.

The shift from Wilson to Boas symbolizes also a more deeply rooted, longer-run and somewhat complex shift in the anthropological attitude toward missionary ethnographers. In the pre-evolutionary era, James Cowles Prichard— another armchair speculator who, from a somewhat different theoretical viewpoint, was also concerned with the quality of his data—had preferred information collected by missionaries to that of "naturalists" because the latter made only brief visits and never learned the native language (1847:283; cf. GS 1973). The centrality of religious belief in the evolutionary paradigm tended, however, to compromise data collected by those whose primary commitment was to the extirpation of "heathen supersition," and Tylor's orienting commentary in Notes and Queries had clearly been intended to facilitate the careful observation of savage religion by people whose prejudices might predispose them to distort it (BAAS 1874:50). It was not until two anthropological generations later, when a corps of researchers actually trained academically in anthropology had entered the ethnographic arena, that the modern opposition between missionary and ethnographer was established in the ateliers of Boas and of Malinowski (Stipe 1980)—although the latter did in fact get on well with missionary leaders active in the International African Institute (GS 1979b). Most of the earlier British natural scientists-cum-anthropologists still maintained a working ethnographic relationship with missionaries. Nevertheless, this intermediate generation contributed significantly to the emergence of an ethnographic method that (whatever its underlying analogies to the missionary experience) was perceived by its practitioners as characteristically "anthropological."

Although the key figure in the early phase of this process was Alfred Cort Haddon, his career line was followed, up to a point, by another naturalist/ethnographer: Walter Baldwin Spencer. Both were part of that post-Darwinian generation for whom it first became a marginally realistic option as an undergraduate to decide "I want to become a scientist" (cf. Mendelsohn 1963). Spencer was a protégé of the zoologist Henry Moseley at Oxford (Marett & Penniman eds. 1931:10–46); Haddon, of the physiologist Michael Foster at Cambridge (Quiggin 1942; Geison 1978). Both began their careers as zoologists in universities at the imperial periphery—although it was a good deal easier for Haddon to return to the academic center from Dublin than it was for Spencer off in Melbourne. Both became interested in ethnographic data while carrying on zoological fieldwork; capitalizing permanently on their new-found interest, both ended their careers as anthropologists.

HADDON IN THE TORRES STRAITS: 1888–1899

Haddon first went out to the Torres Straits in 1888 in the hope that an important scientific expedition might help him escape what seemed after seven years the dead end of a provincial professorship. His scientific goals were archetypically Darwinian: to study the fauna, the structure, and the mode of formation of coral reefs. Having been told "that a good deal was already known" about the natives of the area, he "had previously determined not to study them" (1901:vii)—although he did take along the *Questions on the Customs, Beliefs and Languages of Savages* James Frazer had privately printed in 1887 to facilitate research on *The Golden Bough*. Haddon had barely arrived, however, before he began collecting "curios" he apparently hoped to sell to museums to recoup some of the expenses of the trip. On the island of Mabuaig, where he settled for a longer stay, he would join the already missionized natives round their campfire for evening prayers, and as they talked on into the night in pidgin, he asked them what life had been like before the white men came. As the older men "yarned," Haddon became convinced that if he neglected this ethnographic opportunity, it was likely to be lost forever (Quiggin 1942:81–86). Although he continued his zoological research, he filled every spare moment with ethnography, and before his departure his primary interest had clearly shifted to anthropology. As a biologist concerned with the geographical distribution of forms over a continuous area (in the manner of Darwin in the Galapagos) his most systematic ethnological concern was with material culture—the provenience and distribution of those "curios" he had been collecting. But he also recorded a considerable amount of general ethnographic data, which upon his return was published in the *Journal of the Anthropological Institute*, organized in terms of the categories of "that invaluable little book," *Notes and Queries on Anthropology* (1890:297–300).

In the context of the ethnographic reorientation already evidenced in the British Association, it is not surprising that Haddon's data were of interest to leading anthropologists (Quiggin 1942:90–95). As an academic man with field experience in ethnography, he was a rarity in British anthropology, and soon made his way to its front ranks by the same process through which he trained himself in the research orientations then dominating it: physical anthropology and folklore. Taking over as the principal investigator in Ireland for the British Association's Ethnographic Survey of the British Isles, which the anthropologists and folklorists co-sponsored in the 1890s (ACH 1895b), he soon won an appointment as lecturer in physical anthropology at Cambridge, a position which for some years he held jointly with his Dublin chair. Although he drew on his Torres Straits material for a volume on *Evolution in Art* (1895a), however, he felt that his data were inadequate for an ethnographic monograph he had outlined in the early 1890s (ACHP [1894]). To complete them, and to expand his Cambridge foothold into a "School of Anthropology," he began to plan for a second and strictly anthropological expedition (ACHP: ACH/P. Geddes 1/4/97).

For Haddon, "anthropology" still had the embracive meaning it had gained in the nineteenth-century Anglo-American evolutionary tradition, and which it might also be expected to have for a field naturalist, to whom the behavior, cries, and physical characteristics of animals were all part of a single observational syndrome. Aware, however, that some areas of anthropological inquiry had developed a technical elaboration beyond the limitations of his own competence, and anxious to introduce the methods of experimental psychology to accurately "gauge the mental and sensory capacities of primitive peoples," Haddon took as his model the great nineteenth-century multidisciplinary maritime exploring expeditions—on the basis of one of which Moseley had made his reputation and won his position at Oxford (Moseley 1879). He therefore sought "the co-operation of a staff of colleagues, each of whom had some special qualification," so that they could divide the labor of anthropological inquiry, one doing physical measurement, another psychological testing, another linguistic analysis, another sociology, and so forth (1901:viii).

As it happened, Haddon ended up with three experimental psychologists. His first choice had been his Cambridge colleague W. H. R. Rivers, who after early training in medicine had come under the influence of the neurologist Hughlings Jackson and gone on to study experimental psychology in Germany. Upon his return, Rivers was asked by Foster to lecture on the physiology of the sense organs at Cambridge, and there introduced the first course of instruction in experimental psychology in Britain (Langham 1981; Slobodin 1978). Unwilling at first to leave England, Rivers proposed his student Charles Myers to take his place; another student, William McDougall, volunteered himself before Rivers decided after all to come along (ACHP: WHR/ACH 11/25/97; WM/ACH 5/26/97). At Codrington's suggestion, Haddon had been working since 1890 on his linguistic data with Sydney Ray, a specialist in Melanesian languages who made his living as a London schoolteacher, but who managed now to get an unpaid leave (RHC/ACH 4/9/90; SR/ACH 6/6/97). Haddon's own student Anthony Wilkin—still an undergraduate—was recruited to handle the photography and assist with physical anthropology (AW/ACH 1/27/98). Charles Seligman, a doctor friend of Myers and McDougall who also volunteered his services, rounded out the group as specialist in native medicine (CGS/ACH 10/28/97).

Supported by money from the University, various scientific societies, and the British and Queensland governments, the members of the expedition arrived by commercial steamer in the Torres Straits late in April, 1898. They all began work on Murray (Mer) Island in the eastern straits, where the three psychologists continued testing the natives until late August, when Myers and McDougall went off as advance guard for research in Sarawak, to which the expedition had been invited by Rajah Brooke (at the instigation of district officer Charles Hose). Within three weeks of their arrival on Mer, however, Haddon, Ray, Wilkin, and Seligman were off for a two-month trip to Port Moresby and several nearby districts on the Papuan coast. Leaving Seligman to work northwest along the mainland, the other three rejoined Rivers on Mer late in July. Early in September all four sailed from Mer to meet Seligman in the Kiwai district, where they left Ray to work on linguistics, while the others went southwest for a month's work on Mabuaig. Late in October, Rivers and Wilkin left for England, while Haddon, Ray, and Seligman took a three-week jaunt to Saibai and several smaller islands, and then back to the Cape York Peninsula, whence they departed in late November for four months' work in Sarawak and Borneo (ACH 1901:xiii–xiv).

Detailing the itinerary is to the point, since it was on the basis of this rather hurried research, carried on entirely in pidgin English, that there were to be produced eventually six large volumes of ethnographic data—not to mention Haddon's popular narrative account (1901), materials incorporated into later books by Seligman on *The Melanesians of British New Guinea* (1910) and by Hose and McDougall on *The Pagan Tribes of Borneo* (1912), and numerous journal articles. Of course, Haddon drew also on materials he had collected in 1888, but much of his ethnography was frankly carried on at second hand: he culled extensively from missionary and travel accounts, and relied heavily on material provided by traders, missionaries, and government employees, either on the spot, or in his extensive subsequent ethnography-by-mail (ACHP:passim). His most important ethnographic intermediary, a government schoolmaster named John Bruce who had lived for a decade on Mer, was the acknowledged source of perhaps half of the information recorded in the volume on Mer sociology and religion (ACH ed. 1908:xx). This is not to minimize the labors of Haddon and his colleagues, who surely produced a large amount of data in relatively short ethnographic episodes (including, one may note, some of the very earliest ethnographic cinematography [Brigard 1975]), and who at many points evidenced a considerable thoughtfulness and sensitivity about problems of ethnographic method. It is simply to emphasize that there was still some distance from Torres Straits to fieldwork in the classic anthropological mode.

OBSERVING THE STONE AGE AT FIRST HAND
IN AUSTRALIA

Spencer's ethnography is much closer in style to that of later social anthropology. Like Haddon's, however, it developed as a deviation from zoological research. While still at Oxford, Spencer had attended Tylor's lectures, watched him demonstrate the making of stone tools, and helped Moseley and Tylor begin the installation of the Pitt Rivers collection of material culture in a new annex to the University Museum (WBSP: WBS/H. Govitz 2/18/84; 6/ 21/85). During his early years at Melbourne, Spencer was too preoccupied with teaching biology for research of any sort, and when he joined the Horn Expedition to the Central Australian desert in 1894, it was as zoologist—the anthropological work being delegated to E. C. Stirling, a lecturer in physiology at Adelaide. Stirling, however, was more interested in physical anthropology and material culture than in Australian marriage classes, and he seems not to have risen to the opportunity when at Alice Springs the expedition came upon the local equivalent of Haddon's Murray schoolmaster (Stirling 1896). Frank Gillen was an outgoing Irish republican who for twenty years had served as station master of the transcontinental telegraph and "subprotector" of the local aborigines. Although he habitually referred to them as "niggers," and to fieldwork as "niggering," Gillen got on very well with the Arunta, and had already been collecting information on their customs, a portion of which was published in the report of the expedition (Gillen 1896). He did not get along so well with Stirling, but Gillen took to Spencer, and the two became fast friends—despite Gillen's occasional irritation when Spencer reproved his racial epithets (Gillen once berated Spencer for his own "arrogant assumption of superiority so characteristic of your Nigger-assimilating race" [WBSP: FG/WBS 1/31/96]).

On returning from central Australia, Spencer put Gillen in touch with Fison, the leading authority on Australian marriage classes, who by this time had retired to Melbourne (WBSP: FG/WBS 8/30/95). Soon, Spencer and Gillen had joined forces for further research—Spencer writing from Melbourne to pose evolutionary questions about marriage classes; Gillen writing back with the ethnographic data he obtained. Gillen, however, soon became dissatisfied with what he felt was "only a splendid verification" of work previously done by Fison and Howitt (1880). Complaining that "getting at the 'why' of things is utterly hopeless" because "when driven into a corner they always take refuge in the alcheringa," Gillen reported to Spencer that he was "on the track of a big ceremony called Engwura" (7/14/96). By offering the rations necessary to support a gathering of far-flung clansmen, he was able, "after much palaver," to convince the Arunta elders to hold the great periodic initiation ceremony one more time (8/n.d./96).

When Spencer arrived in November 1896, Gillen introduced him as his younger classificatory brother, thereby entitling him to membership in the same Witchity Grub totem to which Gillen himself belonged. Fison and Howitt, as great Oknirabata (men of influence) in southeastern Australian tribes, and ultimate recipients and judges of the information to be collected, were assigned to the lizard and wildcat totems, on the basis of sketch portraits drawn by the two ethnographers (WBSP: FG/WBS 2/23/97). Although Gillen had expected the ceremonies to last only a week, they went on for three months, during which he and Spencer lived at or near the Arunta camp, observing the ceremonies, discussing with the natives (in pidgin and Gillen's somewhat limited Arunta) the associated myths and religious beliefs (Spencer & Gillen 1899). Their racial attitudes and evolutionary theoretical assumptions seem not to have inhibited a considerable degree of empathetic identification: finally discovering the profound religious significance of the churingas, and assimilating aboriginal belief to his own lost Roman Catholicism, Gillen expressed bitter regret for his previous casual treatment of these sacred objects (7/30/97).

When the ceremonies ended, Spencer and Gillen had a wealth of ethnographic detail about native ritual life of a sort that armchair anthropologists had never previously experienced. Frazer, who soon became Spencer's own mentor-by-correspondence, had never felt himself so close to the Stone Age (1931:3; Marett & Penniman eds. 1932). But despite the evolutionary framework in which it had been conceived and into which it was received, the monograph that appeared in 1899 was recognizably "modern" in its ethnographic style. Rather than running through the categories of Notes and Queries or some other armchair questionnaire, The Native Tribes of Central Australia was given focus by a totalizing cultural performance. Coming at a point when evolutionary theory was already somewhat in disarray, and offering data on totemism that conflicted with received assumption, it had tremendous impact. Malinowski suggested in 1913 that half of the anthropological theory written since had been based upon it, and all but a tenth heavily influenced by it (1913c).

Malinowski no doubt also recognized an ethnographic style that was closer to his own than Haddon's—whose expedition had not yet returned from the Torres Straits when Native Tribes was published. Its status as an ethnographic innovation (and perhaps an alternative model: the ethnographic "team") was compromised, however, by Spencer's failure to leave significant academic progeny. Rather than creating an anthropological school, he was incorporated into an already established line of Australian ethnologists (Mulvaney 1958, 1967). As Fison had been to Tylor, so he became one of Frazer's "men-on-the-spot." Although Frazer never left the armchair, he was a great encourager of anthropological fieldwork. For several decades he worked hard to sustain the researches of John Roscoe, a missionary among the Baganda who had responded to his questionnaire. In 1913 he even tried to get the Colonial Office to appoint Roscoe Government Anthropologist in East Africa (JGFP: JGF/JR 11/27/13; cf. Thornton n.d.). Frazer often said that the efforts of fieldworkers would long outlast his own theoretical musings. But his insistence on a sharp separation of ethnography and theory (which should "regularly and rightly be left to the comparative ethnologist" [1931:9]) ran counter to the emerging tradition of fieldworker academics, and his hermetic style prevented him from leaving academic anthropological offspring. Accepting a role as Frazer's ethnographic agent in Australia, Spencer also died heirless. Left hanging on a collateral branch off in the colonies, he was effectively removed from the myth-making process in British anthropology, where lineage relations have played a much more powerful role than in the pluralistic American academic institutional structure (Kuper 1973).

THE "INTENSIVE STUDY OF LIMITED AREAS" BEFORE THE GREAT WAR

In the meantime, Haddon and his colleagues were becoming recognized as "the Cambridge School" (Quiggin 1942:110–30). Although the early Torres Straits volumes contained data on physiological psychology, social organization, and totemism that were significant for contemporary theoretical discussions, it was less the empirical data it collected than the expedition itself as a symbol of ethnographic enterprise that established the group's reputation. And it took several years to achieve a solid institutional base in the University. Frazer's effort, shortly after the expedition's return, to memorialize the Board of General Studies for the establishment of regular instruction in ethnology produced for Haddon only a poorly paid lectureship to replace the one in physical anthropology to which W. L. Duckworth had been appointed in his absence (ACHP: JGF/ACH 10/17, 10/28/99). It was not until 1904 that a Board of Anthropological Studies was set up, and not until five years later that a Diploma course was established and Haddon given a Readership (Fortes 1953).

From the time of his return, however, Haddon busily propagandized for more anthropological "field-work" (a term, apparently derived from the discourse of field naturalists, which Haddon seems to have introduced into that of British anthropology). In his presidential addresses to the Anthropological Institute and in popular articles, he spoke of the pressing need of "our Cinderella Science" for "fresh investigations in the field" carried on by men trained as "field-anthropologists" (1903b:22). Warning against the "rapid collector," he emphasized the urgent necessity not simply to gather "specimens" but to take the time to "coax out of the native by patient sympathy" the deeper meaning of the material collected. Always inclined to view scientific work in the same spirit of rationalized cooperative endeavor that characterized his mildly socialist politics, Haddon suggested that "two or three good men should be always in the field" supported by an international council that would set research priorities (1903a:228–29). His own conception of these priorities was captured in the slogan "the intensive study of limited areas."

It is not clear, however, that Haddon meant by this the sort of intensive study that was shortly to emerge. Coming from zoology, he was oriented toward the study of "biological provinces." His proposal for a steamer expedition to Melanesia that would drop off investigators on different islands, returning to pick them up several months later, was intended to clarify the distribution and variation of forms in a region, with emphasis particularly on transitional forms and areas. His ultimate ethnological goal was still the elucidation of the "nature, origin and distribution of the races and peoples" of a particular region, and the clarification of their position in evolutionary development (1906:87). Even so, the movement was clearly toward a more focussed, extended, and intensive ethnography—and towards a distinction between "survey" and "intensive" work.

Haddon was not the only Torres Straits alumnus to contribute to the reputation of the "Cambridge School." For a number of them the expedition was either the beginning or a significant turning point in a quite distinguished career. Ray's reputation as a brilliant Melanesian linguistic scholar never managed to provide a paying alternative to his London schoolteacher's job (ACH 1939), and within two years of his return Wilkin died of dysentery contracted while doing archeological research in Egypt. McDougall and Myers, however, went on to become leaders in psychology—authoring, respectively, influential early textbook introductions to social and experimental psychology (Drever 1968; Bartlett 1959). Before leaving anthropology, Myers did further fieldwork in Egypt, and Seligman and Rivers were of course the leading field anthropologists of their generation in Britain. After Torres Straits, Seligman (teaming later with his wife Brenda) worked successively in New Guinea and Ceylon (1910, 1911; Firth 1975) before beginning a long series of investigations in the Anglo-Egyptian Sudan in 1910 (1932; Fortes 1941). Rivers went on to do research in Egypt, then among the Todas in India, and came back twice for further work in Melanesia before returning to psychology during World War I (Slobodin 1978). Though much of their own work was of what came to be called the "survey" variety, both men played a role in training a rising generation of field researchers whose work was in an increasingly more "intensive" mode—Rivers at Cambridge in cooperation with Haddon; Seligman at the London School of Economics, where he joined the

Seligman at work, Hula. "The anthropologist must relinquish his comfortable position . . .
on the verandah . . . where . . . he has been accustomed to collect statements from informants
. . . [and] . . . go out into the villages" (Malinowski 1926a:147). Courtesy University Museum
of Archaeology and Anthropology, Cambridge, England.

Anglo-Finnish sociologist Edward Westermarck, who himself did extensive
fieldwork in Morocco (1927:158–96). At Oxford, all three Torres Straits
alumni served occasionally as informal extramural ethnographic mentors to
the several fieldworkers recruited into anthropology by Marett and his colleagues in the Committee on Anthropology established in 1905 (Marett 1941).

Bronislaw Malinowski was a member of this pre–World War I group, and
in fact the last of them actually to get into the field. A. R. Radcliffe-Brown

(not yet, however, hyphenated) was the first; in his case the Torres Straits model was still in evidence, with all the functions of its divided scientific labor to be carried on by one lone investigator. Brown was actually in the field only for a portion of the two years normally listed for his Andaman expedition (1906–1908), and much of his research was apparently carried on among the "hangers-on" around the prison camp at Fort Blair. His attempt to study unacculturated Little Andamanese was frustrated by his difficulties with their language ("I ask for the word 'arm' and I get the Onge for 'you are pinching me'" [ACHP: ARB/ACH n.d.; 8/10/06]). But if his Andaman work is less notable ethnographically than for its later recasting in the mold of Durkheimian theory, it was nonetheless clearly a further step toward a more intensive fieldwork style (Radcliffe-Brown 1922; GS 1971).

The year of Brown's return saw two other young academic ethnographers off to the southwestern Pacific with Rivers on the Percy Sladen Trust Expedition. While Rivers' own work seems mostly to have been done on board the mission ship Southern Cross as it sailed from island to island, Gerald C. Wheeler (from the London School of Economics) and A. M. Hocart (from Oxford) undertook much more intensive study. Wheeler spent ten months among the Mono-Alu in the Western Solomons (1926:vii); Hocart, after working for ten weeks with Wheeler and Rivers on Eddystone Island (1922), settled in Fiji for four years, where as schoolmaster he collected a very rich body of ethnographic data (WHRP: AMH/WHR 4/16/09; cf. AMHP).

In the remaining years before the war, more than half a dozen young anthropologists left English universities for the field. Brown was back in 1910 for a year's work in Western Australia (White 1981). That same year saw Diamond Jenness, an Oxonian from New Zealand whose sister had married a missionary in the D'Entrecasteaux, off to Goodenough Island (Jenness & Ballantyne 1920). Two young Finns followed Edward Westermarck to England to work under Haddon's tutelage in "the intensive study of limited areas" (GS 1979a): Gunnar Landtman went to New Guinea for two years to explore in depth the Kiwai area Haddon and his colleagues had surveyed in 1898 (Landtman 1927); Rafael Karsten worked among three tribes of the Bolivian Gran Chaco in 1911 and 1912 (Karsten 1932). The group included also two Oxford-trained women: Barbara Freire-Marreco, who worked among the Pueblo in the American Southwest (Freire-Marreco 1916), and Marie Czaplička (another Polish emigre) who spent a strenuous year on the Arctic Circle in Siberia working among the Tungus (Czaplička 1916). And when Malinowski went to the southeastern Papuan coast to follow up another Torres Straits survey in the fall of 1914, yet another offspring of the Cambridge School, John Layard, was settling in for two years' work in Atchin off the coast of Malekula (1942).

Thus by the outbreak of the Great War it could already be said that fieldwork was to anthropology "as the blood of martyrs is to the Roman Catholic Church" (Seligman, as quoted in Firth 1963:2). The failure of these other early "intensive studies" to figure more prominently in the myth-history of British anthropology (Richards 1939) is perhaps in part a reflection of biographical accident and institutional circumstance. Both Karsten and Jenness were soon caught up in further "intensive" (and extended) studies in quite different (and difficult) areas—among the Peruvian Jibaro and the Canadian Eskimo, respectively (Karsten 1935; Jenness 1922–23). Landtman's fieldnotes were actually lost in shipwreck; it was only by hiring a diver that he was able to salvage the trunk that contained them (Landtman 1927:ix). Layard returned from Malekula to suffer an extended incapacitation from mental distress (Langham 1981:204). Hocart came back from Fiji to serve four years as captain on active duty in France (Needham 1967). Czaplička died young in 1921 (Marett 1921). Although several of them had successful careers, none of them (save, belatedly, Radcliffe-Brown) established himself in British academic life. Jenness emigrated to Canada, where he eventually succeeded Edward Sapir as director of the anthropological division of the Canadian Geological Survey (Swayze 1960). Karsten and Landtman returned to take up professorial positions in Finland (NRC 1938:157). Hocart, an unsuccessful competitor of Radcliffe-Brown's for the chair in anthropology at Sydney (BMPL: Seligman/BM 3/18/24), came no closer to a major academic position than the chair in sociology at Cairo (Needham 1967). Layard became involved in Jungian psychology (Layard 1944); Wheeler, the co-author with Hobhouse and Ginsberg of the *Material Culture of Primitive Peoples* (1915), seems to have left anthropology for the translation of travel accounts from the Danish (ACHP: CW/ACH 12/23/39). Even Malinowski had trouble finding a place in academic life; as late as 1921 he was considering returning to Poland (BMPL: Seligman/BM 8/30/21), and it was only with Seligman's help (including a quiet subvention of his salary) that he was able to establish himself at the London School of Economics (CGS/BM 1921–24).

Something more than delayed or institutionally marginal careers would seem to be involved, however, in the lapsed remembrance of these other academic ethnographers of Malinowski's generation. Although some of them (notably Hocart) are revealed in their fieldnotes as extremely sensitive and reflective practical methodologists (AMHP:reel 9, passim), their early monographs did not present them as self-conscious ethnographic innovators. The closest approximation to Malinowski's *Argonauts* is Landtman's flat-footedly descriptive (and rather cumbrously titled) *Kiwai Papuans of British New Guinea: A Nature-Born Instance of Rousseau's Ideal Community* (1927). Insofar as one can infer from its photographic representation, and from his long letters to Haddon from the field, Landtman's ethnographic situation seems roughly analogous to that of Malinowski in the Trobriands. But although he recorded observational data, Landtman conceived his method primarily in terms of working closely with individual (and paid) informants (or, more aptly in one letter to Haddon, "teachers" [ACHP: GL/ACH 8/28/10]). Although he did learn some Kiwai, and wrote a perceptive little essay on the nature of pidgin as a language in its own right (1927:453–61), the many quoted passages in his ethnography make it clear that he worked primarily in the latter tongue. His efforts, nonetheless, were favorably viewed by the Kiwai ("this white man he another kind, all same me fellow" [ACHP: GL/ACH 4/4/11]), and ultimately received Malinowski's imprimatur as well. If Malinowski failed to mention in his review (1929b) that this "master of the modern sociological method in fieldwork" had entered the field five years before his own arrival in the Trobriands, his neglect was perhaps understandable. By this time Professor of Anthropology at the London School of Economics, Malinowski had succeeded to Haddon and Rivers as the leading exponent of the "intensive study of limited areas." With *Argonauts* by then five years in print, the transformation of a research strategy into a methodological myth had already been accomplished.

RIVERS AND THE "CONCRETE" METHOD

To place Malinowski's achievement in context, however, it is necessary to look more closely at the evolution of "intensive study." If the actual ethnographic practice of the initiates of the Cambridge School is only indirectly accessible, we can say with some certainty what "intensive study" was intended to be, because the man who did the most to define it published, on the eve of Malinowski's departure for the field, several fairly explicit statements of what such work involved. That man was not Haddon, of course, but Rivers. Coming to ethnology from experimental psychology—one of the more methodologically explicit areas of the human sciences—Rivers brought with him a high degree of self-consciousness about problems of method; but he also possessed an uninhibited (Mauss said "intrepid") explanatory imagination (1923), and was quite capable of pursuing a pet hypothesis well beyond the limits to which rigorous method could carry him. As manifested in the far-fetched migration-theories of his *History of Melanesian Society* (1914a), and in his subsequent association with the hyperdiffusionism of William Perry and Grafton Elliot Smith, the latter tendency was seriously to compromise his historical reputation (Langham 1981:118–99). But during the decade or so before his death in 1922, he was the single most influential British anthropologist. Haddon described him in 1914 as "the greatest field investigator of primitive sociology there has ever been" (ACHP: ACH Rept. Sladen Trustees), and his "concrete method" provided for Malinowski, as for many others, the exemplar of sound ethnographic methodology.

Rivers' methodological contributions tend in disciplinary memory to be subsumed within a rather narrow conception of the "genealogical method" he developed in Torres Straits, as if all he provided was a convenient (and some would now say questionable [Schneider 1968:13–14]) means for gathering kinship data. For Rivers, however, the study of kinship was a derived advantage, and by no means marked the limits of the usefulness of genealogies. Although he was not the first ethnographer to collect them, Rivers' interest seems to have stemmed from his psychological work, rather than from any ethnographic precursors. His model was apparently the research into human heredity carried on by the polymathic psychologist/statistician/eugenicist Sir Francis Galton, who as anthropometrist was also one of the leading figures in British anthropology (Pearson 1924:334–425). Prior to departing for the Torres Straits, Rivers had consulted with Galton (FGP: WHR/FG 1/4/97), and his original goal in collecting genealogies was much the same as that which had previously motivated Galton's *Inquiries into Human Faculty* (1883): "to discover whether those who were closely related resembled one another in their reactions to the various psychological and physiological tests" (WHR 1908:65). Upon realizing, however, that the genealogical memories of the islanders went back as far as three or even five generations, Rivers "with the stimulus of Dr. Haddon's encouragement" began to collect the data for its potential sociological utility as well (1900:74–75).

Using only a few basic English categories ("father," "mother," "child," "husband," "wife"), Rivers tried in pidgin English, sometimes clarified (or further complicated) by a native interpreter, to get from each informant the personal names and marital connections of his parents, siblings, children, and grand-relatives: "what name wife belong him?", "what piccaninny he got?"; making sure that the terms were used in their "real" or "proper" English (i.e., biological) sense, and did not elicit some classificatory or adoptive relative—"he proper father?", "he proper mother?" (ACH 1901:124–25). In the context of a later sophistication as to the ambiguities of social and biological kinship, and the problematic character of all such ethnographic elicitation, the image of Rivers' ethnography-in-process given to us by Haddon is likely itself to elicit a smile. Who knows just what meaning "proper" conveyed in the semantics of pidgin English as applied to the categories of Mabuaig kinship? (Howard 1981). To Rivers, however, the method seemed self-correcting against error or even deliberate deception, because the same set of relationships could be elicited on separate occasions (and even by different observers) from different informants in the same (or overlapping) genealogies (1899). Thus even after Rivers had returned to England, the "chief" of Mabuaig, anxious to draw up his own record "for the use and guidance of his descendants," created another version (recorded and sent along by the local trader) which save for "minor discrepancies" confirmed information previously collected by Rivers (1904:126). At the very least, there would seem to have been some agreement among informants as to what "proper" meant.

Rivers, however, felt no need for such benefit of doubt. Despite occasional acknowledgments of the difficulties of "exact" translation, he managed to convince himself that he was dealing with "bodies of dry fact . . . as incapable of being influenced by bias, conscious or unconscious, as any subject that can be imagined" (1914a, 1:3–4). Furthermore, they provided the basis for a "scientific" approach to the reconstruction of the history of human social forms. Although in principle the genealogical method required the exclusion of native kinship categories, which tended to obscure the "real" biological relationships, Rivers' attention was inevitably focussed on the systematic aspect of the native terms he was excluding. Thus when it came to summarizing the various personal-name genealogies for all the Mabuaig Islanders, he used native kin terms to draw up "the genealogy of an ideal family" which illustrated a kinship system "of the kind known as classificatory" (1904:129). In this context he was quickly led to the "rediscovery" (Fortes 1969:3) of Lewis H. Morgan's Systems of Consanguinity (1871; cf. WHR 1907)—if such a term is appropriate for assumptions that had been the common currency of Australian ethnography from the time of Fison and Howitt. Rivers became committed to the idea that the elemental social structure of any group would be systematically revealed in its kinship terminology. While later writers have emphasized the utility of paradigmatic models of such systems for comparative purposes (Fortes 1969:24), Rivers himself was more impressed that he had found an area of human behavior where "the principle of determinism applies with a rigor and definiteness equal to that of any of the exact sciences"—since "every detail" of systems of relationship could be traced back to some prior "social condition arising out of the regulation of marriage and sexual relations" (1914b:95). Even after he had abandoned his early "crude evolutionary point of view" for the "ethnological [historical] analysis of culture" (1911:131–32), he continued to feel that his methods provided the basis for reliable reconstructions of major historical sequences of human social development (1914a).

Our concern here, however, is less with how Rivers' "invention" of the genealogical method led to a set of theoretical concerns which, subsequently dehistoricized by Radcliffe-Brown, were to be central to later British social anthropology (GS 1971). It is rather, insofar as it can be kept separate, with his somewhat paradoxical contribution to the development of ethnographic method. On the one hand, Rivers' elaboration of the genealogical method offered a staunchly positivistic approach, a kind of "quick methodological fix," by which scientifically trained observers, "with no knowledge of the language and with very inferior interpreters," could "in comparatively short time" collect information that had remained hidden from the most observant long-term European residents, even to the point of laying bare the basic structure of the indigenous society (1910:10). The model here is Rivers on the deck of the Southern Cross interrogating an informant through an interpreter, during one of the brief stops of its mission circuit. But there were other aspects of his ethnographic experience that led toward a more sophisticated longer-term "intensive study," one that might enable the scientific observer to achieve something analogous to the more empathetic, extensively detailed, and broadly penetrating knowledge that had previously characterized the very best missionary ethnographers.

In his more confidently positivistic moments, Rivers tended to see the genealogical (generalized as the "concrete") method as the solution to almost every ethnographic problem. It provided a framework in which all members of a local group could be located, and to which could be attached a broad range of ethnographic information on "the social condition of each person included in the pedigrees"—data on residence, totems, and clan membership, as well as miscellaneous behavioral and biographical information (1910:2). In addition to its utility in collecting sociological data, however, it could be used in the study of migrations, of magic and religion, of demography, of physical anthropology, and even of linguistics. Most important, it enabled the observer "to study abstract problems, on which the savage's ideas are vague, by means of concrete facts, of which he is a master" (1900:82). It even made it possible "to formulate laws regulating the lives of people which they have probably never formulated themselves, certainly not with the clearness and definiteness which they have to the mind trained by a more complex civilization" (1910:9). Not only could the observing scientist delineate the actual social laws of a particular group, he could detect also how far its ostensible social laws "were being actually followed in practice" (1910:6). The power of the genealogical method was attested by independent observers—"men on the spot" such as G. Orde Brown, who after telling Rivers that kinship data were unobtainable among a particular Kenyan group, was urged to try Rivers' method: "and now I find that he was right, and that I was completely wrong, in spite of my then three years experience of these people" (ACHP: GOB/ACH 2/8/13). It was also evident in Rivers' fieldwork, which although for the most part frankly of the survey variety, did indeed provide a large amount of data in a relatively short time.

No doubt Rivers' insouciant assurance of the power of positivistic thinking was buttressed both by traditional ethnocentric assumptions about the evolution of the capacity for abstract thought and by the experimental psychological studies he carried on in these terms (Langham 1981:56–64). But it is worth noting that at some points he interpreted savage concreteness as due to lexical rather than cognitive deficiency, and suggested that "he certainly cannot be expected to appreciate properly the abstract terms of the language of his visitor" (1910:9). At such moments, one feels the pull of Rivers' actual experience toward a somewhat different ethnographic style, which while ultimately perhaps no less scientistic, implied a greater sensitivity to the difficulties of cultural translation and the necessity for long-term intensive study to overcome them.

Rivers did attempt one piece of fieldwork that verged on such "intensive study." In 1902, he went to the Nilgiri Hills of southern India to study the Todas, whose polyandry had long made them an important ethnographic case for the evolutionary paradigm (Rooksby 1971). Although his difficulties in fitting Toda data within an evolutionary framework seem to have been a factor in his subsequent "conversion" to diffusionism, Rivers presented his results merely as a "demonstration of anthropological method" in the "collecting" and "recording" of ethnographic material (1906:v). He planned only a six-month stay, and worked through interpreters, but his brief methodological introduction suggests that he intended his work as an "intensive study." His many interpolated comments on how he obtained particular bits of information indicate that most of his accounts of Toda ceremony were narratives obtained through informants in "public" morning and "private" afternoon sessions. But he made it a point to obtain as many independently corroborating accounts as he could and to pay only for an informant's time rather than for particular items of information (7–17). He also moved about observing for himself, and in at least one instance was allowed to witness one of the most sacred Toda ceremonies. Within days, however, the wife of the man who arranged this died. This and similar misfortunes befalling two other Toda "guides" were ascribed by their diviners to "the anger of the gods because their secrets had been revealed to the stranger." Rivers' sources of information ran dry, and he came away from India "knowing that there were subjects of which [he] had barely touched the fringe," and suspecting that there were "far more numerous deficiencies" of which he was not even aware (2–3; cf. Langham 1981:134–35, where Rivers' increasing "ethnographic empathy" is linked to the experience of his 1908 expedition).

THE 1912 REVISION OF *NOTES AND QUERIES*

When the British Association established a committee to prepare a revised edition of *Notes and Queries* the year after *The Todas* was published, Rivers, Haddon, and Myers (joined later by Seligman) were all members. The publication that eventuated in 1912, apparently after some conflict between the young turks and the old guard (Urry 1972:51), was in many respects a new departure. The book was ostensibly still directed to "travellers" and non-anthropologists who might "supply the information which is wanted for the scientific study of anthropology at home" (BAAS 1912:iii–iv). Despite the urging of "friendly critics" who had argued the virtues of a "narrative form," many sections still reflected the "old lists of 'leading questions'" that had characterized the three Tylorian editions. Nevertheless, the "friendly critics" had clearly had a major impact. J. L. Myres, the Oxford archaeologist who was the only contributor to author more pages, described Rivers' contribution as "a revelation" that set a new "standard for workmanship in the field" (Urry 1972:51). It is quite evident that the "workers in the field" for whom Rivers wrote, although lacking perhaps an "advanced knowledge in anthropology," were not casual travellers but people in a position to undertake "intensive study."

The centerpiece of the whole volume, Rivers' "General Account of Method," may be regarded as a programmatic systematization of the ethnographic experience of the "Cambridge School." The distinction between "intensive study" and "survey" was here recast in linguistic terms. Because (as it was suggested elsewhere in the volume) "language is our only key to the correct and complete understanding of the life and thought of a people" (BAAS 1912:186), the investigator's first duty was "to acquire as completely as possible" a knowledge of their language (109). To that end the volume incorporated "Notes on Learning a New Language" by the American linguistic anthropologist J. P. Harrington—although Rivers still felt it was better to rely on an interpreter, supplemented by native terms, than on "an inadequate knowledge of the language" (124). While Rivers gave special prominence to the genealogical method, its justification was now cast in rather different terms: by enabling the inquirer "to use the very instrument which the people themselves use in dealing with their social problems," it made it possible to study "the formation and nature of their social classifications," excluding "entirely the influence of civilised categories" (119).

Although the nature of "the thought of people of the lower culture" was still used to justify Rivers' first rule of method ("the abstract should always be approached through the concrete"), he now placed great emphasis on the problem of category differences: "native terms must be used wherever there is the slightest chance of a difference of category," and "the greatest caution must be used in obtaining information by means of direct questions, since it is probable that such questions will inevitably suggest some civilised category" (110–11). Similarly, special attention must be paid to volunteered information, even if it interrupted one's train of thought: instead of complaining of the difficulty of keeping an informant to the point, the investigator should recognize that "the native also has a point, probably of far more interest than his own" (112).

Rivers' "investigator" was still more an "inquirer" than an "observer," but he was strongly encouraged to get the corroboration of "two or more independent witnesses," and cautioned also that disagreements among them were "one of the most fruitful sources of knowledge"—"a man who will tell you nothing spontaneously often cannot refrain from correcting false information" (113). Wherever possible he was to supplement verbal accounts with the actual witnessing of ceremonies, and "to take advantage of any events of social importance which occur during your stay," since "the thorough study of a concrete case in which social regulations have been broken may give more insight . . . than a month of questioning" (116). Last but not least, the inquirer was to develop "sympathy and tact," without which "it is certain that the best kind of work will never be done." Although urged on grounds of expedience ("people of rude culture are so unaccustomed to any such evidence of sympathy with their ways of thinking and acting" that it would "go far to break down their reticence"), Rivers cautioned that natives would be "quick to recognize whether this sympathy was real and not feigned" (125).

To suggest that the new ethnographic orientation embodied in the 1912 *Notes and Queries* clearly reflected the field experience of a new breed of academician-cum-ethnographer is not to say that it was unrelated to developments in anthropological theory. A sense of crisis in evolutionary theory had been evident in Great Britain as early as the mid-1890s, when Tylor, responding to Boas' critique of "The Comparative Method of Anthropology," had suggested the need for "tightening the logical screw" (GS 1968b:211). The malaise was particularly evident in relation to the study of religion, where Andrew Lang's defection from the Tylorian camp (1901), R. R. Marett's interpretation of Codrington's Melanesian "mana" as a pre-animistic religious phenomenon (Marett 1900), and the debates precipitated by Spencer and Gillen's Arunta data (Frazer 1910) all contributed to a strong feeling that something was wrong with both the categories and the data in terms of which armchair anthropologists were interpreting primitive religion. This discomfort was reflected in the revised *Notes and Queries* in an essay by Marett (never himself a field ethnographer) on "the study of magico-religious facts" (BAAS 1912:251–60). The hyphenation was both a reflection of the fact that "framers of general theory" were "in dispute" and an exhortation to the ethnographer to collect data from the "point of view" of primitive folk, "uncoloured by his own" (251). Eschewing questionnaires, Marett argued that "the real scheme of topics . . . must be framed by the observer himself to suit the social conditions of a given tribe" (255). The observer must not ask "why" but "what," focussing on the rite in all its complex concrete detail—"at the same time keeping at arm's length our own theological concepts, as well as our anthropological concepts, which are just as bad, since they have been framed by us to make us understand savagery, not by savagery to enable it to understand itself" (259). In this context, then, the "concrete method" was not simply a means of getting at abstractions that the savage could not himself articulate, but a way of collecting "concrete facts" uncontaminated by European evolutionary abstractions that had come to seem more than a bit problematic.

As a kind of footnote to the new edition of *Notes and Queries*, Rivers in 1913 published a statement on the needs of ethnography in which he further elaborated certain aspects of "intensive study" that may have seemed inappropriate to argue in the earlier collaborative effort. In specifying just what type of anthropological research was most pressingly urgent, Rivers narrowed and refined the conception of intensive study that had emerged in the work of the Cambridge School. On the one hand, he explicitly subordinated certain traditional concerns of a general anthropology, either because their data were less immediately endangered (in the case of archeology) or because pursuing them risked destroying the rapport necessary for intensive sociological study (in the case of material culture and physical anthropology [WHR 1913:5–6, 13]). Similarly, because of the "disturbance and excitement produced among natives by the various activites of the different members of an expedition," he now urged that ethnographic work should be carried on by single investigators "working alone" (10–11). As further justification, he argued that the labor of ethnography should be undivided because its subject matter was indivisible. In a rude culture (and there are several indications that he now thought of culture in the plural), the domains civilized men designated as politics, religion, education, art, and technology were interdependent and inseparable, and it followed that "specialism in the collection of ethnographic details must be avoided at all costs" (11). Rivers did insist, however, on the specialization of the ethnographer's role itself: because government officials and missionaries had little time after the performance of their regular duties, because they lacked appropriate training, and because their occupations brought them into conflict with native ideas and customs (even, in the case of missionaries, to the point of embracing the "duty to destroy" them), Rivers now felt that ethnography was best carried on by "private workers," preferably with special training or experience "in exact methods in other sciences" (9–10). Such were the preconditions of "intensive work," which Rivers defined as that "in which the worker lives for a year or more among a community of perhaps four or five hundred people and studies every detail of their life and culture; in which he comes to know every member of the community personally; in which he is not content with generalized information,

but studies every feature of life and custom in concrete detail and by means of the vernacular language" (7).
That, one might suggest, was just what Malinowski did in the Trobriands. Malinowski's enactment of Rivers' program was, however, more than a matter of taking the new *Notes and Queries* into the field and following instructions. It involved a shift in the primary locus of investigation, from the deck of the mission ship or the verandah of the mission station to the teeming center of the village, and a corresponding shift in the conception of the ethnographer's role, from that of inquirer to that of participant "in a way" in village life. It also required a shift in theoretical orientation, since as long as "the aim of anthropology [was] to teach us the history of mankind" (WHR 1913:5) the bustle of village activity could have only mediate rather than intrinsic interest. And finally, it required not only enactment but embodiment—or precisely the sort of mythic transformation Malinowski provided.

MALINOWSKI FROM THE BRITISH MUSEUM TO MAILU

Before his mythopoeic ethnographic experience in the Trobriands, Malinowski himself had served an apprenticeship as armchair anthropologist. His introduction to anthropology had in fact come when, during a period of medically enforced withdrawal from chemical and physical research, he read (or had read to him by his mother [JGFP: BM/JGF 5/25/23]) the second edition of Frazer's *Golden Bough* (1900). Complicated as it is by a complexly motivated rhetorical inflation, Malinowski's debt to Frazer has been a matter of debate (Jarvie 1964; Leach 1966; cf. BM 1923, 1944). He later spoke of having been immediately "bound to the service of Frazerian anthropology"—"a great science, worthy of as much devotion as any of her elder and more exact sister studies" (1926a:94). There is no doubt a link between the epistemological concerns of Malinowski's doctoral dissertation at the University of Cracow (Paluch 1981) and the warp threads of magic, religion, and science on which Frazer wove his rich tapestry of transfigured ethnographic detail. But Malinowski had chosen Frazer as a "masterpiece" of English literary style, and his more convincing acknowledgments reflect his appreciation of Frazer's compelling representation of exotic but generically human experience within a vividly recreated landscape (JGFP: BM/JGF 10/25/17)—the "scene/act ratio" which, according to the literary critic Stanley Hyman (1959:201, 225, 254), provided the "imaginative core" of Frazer's work, and was later strikingly evident in Malinowski's *Argonauts*.

From a literary viewpoint Malinowski's anthropology may be regarded as a seedling of the *Golden Bough*. And there are no doubt also substantive and even theoretical concerns in which the bond to Frazerian anthropology is evident (BM 1944). But from a more general methodological and theoretical viewpoint, the differences are clear enough. Carrying forward the tradition of armchair speculation from within the very precincts of the Cambridge School, Frazer defended his questionnaire in the face of Rivers' "concrete method" (JGFP: JGF/J. Roscoe 5/12/07). During the decade after 1900 when his (somewhat disapproving) master Tylor had begun to withdraw into senescence, theoretical debate in British anthropology swirled around the issues Frazer used to give thematic focus to his literary efforts: the nature of primitive religion, and particularly the problem of totemism—on which Frazer by 1910 had offered three different "theories," all of which were incorporated into his four-volume compendium on *Totemism and Exogamy* (cf. Hyman 1959:214–15). By that time, the theoretical malaise in British anthropology was becoming acute. One consequence was a generally heightened sense of ethnographic urgency—the previously noted feeling that received ethnographic categories were somehow inadequate, and that what was needed was a new body of data unencumbered by theoretical assumption. But evolutionary theory itself had by now been called into question. Rivers was shortly to announce his "conversion" to an "historical" diffusionary point of view (1911), and Radcliffe-Brown had already begun the Durkheimian reworking of his Andaman data which, in the context of subsequent debates with Rivers, led him to turn away from diachronic problems almost entirely (GS 1971).

At this point Malinowski, after a year at Leipzig where he studied with the psychologist Wilhelm Wundt and the economic historian Karl Bücher, came to England to study anthropology (KS 1958–60). Introduced by Haddon to Seligman, he entered the more cosmopolitan (and sociological) London School of Economics, where he became a student of both Seligman and Westermarck. Carrying on extensive library research in the British Museum, Malinowski entered actively into the ongoing discussion of totemism, starting with a critique of Frazer's interpretation of the *intichiuma* ceremony (1912), continuing with a brief review of Durkheim's *Elementary Forms* (1913b), and culminating with his still untranslated Polish publication on *Primitive Beliefs and Forms of Social Organization: A View on the Genesis of Religion with Special Respect to Totemism* (1915b). While these pieces are all still contained within the general framework of evolutionary assumption, there is another that reflects the ongoing shift from ultimate origins and long-term diachronic development toward more specifically historical or purely synchronic problems.

Regarded from a substantive point of view, Malinowski's *Family among the Australian Aborigines* (1913a) is an attempt, following the line pioneered by his teacher Westermarck (1891), to attack such evolutionary warhorses as "primitive promiscuity" and "marriage by capture," as well as the whole Morganian notion of the "classificatory system of kinship," on the basis of a systematic analysis of all the available literature from the ethnographic realm that provided evolutionists like Frazer with their type case of *truly* "primitive man." Constructively, the book is Malinowski's most Durkheimian work: his primary concern is to demonstrate the interrelation both of the idea of kinship and of the family as a social institution with "the general structure of society" (1913a:300). At the same time, it may also be regarded as a methodological exercise—another attempt to tighten Tylor's "logical screw." Malinowski shows a notable (some would say uncharacteristic) concern with the definition of analytic categories not "directly borrowed from our own society" (168). And he is even more systematically concerned with developing rigorous method in the evaluation of ethnographic evidence. In doing so, he turns to history in a quite technical and professional sense, using Langlois and Seignobos' historiographical text (1898) as a model for the treatment of the major Australian ethnographic sources by "the strict rules of historical criticism," and analyzing conflicting testimony so that future fieldwork might be focussed on key issues of fact (1913a:19). That same focus toward the field is evident in his already somewhat critical view of Durkheimian sociology, which he tended to regard as a closet philosophy hypostatizing a metaphysical "collective mind" to the neglect of the activities of real human individuals (1913b). Malinowski felt that Durkheimian interpretation was constrained by the "complete absence in our ethnographic information of any attempt to connect the data of folk-lore and the facts of sociology" (1913a:233), or as he sometimes was inclined to pose it, "social belief" and "social function"— a term which in Malinowski's often rather *un*Durkheimian usage tended to mean "actual behavior." From this point of view, the Australian monograph is not so much an armchair exercise as the prolegomenon to Malinowski's future fieldwork.

His entry into the field, however, was delayed by exigencies of funding. From 1911 on Seligman, along with Haddon and Rivers (from both of whom Malinowski also received guidance), pursued various possible fieldwork sites, including the Sudan, to which Seligman's own interests had shifted (BMPL: BM/CGS 2/22/12), and *faute de mieux*, back in Poland "among our peasants" (ACHP: BM/ACH 11/12/11). However, it was not until 1914, when the British Association met in Australia, that Seligman got Malinowski a travelling fellowship, and he received his fare to the Orient as secretary of the Association's anthropological section. His introduction to the field after the August meetings was clearly designed by Seligman to focus more intensively on the boundary region between two major ethnic groups his own earlier survey work had distinguished (1910:2, 24–25; Firth 1975). Malinowski began by working in Port Moresby with Ahuia Ova, a village constable who had served as Seligman's primary informant in conversations "held on the verandah of the house where he lived with his uncle Taubada, the old chief of Hododai" (Seligman 1910:ix; BMPL: BM/CGS 9/10/14; Williams 1939).

Malinowski quickly became dissatisfied, however, with these "ethnographic explorations," on grounds that foreshadow his later ethnographic mode: "(1) I have rather little to do with the savages on the spot, do not observe them enough and (2) I do not speak their language" (1967:13). The latter defect he seems to have remedied when he settled down for more intensive research on the island of Mailu. By the time he left in late January he was quite fluent in the lingua franca of the area (Motu)—an accomplishment sufficiently remarkable that, lest it be discredited, he felt it necessary in his published account "to explicitly boast of my facility for acquiring a conversational command of foreign languages" (1915a:501). The problem of observation "on the spot" was not so easily solved: throughout the Mailu diary, Malinowski's days begin with the phrase "went to the village." There are momentary glimpses, however, of a more intimate ethnographic style. On a trip he made in early December surveying groups along the far southeastern coast, he stayed in several villages in the *dubu* or men's house—on one occasion for three successive nights during a native feast. Although "the stench, smoke, noise of people, dogs and pigs" left him exhausted, Malinowski clearly had a sense of the ethnographic potential of a more direct involvement, and returned to Mailu resolved that he "must begin a new existence" (1967:49, 54–55).

Malinowski later suggested that the next few weeks on Mailu, when the absence of the local missionary left him "quite alone with the natives," were his most productive period on Mailu (1915a:501). One would hardly guess this from his diary, where he recounts being left with "*absolutely* nobody" for more than a week because he foolishly refused to pay the 2£ the Mailu demanded to allow him to accompany them on a trading expedition (1967:62). But one must pose against such private records of frustration some of the material from the published Mailu ethnography—which, one may note in passing, still strongly reflects the categories of the new edition of *Notes and Queries* Malinowski carried with him into the field. Recounting how he overcame difficulties in getting at "magico-religious" beliefs, Malinowski tells how at a certain point the Mailu became convinced that the deserted mission house in which he stayed was ghost-ridden. His "cook boy" and some village men who used to sleep there stopped doing so. Later, when one evening the conversation turned to ghosts, Malinowski, professing his ignorance of such matters, asked their advice, and got a great deal of information about topics previously closed to him. Generalizing in the published account, he commented: "My experience is that direct questioning of the native about a custom or belief never discloses their attitude of mind as thoroughly as the discussion of facts connected with the direct observation of a custom or with a concrete occurence, in which both parties are materially concerned" (1915a:650–52). Implicit in that last phrase was the essence of a fieldwork style significantly different from that formalized by Rivers in *Notes and Queries*.

Malinowski was by no means entirely satisfied with his Mailu research (ACHP: BM/ACH 10/15/15). Analyzing his data in Melbourne in the spring of 1915, he decided that work done alone with the natives was "incomparably more intensive than work done from white men's settlements, or even in any white man's company; the nearer one lives to a village and the more he sees actually of the natives the better" (1915a:501). The obvious conclusion was that he should live in the village. But as those nights in the *dubu* testify, total immersion was not easy for him. It has been argued that a solution was suggested to him during his brief stay on Woodlark Island early in 1915 (Wax 1972:7), where he lived "in a tent of palm leaves" only sixty meters from the village—"happy to be alone again with N. G. boys[,] particularly when I sat alone . . . gazing at the village . . . " (1967:92). The ethnographer's tent—fragile canvas artifact of civilized Europe—embodied a similar ambivalence. Pulling its flaps behind him, he could to some extent shut out the native world and retire to his novels when the strain of the very intensive study of a very limited area became too great.

THE TROBRIANDS: FROM RIDER HAGGARD
TO CONRAD

With financial support from the Australian government that had nominally interned him (Laracy 1976), Malinowski was off to the field again in June 1915. Although Seligman wanted him to go to Rossel Island to examine another of the "three points of the Massim triangle" (BMPL: CGS/BM n.d.), Malinowski set off for the Mambare district on the northern coast of New Guinea (BM/CGS 5/6/15). He decided, however, to stop on the way on Kiriwina in the Trobriands, where Seligman had once worked briefly, because they were "the leaders of the whole material and artistic culture" of the area (BM/CGS 6/13/15). Although totally "pacified" for more than a decade, the Trobriands were, compared to many island and coastal areas of New Guinea, relatively unacculturated. Malinowski arrived during the season of the *milamala* festival, the ceremonial high point of the annual cycle, and his attention was immediately engaged by the phenomena that were to be the subjects of his later monographs: the "ceremonial gardening," the "beliefs and ceremonies about the spirits," and their "peculiar and interesting" system of trading (BM/CGS 7/30/15). In the Trobriands—in contrast to the islands of the

Torres Straits—these did not have to be *recaptured* from the memories of elders, or *reconstructed* from fragmentary data surviving into the present, or *recreated* by people cajoled into performing defunct ceremonies. Here they could be directly observed. More than that, this was apparently one of those cases where there was a close "fit" between ethnographer and subject—Malinowski later contrasted the relative ease of his work in Kiriwina with difficulties he encountered elsewhere (1967:227). At the time, he was clearly captivated. When he received news of the unexpected departure of the Mambare missionary from whom he had hoped to get an ethnographic orientation, he extended his Trobriand stay, apologizing to Seligman for remaining in an area he had already covered. By mid-October, when he fired his interpreter, Malinowski already had enough Kiriwinian that for three weeks he had only used pidgin English "a sentence or so per diem." Having moved inland from the government station to the village of Omarakana, he wrote to Seligman that he was "absolutely alone amongst niggers [sic]." Denying himself both whiskey and "the other 'white man's solace,'" he was getting "such damned good stuff" that he had decided not to go to Mambare after all (9/24, 10/19/15). Save for any fortnightly "Capuan days" he may have enjoyed back on the coast in Gusaweta (1967:259), he apparently remained in Omarakana for almost six months.

This is not the place to attempt to answer all the questions raised about Malinowski's fieldwork by the "revelations" of his diaries—Joycean documents whose adequate interpretation awaits a detailed indexing and contextualization with other materials. Perhaps because they are not primarily "about" his fieldwork, they do not in any case treat his first Trobriand expedition (1967:99). The present account will depend primarily on other source materials. We know from later reflections that despite dispensing with an interpreter, Malinowski was not yet able to "follow easily conversations among the natives themselves" (1935, 1:453). We know also that he was still very much under Rivers' methodological influence: "it was my ambition to develop the principle of the 'genealogical method' into a wider and more ambitious scheme to be entitled the 'method of objective documentation'" (1935, 1:326; WHRP: BM/WHR 10/15/15). For contemporary evidence of his methodological concerns, the best source is *Baloma: The Spirits of the Dead in the Trobriands* (1916), which he wrote during the interval between his first and second Trobriand trips.

Despite the suggestion of one critic that Malinowski's (actually, Marett's) slogan was "study the ritual and not the belief" (Jarvie 1964:44), and despite his characterization as an "obsessional empiricist" (Leach 1957:120), what is striking in *Baloma* is precisely the attempt to penetrate native belief, and his insistence on the inadequacy of any uninterpreted "pure facts"—and by implication Rivers' "concrete method"—to the task (cf. Panoff 1972:43–45).

Baloma reveals Malinowski as an aggressively interactive fieldworker. In contrast to *Notes and Queries,* he defends the use of leading questions under certain circumstances (1916:264); he questions beliefs the natives take for granted (208); he suggests alternative possibilities (227–28); he forces them on apparent contradictions (167); he pushes them, as he says, "to the metaphysical wall" (236)—and is upon occasion pushed towards it himself. Rejecting the notion that it was "possible to wrap up in a blanket a certain number of 'facts as you find them' and bring them all back for the home student to generalize upon," he insists that "field work consists only and exclusively in the interpretation of the chaotic social reality, in subordinating it to general rules" (238). In at least one critical instance, this approach seems to have led Malinowski astray: his trader friend Billy Hancock later wrote him indicating that the natives never corrected an early interpretation of the reincarnation of the *Baloma* because they were afraid to "contradict the doctor" (GS 1977). But Malinowski's ethnographic style seems also to have generated a large and variegated body of data. In marked contrast to the ethnographic notes of Haddon, which contain a disproportionate amount of second-hand material, derived either from printed sources or correspondence with "men on the spot" (ACHP:passim), and with those of Rivers, which tend to have the schematic character one might expect of the "concrete method" (WHRP:passim), Malinowski's fieldnotes are richly documented in the materials of his own observation, recorded to a considerable extent in the native language (BMPL:passim).

From a substantive point of view *Baloma* is a treatise on the relation of individual to collective belief; viewed methodologically, it is an attempt to deal in a general way with the problems posed by this mass of information, and particularly with the problem of informant variation—a problem that in the positivistic Riversian mode was reduced to insignificance. How was one to synthesize as one "belief" the "always fragmentary" and "at times hopelessly inadequate and contradictory" answers to the question "How do the natives imagine the return of the *baloma?*" (1916:241) Temperamentally disinclined to allow them to contradict him rather than each other, Malinowski's solution—arrived at ex post facto in the analysis of his field data—was to distinguish between "social ideas or dogmas" (beliefs embodied in institutions, customs, rites, and myths, which, "believed and acted upon by all," were absolutely standardized), "the general behavior of the natives towards the object of a belief," and opinions or interpretations that might be offered by individuals, groups of specialists, or even the majority of the members of a community (245, 252–53). Some such distinction between cultural idea and individual opinion, often overlaid with one between "rules and regularities" and actual behavior, was characteristic of all Malinowski's later methodological prescriptions, as well as his more theoretically oriented ethnographic writings (cf. 1922:24). Often seen as anti-Durkheimian, it was anti-Riversian as well. Though it apparently privileged a customary or institutional realm where native belief was homogeneous, it gave tremendous weight to the conflict of cultural rule and individual impulse which made savage society "not a consistent logical scheme, but rather a seething mixture of conflicting principles" (1926b:121).

After a year and a half in Australia, Malinowski left for the Trobriands again late in October 1917. The fact that he returned is itself methodologically significant. Shortly after arriving back in Sydney in 1916, Malinowski was still thinking in terms of pursuing Seligman's Rossel Island project as soon as he "worked out the Trobriand material" (ACHP: BM/ACH 5/25/16). But it is clear that his understanding of the demands of "intensive study" evolved in the interim, and when official permission to visit Rossel was denied, he was free to return to Kiriwina (Laracy 1976). Writing to Frazer en route back, he noted how "whilst in the field, . . . the more elementary aspects" of many subjects "become soon so familiar they escape notice"; at the same time, "once away from the natives," memory could not take the place of "direct observation." He had therefore spent much of the Australian interim going through all his material to create a "condensed outline," which had opened "a whole series of new questions" he now needed to pursue (JGFP: BM/JGF 10/25/17).

Although he did not settle this time in Omarakana, Malinowski's return to the same area, after having left it for an extended period, may also (if the experience of many other anthropologists applies) have helped to cement more closely his relationships with Trobriand informants. These were scarcely the relationships of "social parity" that one retrospective (and distinctly American democratic) commentator has suggested are a condition of participant-observation (Wax 1972:8). Malinowski's retinue of two or three New Guinean "boys" (one of whom on at least one occasion he seems to have struck [BM 1967:250]) does indeed call up images of the colonial "petty lordship" manifest also in some of his diary fantasies (140, 167, 235). But in a stratified society like the Trobriands (where the chief sat upon a platform so commoners need not crawl upon the ground in passing [Wax 1972:5; cf. BM 1929a:32–33]), social parity—which bears a problematic relationship to understanding—is itself a rather problematic notion. That Malinowski, in return for half a tobacco stick a day, was allowed to pitch his tent in the restricted central area of Omarakana (1935, 1:41), that he was apparently addressed in terms connoting high rank (1929a:61), and doubtless did not walk bent-backed in front of his next-door neighbor, the village chief To'uluwa, may have opened up more areas of Trobriand life to him than any other readily available status—even as it also may have in some respects distorted his perspective (cf. Weiner 1976).

Malinowski at work, Omarakana. "Feeling of ownership: it is I who will describe them or create them. . . . This island, though not 'discovered' by me, is for the first time experienced artistically and mastered intellectually" (Malinowski 1967:140 [December 1, 1917], 236 [March 26, 1918]). Courtesy Mrs. Helena Wayne and the London School of Economics.

The critical issues would seem to be the mode of interaction and the quality of relationships he was able to establish. Insofar as the activity of the fieldworker may be divided into different modes (participation, observation, and interrogation [Wax 1972:12])—or perhaps more neutrally, doing, seeing, and talking), it is certainly true that Malinowski (like every other fieldworker since?) gathered more information by the last two than by the first. But one might argue that from the point of view of gathering information, participation is to some extent a contextual phenomenon—as the often very brief references to his actual fieldwork in the diary of the second Trobriand trip suggest: "I went to a garden and talked with the Teyava people of gardening and garden magic" (1967:276). In the case of frequently sparer references such as "*buritila'ulo* in Wakayse-Kabwaku" (291), it is even harder to say just what went on. That is the sole reference in the diary to a major event in his fieldwork, a competitive food-display recounted in some detail in *Coral Gar-*

dens and Their Magic (1935, 1:181–87). Although the diary indicates that a good bit of Malinowski's "talking" was in one-to-one sessions with informants compensated by tobacco, it is evident throughout his ethnographies that much of it was in the context of events he observed and ceremonies at which he "assisted"—a vague term, perhaps reflecting the meaning of the French *assister*, but appropriately chosen by Malinowski to imply a certain degree of participation. There were many situations in which his participation was severely limited indeed. His diary reveals him as always left on the beach when the natives left on a Kula expedition (1967:234, 245)—and *Argonauts* suggests why: when an expedition Malinowski had been allowed to join late in 1915 was forced back by adverse winds, To'uluwa attributed this bad luck to his presence (1922:479). But if he was sometimes forced to rely on simple question and answer, Malinowski clearly regarded this as a distinctly inferior style of work. Although he felt that concrete documentation and the collection of texts were essential components of a correct style, his methodological ideal—frequently realized in practice—remained that established in Mailu: discussion with one or more informants of a mutually (if differently) experienced activity or event. Only thus could one "integrate native behavior into native significance" (1935, 1:86).

As far as the quality of his relationships with the Trobrianders is concerned, it is a serious mistake to judge these simply on the basis of a selective reading of the more negative sections of the diary (Hsu 1979). Without minimizing the pervasive tone of loneliness, frustration, and aggression or the evolutionary racial terms in which these feelings were often expressed, without denying the explicit racial epithets,[2] one must keep in mind, as I have argued elsewhere (1968a), that the diary functioned as a safety valve for

2. On the basis of the facsimile page of the Polish original reproduced as frontispiece of the published translation of Malinowski's diaries (BM 1967), it has been argued (Leach 1980) that "nigger" is an inappropriate translation of the actual term Malinowski used: *nigrami*. I was assured by my one-time student Edward Martinek, who did research on Malinowski in a number of archives in Cracow, Poland, that *nigrami* is not properly a Polish word. What Malinowski seems to have done is to render the English racial epithet phonetically ("nigr") and add the Polish ending "-ami," which I am told by Norbert Guterman, the translator of the diaries, indicates the instrumental case (cf. KS 1982). That Malinowski knew and used the English epithet at the time of the Trobriand diary is evident in several sources quoted in this paper. The significance of his usage is a complex matter (cf. GS 1968b). It is certainly not to be taken casually as "proof" of thoroughgoing racism. But neither will it do to argue that the word did not then have derogatory racial meaning. Spencer's reaction to Gillen's usage suggests otherwise. An unpublished fragment of Haddon's from the 1890s speaks of "niggers" as "a term of reproach which implies a hatred and superciliousness similar to that with which the Jews regard the Gentiles, the Greeks the Barbarians, and which the Chinese still hold for 'foreign devils'" (ACHP:[1894]). Indeed, as early as 1858 Sir Henry Maine reproved those who "contemned the idiosyncracies of their dark-skinned fellow-creatures: If an Englishman thinks and talks of a Hindoo as a Nigger, what

feelings Malinowski was unable or unwilling to express in his daily relations. At the level of methodological principle, Malinowski insisted on the critical importance of "personal friendships [to] encourage spontaneous confidences and the repetition of intimate gossip" (1929a:282–83). How "real" these friendships were is too complex an issue to venture on here. One may assume that they shared the inherent ambiguity and asymmetry of almost all ethnographic relations (cf. the suggestive remarks of Forge 1967). But it is surely presuming a great deal to characterize him as "an anthropologist who hates the natives" (Hsu 1979:521).

As for the Trobrianders' reaction to him, we can be sure that when they were wearied by his questions or hurt by his occasional angry outbursts, they rebuffed him. But any number of details in both the diary and the ethnographies—particularly *The Sexual Life of Savages,* which is the most revealing of the imponderabilia of his daily ethnographic behavior—testify that he was usually on fairly good terms with them. Clearly, it would be a mistake to take at face value the ironic passage in *Argonauts* where he suggests that he was accepted as a necessary nuisance "mitigated by donations of tobacco" (1922:6; cf. Young 1979:14–15). The number of his informants (who frequently appear, one may note, as identifiable individuals in the ethnographies), the *kayaku* or congregations in his tent (1967:103), the magic offered for him during illness (1922:244), the numerous sexual confidences (1929a:passim), suggest something more than a necessary nuisance. No doubt he remained in Trobriand minds a European, set apart from them by many things—some of them rather subtle and even paradoxical, like his encyclopedic collection of private magic, of which no Trobriander commanded more than a small fragment (1929a:373). But he was clearly a European of a special sort—as was evident in their surprise that he, so unmissionary in other respects, should have argued the "missionary view" of physiological paternity (1929a:187). It was evident even after his death, when he was still remembered as "the man of songs" (Hogbin 1946)—doubtless from the times when in order to frighten away *mulukwausi,* or flying witches, he sang "kiss my ass" to melodies from Wagner (1967:157).

Distracted by all that venting of negative affect, one may neglect the insights his diaries offer into Malinowski's ultimate ethnographic purpose. In the Mailu diary, Malinowski was still greatly under the influence of Rivers, whom he described to Haddon in 1916 as his "patron sain[t] in fieldwork"

---

will be his ideas of a Bheel or a Khond?" (Maine 1858:129). These examples suggest that the key to usage lies in the geography of race relations. *Nigrami* does not appear in Malinowski's first New Guinea diary, nor does "niggers" in the letters of this period, but only after he had spent several years on the colonial periphery.

(ACHP: BM/ACH 5/25/16). In contrast, the second Trobriand diary reveals Malinowski frequently in debate with Rivers, not only in his "concrete" methodological but also in his "historical" interpretive mode (1967:114, 161, 229, 254, 280). If the *History of Melanesian Society* was to be the outcome of the turn from evolution to history, then the place of diachronic approaches in ethnological inquiry seemed problematic indeed. Unlike Rivers, who was (at this point in his career) willing to put aside psychological problems (1916), Malinowski both by temperament and ethnographic experience was impelled toward them. He did not reject history entirely—as late as 1922 he was still talking about doing a migration study in the Riversian mode (1922:232). But it is clear already in *Baloma,* and quite explicit in the early pages of the Trobriand diary, that psychological problems were "the deepest essence of [his] investigations": "to discover what are [the native's] main passions, the motives for his conduct, his aims, . . . his essential deepest way of thinking" (1967:119). At this point, he saw himself "back to Bastian"—or, in an English context, perhaps to Frazer. But in contrast to the evolutionists, Malinowski's social psychology was grounded not in some hypothetical diachronic sequence, but in the ongoing events of a contemporary ethnographic situation, closely observed by a method that sought to probe more deeply than Rivers ever had. The contrast was suggested in ideas he recorded for the preface to his planned ethnography: "[Jan] Kubary as a concrete [i.e., Riversian] methodologist; Mikluho-Maclay as a new type. Marett's comparison: *early ethnographers as prospectors*" (1967:155; cf. Tumarkin 1982). It is in the context of this implied contrast between the surveying of an ethnographic surface and the mining of its deeper psychological meaning—as well as that of transforming national identity—that one must gloss Malinowski's reported proclamation of his ultimate anthropological ambition: "Rivers is the Rider Haggard of anthropology; I shall be the Conrad" (Firth ed. 1957:6; cf. BMPY:BM/B. Seligman 6/21/18; cf. Kirschner 1968; Langham 1981:171–77).

ARGONAUTS AS EUHEMERIST MYTH

That self-proclaiming epigram is of course multiply meaningful, and one may find in it also perhaps a clue to the method of Malinowski's ethnography—taking that word now not in the sense of recording ethnographic data in the field, but in the sense of its subsequent representation in a published monograph (cf. Marcus 1982). Malinowski (whose choice of adjectives can scarcely have been accidental) was himself acutely conscious of the chasm between "the *brute* material of information . . . and the final *authoritative* presentation of the results" (1922:3)—or, as he elsewhere equally revealingly phrased it,

between "the slight dust of little bits of information—here and there, chaotic, unequal even in their credibility" and the "final ideals of knowledge":
"the essential nigger [sic] as an illustration and document to our Conception
of Man" (BMPL: "Method" n.d.). The problem was how "to convince my
readers" that the ethnographic information offered them was "objectively
acquired knowledge" and not simply "a subjectively formed notion" (ibid.).
At the level of explicit formulation, Malinowski usually tended to discuss the
issue in terms one might expect of a physicist-turned-ethnographer under the
methodological shadow of Rivers. Just as in "an experimental contribution
to physical or chemical science," the critical thing was to be "absolutely can-
did" about one's method (1922:2). But although Malinowski devoted detailed (if not fully revealing) attention to certain aspects of his method, his
consciousness of other aspects is only infrequently and implicitly evident. We
may assume from his epigrammatic proclamation an awareness that the ethnographer was ultimately a literary artificer. Nevertheless, his explicit models
are all from Science, and we are left to our own literary critical devices to
explicate the method of his artifice (cf. Payne 1981)—and thereby to appreciate fully the manner in which he constituted his authority, which may be
regarded as the prototype for the authority of all of modern ethnography, in
both the senses I have suggested (cf. Clifford 1983).

The most explicit attempt to validate that authority is in the introductory
chapter of *Argonauts* (1922:1–25). There Malinowski groups the "principles
of method" under three main headings: "proper conditions for ethnographic
work" (6); knowledge of the "principles," "aims," and "results" of modern
"scientific study" (8); and the application of "special methods" of "collecting,
manipulating, and fixing" evidence (6). The latter are also grouped under
three rubrics: "statistic documentation by concrete evidence" of the "rules
and regularities of tribal life" (17, 11); collecting "the imponderabilia of actual life and of typical behavior" in order to put "flesh and blood" on the
"skeleton" of the tribal constitution (20, 17); and the creation of a *corpus
inscriptionum* of native opinion and utterance to illustrate "typical ways of
thinking and feeling" (23–24). Viewed in terms of specific methodological
canons, Malinowski's introduction offers little Rivers had not proposed in
Notes and Queries. His method is less a matter of disembodied rules, however,
than of total personal style. His apparently more innovative methodological
injunctions—the keeping of an "ethnographic diary," the making of "synoptic charts," and the preliminary sketching of results—all emphasize the constructive problem-generating role of the ethnographer. But what is really critical is to place this "active huntsman" in a certain situation. Cut off from
"the company of white men," he will "naturally" seek the society of natives
not his "natural companions," engaging in "natural intercourse" with them
rather than relying on "paid, and often bored, informants." Waking up "every

morning to a day presenting itself more or less as it does to the native," he
finds that his life "soon adopts quite a natural course very much in harmony
with his surroundings." Corrected for repeated "breaches of etiquette," he has
"to learn how to behave." Taking part "in a way" in village life, he ceases "to
be a disturbing element in the tribal life" (7–8). Loneliness thus becomes
the sine qua non of ethnographic knowledge, the means by which one becomes able in a *natural* way to observe a culture from the inside, and thereby
"grasp the native's point of view, his relation to life, and realize *his* vision of
his world" (25).

   Although Malinowski tried to formulate the "ethnographer's magic" as a
prosaic "application of a number of rules of common sense and well-known
scientific principles" (6), his real problem was not so much to tell his readers
how to accomplish the ultimate divinatory task, as to convince them that it
could be done, and that he had done it. If "empty programme" were to be
translated into "the result of personal experience" (13), then his own experience of the native's experience must become the reader's experience as well—
a task that scientific analysis yielded up to literary art.

   In this context, Malinowski's Frazerian apprenticeship (and perhaps also
those tent-bound bouts of novel reading in the Trobriands) served his ethnography very well indeed. As early as 1917, he confided in Frazer that it
was "through the study of your works that I have come to realize the paramount importance of vividness and colour in descriptions of life" (JGF: BM/
JGF 10/25/17). Throughout his book Frazer's "scene/act ratio" is employed to
place the reader imaginatively within the actual physical setting of the events
Malinowski reconstructs: "When, on a hot day, we enter the deep shadow of
fruit trees and palms, and find ourselves in the midst of the wonderfully
designed and ornamented houses hiding here and there in irregular groups
among the green . . . " (1922:35). More important still, perhaps, is a device
one might call the "author/reader equation": "Imagine yourself suddenly set
down surrounded by all your gear, alone on a tropical beach close to a native
village while the launch . . . which has brought you sails away out of sight
. . . " (4). Introduced to Malinowski's opening methodological excursus in
this ambiguously autobiographical fashion, we are encouraged not only to
share his ethnographic "tribulations," but—partaking of the authority his
experience legitimated—to come along with him as he follows the Trobrianders on their "perilous and difficult enterprises." As Malinowski's original
title (*Kula: A Tale of Native Enterprise and Adventure in Eastern New Guinea*
[ACHP: BM/ACH 11/25/21]) suggested, his ethnography has essentially a
narrative structure. Beginning with the construction of the waga or canoe,
through its launching and departure, we are taken on an ambitious overseas
expedition across the sea arm of Pilolu (with a pause for the account of a
mythical shipwreck), on to the Amphletts, Tewara, and Sanaroa, stopping

for magical ceremonies on the beach of Sarubwoyna, to the climactic kula exchanges in Dobu and the journey home—where we witness a return visit from the Dobuans, and tie up the loose ends of the "inland Kula" and its "remaining branches and offshoots." With Malinowski at our side intervening when necessary to explain particular ethnographic details or to provide more extended disquisitions on the sociology, mythology, magic, and language of the Kula, we have followed the Trobrianders through the epic event that periodically focusses all the energies of their existence. At the end we are prepared to believe that we have glimpsed their "vision of the world," and "the reality which [they] breathe and by which [they] live" (517).

This is by no means all that Malinowski's narrative style has accomplished. Characteristically, chapters open with references to a present action or situation: "the canoe, painted and decorated, stands now ready to be launched" (146); "our party, sailing from the north, reach first the main island of Gumasila" (267). True, there are occasional contrasts between "nowadays" and "olden days," and several chapters in fact end with speculations of an historical diffusionist character (289). Characteristically, however, Malinowski writes in the active voice and present tense, employing what one critic has called a "syntax of agency" (Payne 1981:427). By bringing the reader along as eyewitness to the ongoing Kula events, he establishes the conviction that they exemplify life in the Trobriands to this very day. Previous ethnographies had described reconstructed behavior as if it were present practice, and subsequent ethnographies (including his own) did not emulate the event-narrative form of *Argonauts*. But it was Malinowski's *Argonauts* that validated the temporal context in which modern ethnography is normally situated: the vague and essentially atemporal moment we call "the ethnographic present."

As the homeric (and Frazerian) resonances of its actually published title suggest, something was going on in this primal ethnographic scene besides the narrative re-creation of actual experience. At one point in his discussion of the Trobriand shipwreck myth, Malinowski suggests that it is not always easy "to make a distinction between what is mere mytho-poetic fiction and what is . . . drawn from actual experience" (1922:236); and despite his professed methodological candor, it is clear that Malinowski himself sometimes blurred that distinction. It takes an attentive reader to realize from the printed narrative that he never actually sailed with a Kula expedition after that ill-fated venture towards Kitava in 1915. At one point he does in fact explicitly tell us that most of his narrative is "reconstructed," arguing that for one who has "seen much of the native's tribal life and has a good grip over intelligent informants," such reconstruction is neither "fanciful" nor "very difficult" (376). But along the way we have been encouraged by ambiguous phrases ("I have seen, indeed followed") to believe that he had done something more than catch up in a cutter (1967:242). Similarly, while attentive readers may note that he did sometimes pay informants (1922:409), without the benefit of his diary one would scarcely guess just how often he retreated to Billy Hancock's compound at Gusaweta for refuge from "sickness and surfeit of native" (6). From that same diary we know that his time reckoning was somewhat unreliable—in general, he was not actually in the field for quite so long as *Argonauts* suggests (cf. 1922:16 and 1967:216).

A certain vagueness as to the situation of events in time is of course one aspect of the myth-making process. Another is the peopling of the mythopoeic moment with characters of archetypical significance. In this context it is interesting to consider the cast of characters of *Argonauts* (cf. Payne 1981). Most numerous, and manifestly central to the account, are the "natives": distinguished often by tribal group or status, frequently named, occasionally subsumed within the category "savage" (and in the privacy of his diary, by the epithet "nigger"), but most explicitly denied the archetypifying capitalization of Primitive Economic Man—a rubric Malinowski was at some pains to destroy (1922:60). Brushed at times with the exotic colors of noble savagery, they are more often painted in rather prosaic tones. Although it is organized around their adventure, and they are on one occasion referred to as "homeric heroes" (1922:295), they are not in fact the heroes of Malinowski's romance. His attitude toward them is often that of "gentle irony"— a literary mode which was to characterize much of modern ethnography (Payne 1981:421; Thornton n.d.). The ethnographer not only is capable of sharing their vision of their world, but he knows things about it that they will never know, and brings to light phenomena which "had remained hidden even from those in whom they happened" (1922:397).

Such phenomena were also hidden from the second group of characters: "the minor cast of cramped minds" who had "gotten the natives all wrong" in the past—administrators, missionaries, traders, all "full of the biassed and pre-judged opinions inevitable in the average practical man" who had "lived for years in the place . . . and who yet hardly knew one thing about them really well" (Payne 1981:421). Some of them were clearly archetypifications of painful experiences Malinowski had with very real people—notably the Mailu missionary Saville, who had in fact provided him with valuable information, but whose "underhanded dealings" had first provoked his professed "hatred of missionaries" (1967:31, 42). In the methodological introduction to *Argonauts* they all appear briefly as a "stock of strawmen" who by stark contrast highlight the virtues of Malinowski's method. Even previous ethnographers of the concrete Riversian sort are by implication chided for their failure to come down off the verandah.

In contrast to these two sets of characters is a third, who stands apart, capitalized, in heroic singularity: the Ethnographer. Appositional equation to the first person singular leaves no doubt as to his actual identity (1922:34), and the equation is confirmed iconographically in photographs of "the Ethnographer's tent" placed strategically at the beginning and end of the book, before and after the expedition it recounts (16, 481). Marking him off from all other Europeans, the methodological introduction has affirmed his divinatory powers. At its end we know full well that only he, who ventured there alone himself and made his loneliness the instrument of divining knowledge, can now lead us also into the heart of darkness.

Considered in this light, *Argonauts* is itself a kind of euhemerist myth—divinizing, however, not its ostensible Trobriand heroes, but the European Jason who brings back the Golden Fleece of ethnographic knowledge. Long before Susan Sontag used Levi-Strauss as the model of the "Anthropologist as Hero" (1966), Malinowski had created the role for himself. But that his purpose was not simply self-serving is evident in unpublished notes toward his introduction, in which he was concerned not only with the problem of auctorial authority (how to "convince my readers"), but also with the situation of the ethnographic beginner, who enters the field "paralyzed with fear of all sorts of traps and barriers" (BMPL: "Method" n.d.). In this context, it seems clear that the introduction to *Argonauts* was never intended really to be a true description of Malinowski's fieldwork experience. Description was only the device by which he made prescription compelling. Even if the self-advancing striving of his vigorous ego had allowed, it would not have served his confidence-inspiring prescriptive purposes to dwell here upon his own frustrations and failures (cf. the relatively innocuous "Confessions of Ignorance and Failure" [1935, 1:452–82]). He wanted to make the apprentice ethnographer "aware beforehand that we had a method of attacking" all those "initial difficulties which are so very hard to surmount" ("Method," n.d.). More than that, he wanted to legitimate the style of fieldwork upon which that novice was to embark. For novice ethnographers as much as general readers, the problem was not so much to enumerate principles of method, but to convince that the task could be done. In this context, every aspect of *Argonauts*—structure as well as argument, style as well as content, anecdote as well as precept, implication as well as statement, omission as well as inclusion—all contributed to the euhemerist validating myth.

Several years later, in writing on the role of "Myth in Primitive Psychology," Malinowski emphasized the intermingling of its pragmatic and legitimating functions: myth was at once "a warrant, a charter, and often even a practical guide to the activities with which it is connected" (1926a:108). It was "not an explanation in satisfaction of a scientific interest, but a narrative resurrection of a primeval reality, told in satisfaction of deep religious wants, moral cravings, social submissions, assertions, even practical requirements" (101). Expressing, enhancing, and codifying belief, vouching for "the efficiency of ritual," it came "into play when rite, ceremony, or a social or moral rule demands justification, warrant of antiquity, reality, and sanctity" (107). Malinowski had spoken explicitly in his diary of "the revolution" he wanted to "effect in social anthropology" (1967:289), and it is hard to read his later essay, with its final spirited plea for an "open-air anthropology" (1926a:147), without feeling that he had sought more or less consciously in *Argonauts* to provide a mythic charter for its central ritual.

MALINOWSKI'S MYTHIC CHARTER AND MODERN ETHNOGRAPHY

Whether or not he went about it in consciously mythopoeic fashion, Malinowski succeeded in validating the authority of his method to both readers and apprentice ethnographers alike. The world's premier reader of ethnographies, Sir James G. Frazer, gave the work his imprimatur: living "as a native among the natives for many months," Malinowski had portrayed them "in the round and not in the flat"—not like Molière's "dummies dressed up to look very like human beings," but like the "solid" characters of Cervantes and Shakespeare, "drawn not from one side only but from many" (BM 1922:vii, ix). Seligman, whose ethnographic taste was as prosaic as his fieldwork style (Firth 1975), was less impressed. Despite the fact that *Argonauts* was dedicated to him, he continued to regard *Baloma* as Malinowski's best work, tending to view his later writings as compromised by popularizing purpose (BMPL: CGS/BM 8/5/31). With Rivers recently dead, it was Haddon who spoke in public for the Cambridge School, lauding the book as "the high-water mark of ethnological investigation and interpretation," which would "prove of great value for the guidance of future fieldworkers" (ACH 1922).

That it served as such reflects the fact that no other early published work of the prewar cohort paid such explicit and extended attention to ethnographic (as opposed to interpretive) method (cf. Radcliffe-Brown 1922). Their initial ethnographic reports were drably institutional monographic publications (Hocart 1922; Karsten 1923; Landtman 1917) whose manifest level of methodological self-consciousness in one case lent itself to Marett's revealing prefatory comment: "Touring, indeed, proves the ideal method of anthropological research" (Jenness & Ballantyne 1920:7). In this context, the first chapter of *Argonauts* (published, with Haddon's assistance, by a leading commercial publisher [ACHP: BM/ACH 12/20/21]) was the single most accessible statement of the "modern sociological method of fieldwork"—especially for non-anthropologists, who would be unlikely to read Rivers' chapters in *Notes and Queries*. Effectively appropriating to himself experience that had in fact been shared by others (including "The Ethnographer's Tent," which Westermarck, for instance, had taken to Morocco [1927:158]), at once archetypifying it and rendering it in concrete narrative form, Malinowski validated not only his own fieldwork but that of "modern anthropology" (cf. Panoff 1972:54). A man of great ambition and no mean entrepreneurial talent, he was able to make himself the spokesman of a methodological revolution, both within anthropology, and in some ways more important, to the non-anthropological academic and intellectual community.

By 1926, when he was the "star" of the Hanover Conference of the [American] Social Science Research Council, Malinowski had won over a critically important sector of that community: the "philanthropoids" of the Rockefeller Foundation. In the late 1920s he served as their chief informal anthropological advisor, much to the dismay of Grafton Elliot Smith, who could not understand why "the sole method of studying mankind is to sit on a Melanesian island for a couple of years and listen to the gossip of the villagers" (RFA: GES/Herrick 2/13/27). For a time, the seminars of Elliot Smith's diffusionist protégé William Perry at University College rivaled Malinowski's in attracting students to anthropology. But reinforced by the requirement that the Rockefeller-funded fieldworkers of the International African Institute should spend a year in his seminar, Malinowski's methodological charisma soon won out (GS 1979b). Most of those who were to claim the status of social anthropologist in the British sphere served an apprenticeship with Malinowski; and while a number of them were later to turn away from him to find their theoretical inspiration in Radcliffe-Brown, they continued to regard Malinowski as the archetypical fieldworker (Gluckman 1963, 1967). Even in America, which had its own variant of the mythic fieldwork charter, Malinowski's influence was asserted, both from a distance and in person on periodic visits from 1926 on. Despite the fact that the railroad and the Model T facilitated a more transient fieldwork, young ethnographers seem to have measured themselves against a Malinowskian model. Thus Sol Tax, emulating Malinowski's "ideal method of ethnography" (and having no knowledge of those "cook boys" mentioned only in the diary), started out his work among the Fox in the summer of 1932 by living "in a camp of my own in the midst of native camps," only to discover that the Indians felt him silly to "stay out there and cook for myself like a squaw when I could get to town in five minutes" (Blanchard 1979:423).

That the central mythic symbol of the tent could have such potency from afar suggests some final observations. Malinowski seems to have devoted more attention in his seminars to discussing details of fieldwork method than is often now the case, and the correspondence of his students from the field indicates that those synoptic charts were taken very seriously (Richards 1957:25; cf. BMPL: AR/BM 7/8/30). But the fieldwork style he validated was less a matter of concrete prescription than of placing oneself in a situation where one might have a certain type of experience. Like the situations that elicited Trobriand magic, it was one that was initially threatening and could be dangerous, and in which "the elements of chance and accident" often determined success or failure. As Malinowski (echoing Marett) had suggested in "Myth in Primitive Psychology," the function of magic consisted in "the bridging over of gaps and inadequacies in highly important activities not yet completely mastered by man" (1926a:139–40). The gap between the specific methodological prescriptions of fieldwork and the vaguely defined goals of ethnographic knowledge had thus to be filled by what Malinowski himself had called "the ethnographer's magic" (1922:6). And just as in primitive psychology myth functioned "especially where there is a sociological strain" (1926a:126), in anthropological psychology it functioned especially where there was an epistemological strain.

Despite his breezy public confidence that all would be well once anthropologists stepped outside the "closed study of the theorist" and came down from "the verandah of the missionary compound" into the "open air of the anthropological field" (1926a:99, 146–47), it is clear that at times Malinowski felt that strain, and we may assume that so also did those who followed in his footsteps. In retrospect, however, one is struck with the relative dearth of discussion of the fundamental assumptions of fieldwork method (cf. Nash & Wintrob 1972). It is tempting to suggest that Malinowski's ethnographic bravura made it seem unnecessary. Even those whose own research did not live up to (or even model itself upon) his prescriptions were nevertheless sustained by his preemptive archetypification. Thus it was that the problem of instant linguistic competence has rarely been raised either as a general issue (cf. Lowie 1940) or in regard to particular ethnographic monographs—despite the fact that few apprentice ethnographers may be presumed to share Malinowski's remarkable linguistic facility. For almost four decades Malinowski's mythic charter functioned to sustain the ethnographic enterprise, helping several generations of aspiring ethnographers to "get on with the work." By the time his diaries were published, however, changing colonial circumstances had fundamentally altered the ethnographer's situation; and in the context of a protracted epistemological malaise (heightened no doubt by their publication), it has seemed necessary to many anthropologists to examine more systematically all that was so casually subsumed by that deceptively innocent charm phrase: "the ethnographer's magic" (e.g., Rabinow 1977).

ACKNOWLEDGMENTS

Research for this paper was at various points supported by the Center for Advanced Study in the Behavioral Sciences, the Marian and Adolph Lichtstern Foundation for Anthropology (of the Department of Anthropology, University of Chicago), the National Endowment for the Humanities, the National Science Foundation, and the Wenner-Gren Foundation for Anthropological Research. Preliminary versions were given at the meeting of the History of Science Society in Los Angeles, December 1981, and at the March 1982 meeting of the Chicago Group in the History of the Social Sciences (sponsored by the Morris Fishbein Center for the Study of the History of Science and Medicine). I am particularly indebted to James Clifford, Raymond Fogelson, Dell Hymes, David Schneider, Mark Schwehn, and Bruce Trigger for helpful comments. I would like to thank Mrs. Helena Wayne for her kind permission to reproduce the picture of her father, Bronislaw Malinowski, and David W. Phillipson, Curator of the University Museum of Archaeology and Anthropology, Cambridge, for permission to reproduce that of C. G. Seligman. I would also like to express my appreciation to the officers and staffs of the various manuscript archives in which I worked.

REFERENCES CITED

ACH. See under Haddon.

ACHP. See under Manuscript Sources.

AMHP. See under Manuscript Sources.

BAAS. See under British Association for the Advancement of Science.

Bartlett, F. C. 1959. Myers, Charles Samuel. in *Dict. Nat. Biog. 1941–50.*

Blanchard, D. 1979. Beyond empathy: The emergence of action anthropology in the life and career of Sol Tax. In *Currents in anthropology: Essays in honor of Sol Tax,* ed. R. Hinshaw, 419–43. The Hague.

BM. See under Malinowski.

BMPL. See under Manuscript Sources.

BMPY. See under Manuscript Sources.

Brigard, E. de. 1975. The history of ethnographic film. In *Toward a science of man,* ed. T. Thoresen, 33–63. The Hague.

British Association for the Advancement of Science. 1874. *Notes and queries on anthropology, for the use of travellers and residents in uncivilized lands.* London.

———. 1884–. *Report[s] of the . . . 54th [and succeeding] meeting[s].*

———. 1887. Third report of the Committee . . . investigating and publishing reports on the physical characters, languages, industry and social condition of the north-western tribes of the Dominion of Canada. In *Rept. 57th Meeting,* 173–83.

———. 1912. *Notes and queries on anthropology.* 4th ed. London.

Clifford, J. 1983. On ethnographic authority. *Representations.* 1 (2).

Codrington, R. H. 1891. *The Melanesians. Studies in their anthropology and folklore.* Reprint ed. Oxford (1969).

Conrad, J. 1902. Heart of darkness. In *Youth: A narrative and two other stories,* 49–182. Edinburgh.

Czaplička, M. A. 1916. *My Siberian year.* New York.

Drever, J. 1968. McDougall, William. In *Int. Encyclo. Soc. Scis.* New York.

EBTP. See under Manuscript Sources.

Epstein, A. L., ed. 1967. *The craft of social anthropology.* London.

FGP. See under Manuscript Sources.

Firth, R. 1963. A brief history (1913–1963). In *Department of Anthropology* [London School of Economics] *Programme of courses 1963–64,* 1–9.

————. 1975. Seligman's contributions to oceanic anthropology *Oceania* 44:272–82.

————. 1981. Bronislaw Malinowski. In *Totems and teachers: Perspectives on the history of anthropology,* ed. S. Silverman, 103–37. Paperback ed. New York.

Firth, R., ed. 1957. *Man and culture: An evaluation of the work of Bronislaw Malinowski.* Paperback ed. New York (1964).

Fison, L., & A. W. Howitt. 1880. *Kamilaroi and Kurnai: Group-marriage and relationship . . .* Reprint ed. Osterhout N.B., Netherlands (1967).

Forge, A. 1967. The lonely anthropologist. *New Society* 10:221–23.

Fortes, M. 1941. Obituary of C. G. Seligman. *Man* 41:1–6.

————. 1953. *Social anthropology at Cambridge since 1900.* Cambridge.

————. 1969. *Kinship and the social order: The legacy of Lewis Henry Morgan.* Chicago.

Frazer, J. G. 1887. *Questions on the customs, beliefs and languages of savages.* Privately printed pamphlet.

————. 1900. *The golden bough: A study in magic and religion.* 2nd ed., 3 vols. London.

————. 1910. *Totemism and exogamy.* Reprint ed., 4 vols. London (1968).

————. 1931. Baldwin Spencer as anthropologist. In Marett & Penniman, eds. 1931:1–13.

Freire-Marreco, B. 1916. Cultivated plants. In *The ethnobotany of the Tewa Indians,* by W. W. Robbins, J. P. Harrington, and B. Friere-Marreco, 76–118. *Bur. Am. Ethn. Bul.* 55. Washington.

Galton, F. 1883. *Inquiries into human faculty and its development.* London.

Geertz, C. 1967. Under the mosquito net. *N.Y. Rev. Books* (Sept. 14):12–13.

Geison, G. 1978. *Michael Foster and the Cambridge school of Physiology: The scientific enterprise in late Victorian society.* Princeton, N.J.

Gillen, F. J. 1896. Notes on some manners and customs of the Aborigines of the McDonnell Ranges belonging to the Arunta tribe. In *Report of the work of the Horn scientific expedition to central Australia,* ed. W. B. Spencer, vol. 4, 162–86. London.

Gluckman, M. 1963. Malinowski—fieldworker and theorist. In *Order and rebellion in tribal Africa,* 244–52. London.

————. 1967. Introduction. In Epstein, ed. 1967:xi–xx.

Gruber, J. W. 1967. Horatio Hale and the development of American anthropology. *Procs. Am. Phil. Soc.* 111:5–37.

GS. See under Stocking.

Haddon, A. C. 1890. The ethnography of the western tribe of Torres Straits. *J. Anth. Inst.* 19:297–440.

——. 1895a. *Evolution in art.* London.

——. 1895b. Ethnographical survey of Ireland. *Rept. 65th Meeting, Brit. Assn. Adv. Sci.*:509–18.

——. 1901. *Head-hunters: Black, white and brown.* London.

——. 1903a. The saving of vanishing data. *Pop. Sci. Month.* 62:222–29.

——. 1903b. Anthropology: Its position and needs. Presidential address. *J. Anth. Inst.* 33:11–23.

——. 1906. A plea for an expedition to Melanesia. *Nature* 74:187–88.

——. 1922. Ceremonial exchange: Review of B. Malinowski's *Argonauts of the western Pacific. Nature* 110:472–74.

——. 1939. Obituary of Sydney Ray. *Man* 57:58–61.

Haddon, A. C., ed. 1901–1935. *Reports of the Cambridge Anthropological Expedition to Torres Straits.* Vol. 1 (1935); vol. 2 (part 1) (1901); vol. 2 (part 2) (1903); vol. 3 (1907); vol. 4 (1912); vol. 5 (1904); vol. 6 (1908). Cambridge.

Hobhouse, L. T., G. C. Wheeler, & M. Ginsberg. 1915. *The material culture of the simple peoples.* Expanded ed. London (1930).

Hocart, A. M. 1922. The cult of the dead in Eddystone Island. *J. Roy. Anth. Inst.* 52:71–112.

Hogbin, H. I. 1946. The Trobriand Islands, 1945. *Man* 46:72.

Hose, C., & W. McDougall. 1912. *The pagan tribes of Borneo.* London.

Howard, C. 1981. Rivers' genealogical method and the *Reports* of the Torres Straits Expedition. Unpublished seminar paper, University of Chicago.

Hsu, F. L. K. 1979. The cultural problem of the cultural anthropologist. *Am. Anth.* 81:517–32.

Hyman, S. E. 1959. *The tangled bank: Darwin, Marx, Frazer and Freud as imaginative writers.* Paperback ed. New York (1966).

Im Thurn, E. 1883. *Among the Indians of Guiana.* Paperback ed. New York (1967).

Jarvie, I. C. 1964. *The revolution in anthropology.* London.

——. 1966. On theories of fieldwork and the scientific character of social anthropology. *Phil. Sci.* 34:223–42.

Jenness, D. 1922–23. *Life of the Copper Eskimo. Rept. Canadian Arctic Exped.* Vol. 12: Southern party 1913–16. Ottawa.

Jenness, D., & A. Ballantyne. 1920. *The northern D'Entrecasteaux.* Oxford.

JGFP. See under Manuscript Sources.

Kaberry, P. 1957. Malinowski's contribution to field-work methods and the writing of ethnography. In Firth, ed. 1957:71–92.

Karsten, R. 1923. *Blood revenge, war and victory feasts among the Jibaro Indians of eastern Ecuador. Bur. Am. Ethn. Bul.* 79. Washington.

——. 1932. *Indian tribes of the Argentine and Bolivian Chaco.* Societas Scientiarum Fennica. Helsinki.

——. 1935. *The head-hunters of western Amazonas.* Societas Scientiarum Fennica. Helsinki.

Kirschner, P. 1968. *Conrad: The psychologist as artist.* Edinburgh.

KS. See under Symmons-Symonolewicz.

Kuper, A. 1973. *Anthropology and anthropologists: The British school, 1922–1972.* London.

Landtman, G. 1917. *The folk-tales of the Kiwai Papuans.* Societas Scientiarum Fennica. Helsinki.

———. 1927. *The Kiwai Papuans of British New Guinea.* London.

Lang, A. 1901. *Magic and religion.* London.

⌐ Langham, I. 1981. *The building of British social anthropology: W. H. R. Rivers and his Cambridge disciples in the development of kinship studies, 1898–1931.* Dordrecht.

Langlois, C. V., & C. Seignobos. 1898. *Introduction to the study of history.* Trans. G. G. Berry. New York (1926).

⌐ Laracy, H. 1976. Malinowski at war: 1914–18. *Mankind* 10:264–68.

Layard, J. 1942. *Stone men of Malekula.* London.

———. 1944. *Incarnation and instinct.* Pamphlet. London.

Leach, E. 1957. The epistemological background to Malinowski's empiricism. In Firth, ed. 1957:119–37.

———. 1965. Introduction. In Malinowski 1935, vol. 1:viii–xvii.

⌐ ———. 1966. On the "founding fathers." *Cur. Anth.* 7:560–67.

———. 1980. On reading *A diary in the strict sense of the term:* Or the self mutilation of Professor Hsu. *Rain* 36:2–3.

⌐ Lowie, R. H. 1940. Native languages as ethnographic tools. *Am. Anth.* 42:81–89.

McLennan, J. F. 1865. *Primitive marriage.* Edinburgh.

Maine, H. S. 1858. Thirty years of improvement in India. *Sat. Rev.* 5 (Feb. 6):129.

Malinowski, B. 1912. The economic aspect of the Intichiuma ceremonies. In *Festkrift tillegnad Edvard Westermarck,* 81–108. Helsinki.

———. 1913a. *The family among the Australian aborigines.* Paperback ed. New York (1963).

———. 1913b. Elementary forms of religious life. In Malinowski 1962, 282–88.

———. 1913c. Review of *Across Australia,* by B. Spencer and F. J. Gillen. *Folk-Lore* 24:278–79.

———. 1915a. The natives of Mailu: Preliminary results of the Robert Mond research work in New Guinea. *Trans. Roy. Soc. So. Aust.* 39:49–706.

———. 1915b. *Wierzenia pierwotne i formy ustroju społecznego.* [Primitive religion and social differentiation.] Polish Academy of Science. Cracow.

———. 1916. Baloma: Spirits of the dead in the Trobriand Islands. In *Magic, science and religion,* 149–274. Paperback ed. Garden City, N.Y. (1954).

———. 1922. *Argonauts of the western Pacific.* Paperback ed. New York (1961).

———. 1923. Science and superstition of primitive mankind. In Malinowski 1962:268–75.

———. 1926a. Myth in primitive psychology. In *Magic, science and religion,* 93–148. Paperback ed. Garden City, N.Y. (1954).

———. 1926b. *Crime and custom in savage society.* Paperback ed. Paterson, N.J. (1964).

———. 1929a. *The sexual life of savages in northwestern Melanesia.* Paperback ed. New York (n.d.).

———. 1929b. Review of *The Kiwai Papuans of British New Guinea* by G. Landtman. *Folk-Lore* 40:109–12.

———. 1935. *Coral gardens and their magic.* 2 vols. Bloomington, Ind. (1965).

————. 1944. Sir James George Frazer: A biographical introduction. In *A scientific theory of culture and other essays*, 177–222. Paperback ed. New York (1960).

————. 1962. *Sex, culture and myth*. New York.

————. 1967. *A diary in the strict sense of the term*. Trans. N. Guterman. New York.

Marcus, G. & D. Cushman. 1982. Ethnographies as texts. *Ann. Rev. Anth.* 11:25–69.

Marett, R. R. 1900. Pre-animistic religion. *Folk-Lore* 11:162–82.

————. 1921. Obituary of Marie de Czaplička. *Man* 60:105–6.

————. 1941. *A Jerseyman at Oxford*. London.

Marett, R. R., & T. K. Penniman, eds. 1931. *Spencer's last journey: Being the journal of an expedition to Tierra del Fuego by the late Sir Walter Baldwin Spencer with a memoir*. Oxford.

————. 1932. *Spencer's scientific correspondence with Sir J. G. Frazer and others*. Oxford.

Mauss, M. 1923. [Obituary of W. H. R. Rivers.] In *Cohesion sociale et divisions de la sociologie*. *Ouevres*. Vol. 3, ed. V. Karady, 465–72. Paris (1968).

Mendelsohn, E. 1963. The emergence of science as a profession in nineteenth century Europe. In *Management of scientists*, ed. K. Hill. Boston.

Morgan, L. H. 1871. *Systems of consanguinity and affinity of the human family*. Reprint. Osterhout N.B., Netherlands (1970).

Moseley, H. N. 1879. *Notes by a naturalist on the challenger . . .* London.

Mulvaney, D. J. 1958. The Australian aborigines, 1606–1929. Opinion and fieldwork. In *Hist. Stud., Aust. & New Zea.* 8:131–51, 297–314.

————. 1967. The anthropologist as tribal elder. *Mankind* 7:205–17.

Nash, D., & R. Wintrob. 1972. The emergence of self-consciousness in ethnography. *Cur. Anth.* 13:527–42.

N.R.C. [National Research Council]. 1938. *International directory of anthropologists*. Washington.

Needham, R. 1967. *A bibliography of Arthur Maurice Hocart (1883–1939)*. Oxford.

Paluch, A. K. 1981. The Polish background to Malinowski's work. *Man* 16:276–85.

Panoff, M. 1972. *Bronislaw Malinowski*. Paris.

Payne, H. C. 1981. Malinowski's style. *Procs. Am. Phil. Soc.* 125:416–40.

Pearson, K. 1924. *Life, letters and labours of Francis Galton*. Vol. 3: *Researches of middle life*. Cambridge.

Powdermaker, H. 1970. Further reflections on Lesu and Malinowski's diary. *Oceania* 40:344–47.

Prichard, J. C. 1848. *Researches into the physical history of mankind*. Vol 5. London.

Quiggin, A. H. 1942. *Haddon the head-hunter*. Cambridge.

Rabinow, P. 1977. *Reflections on fieldwork in Morocco*. Berkeley.

Radcliffe-Brown, A. R. 1922. *The Andaman islanders*. Paperback ed. Glencoe, Ill. (1964).

RFA. See under Manuscript Sources.

Richards, A. 1939. The development of fieldwork methods in social anthropology. In *The study of society*, ed. F. C. Bartlett, 272–316. London.

————. 1957. The concept of culture in Malinowski's work. In Firth, ed. 1957:15–32.

Rivers, W. H. R. 1899. Two new departures in anthropological method. *Rept.* 69th *Meeting, Brit. Assn. Adv. Sci.*:879–80.

———. 1900. A genealogical method of collecting social and vital statistics. *J. Anth. Inst.* 30:74–82.

———. 1904. Genealogies[,] kinship. In Haddon, ed. 1904, vol. 5:122–52.

———. 1906. *The Todas.* Reprint ed. Osterhout N.B., Netherlands (1967).

———. 1907. On the origin of the classificatory system of relationships. In *Anthropological essays presented to E. B. Tylor,* ed. N. Balfour et al., 309–23. Oxford.

———. 1908. Genealogies[,] kinship. In Haddon, ed. 1908, vol. 6:62–91.

———. 1910. The genealogical method of anthropological inquiry. *Soc. Rev.* 3:1–12.

———. 1911. The ethnological analysis of culture. In *Psychology and ethnology,* ed. G. E. Smith, 120–40. London (1926).

———. 1913. Report on anthropological research outside America. In *Reports upon the present condition and future needs of the science of anthropology,* by W. H. R. Rivers et al., 5–28. Washington.

———. 1914a. *The history of Melanesian society.* Reprint ed., 2 vols. Osterhout N.B., Netherlands (1968).

———. 1914b. *Kinship and social organization.* Reprint ed., London (1968).

———. 1916. Sociology and psychology. In *Psychology and ethnology,* ed. G. E. Smith, 3–20. London (1926).

Rohner, R. P., ed. 1969. *The ethnography of Franz Boas.* Trans. H. Parker. Chicago.

Rooksby, R. L. 1971. W. H. R. Rivers and the Todas. *South Asia* 1:109–21.

Schneider, D. M. 1968. Rivers and Kroeber in the study of kinship. In Rivers 1914:7–16.

Seligman, C. G. 1910. *The Melanesians of British New Guinea.* Cambridge.

Seligman, C. G., & B. Z. Seligman. 1911. *The Veddahs.* Cambridge.

———. 1932. *Pagan tribes of the Nilotic Sudan.* London.

Slobodin, R. 1978. *W. H. R. Rivers.* New York.

Sontag, S. 1966. The anthropologist as hero. In *Claude Lévi-Strauss: The anthropologist as hero,* ed. E. N. & T. Hayes, 184–97. Paperback ed. Cambridge.

Spencer, W. B., & F. Gillen. 1899. *The native tribes of central Australia.* Paperback ed. New York (1968).

Stipe, C. E. 1980. Anthropologists vs. missionaries: The influence of presuppositions. *Cur. Anth.* 21:165–79.

Stirling, E. C. 1896. Anthropology. In *Report of the work of the Horn scientific expedition to central Australia,* ed. W. B. Spencer, vol. 4:1–161. London.

Stocking, G. W., Jr. 1968a. Empathy and antipathy in the heart of darkness. *J. Hist. Behav. Scis.* 4:189–94.

———. 1968b. *Race, culture and evolution.* New York.

———. 1971. Radcliffe-Brown, Rivers and the definition of social anthropology. Typescript.

———. 1973. From chronology to ethnology: James Cowles Prichard and British anthropology, 1800–1850. In Prichard, *Researches into the physical history of man.* Reprint ed. Chicago.

————. 1974. *The shaping of American anthropology, 1883–1911: A Franz Boas reader.* New York.

————. 1977. Contradicting the doctor: Billy Hancock and the problem of Baloma. *Hist. Anth. Newsl.* 4(1):11–12.

————. 1979a. The intensive study of limited areas—Toward an ethnographic context for the Malinowski innovation. *Hist. Anth. Newsl.* 6:9–12.

————. 1979b. Philanthropoids and vanishing cultures: Rockefeller anthropology between the wars. Typescript.

————. 1980a. Innovation in the Malinowskian mode: An essay review of *Long-term field research in social anthropology,* ed. G. Foster et al. *J. Hist. Behav. Scis.* 16:281–86.

————. 1982. Anthropology in crisis? A view from between the generations. In *Crisis in anthropology: View from Spring Hill, 1980,* ed. E. A. Hoebel et al., 407–19. New York.

Swayze, Nansi. 1960. *Canadian portraits: Jenness, Barbeau, Wintemberg; the manhunters.* Toronto.

Symmons-Symonolewicz, K. 1958. Bronislaw Malinowski: An intellectual profile. *Polish Rev.* 3:55–76.

————. 1959. Bronislaw Malinowski: Formative influences and theoretical evolution. *Polish Rev.* 4:17–45.

————. 1960. Bronislaw Malinowski: Individuality as theorist. *Polish Rev.* 5:53–65.

————. 1982. The ethnographer and his savages: An intellectual history of Malinowski's diary. *Pol. Rev.* 27:92–98.

Thornton, R. J. N.d. The rise of the ethnographic monograph in eastern and southern Africa, 1850–1920. Typescript.

Tumarkin, D. 1982. Miklouho-Maclay:Nineteenth century Russian anthropologist and humanist. *Rain* 51:4–7.

Tylor, E. B. 1871. *Primitive culture.* 2 vols. London.

————. 1884. American aspects of anthropology. *Rept. 54th Meeting, Brit. Assn. Adv. Sci.*:898–924.

Urry, J. 1972. *Notes and Queries in Anthropology* and the development of field methods in British anthropology, 1870–1920. *Procs. Roy. Anth. Inst.*: 45–57.

————. N.d. A history of field methods. In *The general conduct of field research,* ed. R. F. Ellen. London. In press.

Wax, M. 1972. Tenting with Malinowski. *Am. Soc. Rev.* 47:1–13.

WBSP. See under Manuscript Sources.

Weiner, A. B. 1976. *Women of value, men of renown: New perspectives in Trobriand exchange.* Austin.

Westermarck, E. A. 1891. *The history of human marriage.* London.

————. 1927. *Memories of my life.* Trans. A. Barwell. New York.

Wheeler, G. C. 1926. *Mono-Alu folklore (Bougainville Strait, Western Solomon Islands).* London.

White, I. 1981. Mrs. Bates and Mr. Brown: An examination of Rodney Needham's allegations. *Oceania* 51:193–210.

WHR. See under Rivers.

Williams, F. E., ed. 1939. The reminiscences of Ahuia Ova. J. Roy. Anth. Inst. 69:11–44.

Wilson, E. F. 1887. Report on the Blackfoot tribes. Rept. 57th Meeting, Brit. Assn. Adv. Sci.:183–97.

⌐ Young, M. W., ed. 1979. The ethnography of Malinowski: The Trobriand Islands, 1915–18. London.

MANUSCRIPT SOURCES

In writing this paper I have drawn on research materials collected since 1969 from various archival sources, which are cited by the following abbreviations:

ACHP   A. C. Haddon Papers, University Library, Cambridge, England.

AMHP   A. M. Hocart Papers, Alexander Turnbull Library, Wellington, New Zealand (nine reels, microfilm, 1970).

BMPL   Bronislaw Malinowski Papers, British Library of Political and Economic Science, London School of Economics.

BMPY   Bronislaw Malinowski Papers, Yale University Library, New Haven, Conn.

EBTP   E. B. Tylor Papers, Library of the Pitt Rivers Museum, Oxford.

FGP   Francis Galton Papers, University College, London.

JGFP   J. G. Frazer Papers, Trinity College, Cambridge, England.

RFA   Rockefeller Foundation Archives, Tarryton, N.Y.

WBSP   W. B. Spencer Papers, Library of the Pitt Rivers Museum, Oxford.

WHRP   W. H. R. Rivers Papers, in the A. C. Haddon Papers, University Library, Cambridge, England.

POWER AND DIALOGUE IN ETHNOGRAPHY

Marcel Griaule's Initiation

JAMES CLIFFORD

In fact, the sociologist and his "object" form a couple where each one is to be
interpreted through the other, and where the relationship must itself be deci-
phered as a historical moment.

—Sartre: Critique de la raison dialectique

Marcel Griaule cut a figure, self-confident and theatrical. He began his career
as an aviator in the years just after World War I. (Later, in 1946, as holder
of the first chair in ethnology at the Sorbonne, he would lecture in his air-
force officer's uniform.) An energetic promoter of fieldwork, he portrayed it
as the continuation—by scientific means—of a great tradition of adventure
and exploration (1948c:119). In 1928, encouraged by Marcel Mauss and the
linguist Marcel Cohen, Griaule spent a year in Ethiopia. He returned, avid
for a new expedition, and his plans bore fruit two years later in the much-
publicized Mission Dakar-Djibouti, which for twenty-one months traversed
Africa from the Atlantic to the Red Sea along the lower rim of the Sahara.
Largely a museum-collecting enterprise, the mission also undertook extended
ethnographic sojourns in the French Sudan (Mali), where Griaule first made
contact with the Dogon of Sanga, and in Ethiopia (the region of Gondar),
where the expedition spent five months. The mission's nine members (some

---

James Clifford is Associate Professor in the History of Consciousness Program, University of California, Santa Cruz. His research has centered on the recent history of
anthropology in France, and he is the author of *Person and Myth: Maurice Leenhardt
in the Melanesian World.* Currently he is working on a study of ethnography and literature in the twentieth century, focussing on problems of authority and textuality.

coming and going en route) included also André Schaeffner, Deborah Lif-
chitz, and Michel Leiris, each of whom would make significant ethnographic
contributions.

Thanks largely to the publicity sense of Georges-Henri Rivière—a well-
connected jazz *amateur* engaged by Paul Rivet to reorganize the Trocadero
Ethnographic Museum—the Mission Dakar-Djibouti was patronized by Paris
high society. The Chamber of Deputies voted a special law, and Griaule and
Rivière skillfully exploited the postwar vogue for things African in soliciting
funds and personnel. The undertaking partook also of a certain technological
bravado reminiscent of the period's famous expeditions, financed by Citroen,
La Croisière Jaune, and La Croisière Noire—each a *tour de force* of mobility
crossing whole continents by automobile. Griaule, an early enthusiast for the
airplane, would be fascinated throughout his career by technological aids to
ethnography: conventional and aerial photography, sound recording devices,
and even the project of a research-boat-cum-laboratory for use on the Niger.

The mission's "booty," in Rivière and Rivet's term (1933:5), included among
its many photos, recordings, and documents, 3,500 objects destined for the
Trocadero Museum, soon to become the Musée de l'Homme. The idea was
only just winning acceptance in England and America, with Rockefeller funding
of the International African Institute, that intensive field studies were in
themselves enough to justify major subventions. Thus collecting was a financial necessity, and the mission brought back whatever authentic objects it
could decently—and occasionally surreptitiously—acquire. The postwar passion for *l'art nègre* fostered a cult of the exotic artifact, and the carved figures
and masks of West and Equatorial Africa satisfied perfectly a European fetish-
ism nourished on cubist and surrealist aesthetics (Clifford 1981; Jamin 1982).

From 1935 to 1939, Griaule organized group expeditions to the French
Sudan, Cameroon, and Tchad, in which museum-collecting played a lesser
role. In annual or biannual visits to West Africa focussing increasingly on
the Dogon, he worked out a distinctive ethnographic "method" that is the
subject of the present essay. For Griaule the collection of artifacts was part of
the intensive documentation of a unified culture area, a region centered on
the bend of the Niger, and particularly on the Bambara and Dogon—with
whom he spent about three years over ten expeditions (Lettens 1971:504).
Griaule's descriptions were cartographic and archeological as well as ethnographic; he was concerned with variations in cultural traits, the history of
migrations, and the overlay of civilizations in West Africa. But increasingly
his interests focussed on synchronic cultural patterns. Over time he established, to his own satisfaction, the existence of a ramified but coherent culture area he later portrayed as one of three major divisions of sub-Saharan
Africa: the Western Sudan, Bantu Africa, and an intermediate zone in Cameroon and Tchad. Each region was characterized by a traditional *sophie* or

science—a mode of knowledge inscribed in language, habitat, oral tradition, myth, technology, and aesthetics. Griaule discerned common principles underlying the three African epistemological fields, and this permitted him to use the Dogon and their neighbors as privileged examples of *l'homme noir*— microcosms of "African" thought, civilization, philosophy, and religion. A characteristic movement from parts to wholes, to more inclusive wholes, was Griaule's basic mode of ethnographic representation. It mirrored, and found confirmation in, Dogon styles of thought, with their encompassing symbolic correspondences of microcosm and macrocosm, of body and cosmos, of everyday details and the patterns of myth.

A number of different approaches are subsumed under the general label of the "Griaule School."[1] The total project spans five decades, falling roughly into two phases: before and after Ogotemmêli. In 1947, in a now legendary series of interviews, the Dogon sage, Ogotemmêli, apparently acting on instructions from tribal elders, instructed Griaule in the deep wisdom of his people (Griaule 1948a). The first decade of research at Sanga had been exhaustively *documentary* in character; now with access to the knowledge revealed by Ogotemmêli and other qualified informants, the task became *exegetical*. Ogotemmêli's elaborate knowledge—reinforced and extended by other sources—appeared to provide a potent "key" to Dogon culture (Griaule 1952c:548). Seen as a kind of lived mythology, it provided a framework for grasping the Dogon world as an integrated whole. This immanent structure— a "metaphysic" as Griaule liked to call it—offered a purely indigenous organization of the complex total social facts of Dogon life.

Full compilations of this *sagesse*, an enormously detailed system of symbolic and narrative correspondences, appeared only after much further research and cross-checking, which continued after Griaule's death in 1956. The masterpieces of the Griaule School's second period are *Le Renard pâle*, co-authored with his closest collaborator Germaine Dieterlen (1965), and *Ethnologie et langage: La parole chez les Dogon* by his daughter, the distinguished ethnolinguist Geneviève Calame-Griaule (1965). In these works one hears, as it were, two full chords of a Dogon symphony: a mythic explanation of the cosmos, a native theory of language and expressivity. More than just native explanations or theories, these superb compendia present themselves

1. There are many personal variants, and one should distinguish the following standpoints. The "core" of the ongoing research on the Dogon and Bambara is that of Griaule, Dieterlen, and De Ganay. Calame-Griaule and Dominique Zahen contribute directly to the project, but from distinct methodological standpoints. Lebeuf, an early co-worker, shares Griaule's general viewpoint, but his work is concentrated in Tchad. Rouch, de Heusch, and various later students remain ambivalently loyal to the "tradition." Paulme, Leiris, and Schaeffner, early contributors to the Dogon project, have always maintained a skeptical distance from the undertaking, and should not be included in the "school."

as coherent arts of life, socio-mythic landscapes of physiology and personality, symbolic networks incarnate in an infinity of daily details.

The work of Griaule and his followers is one of the classic achievements of twentieth-century ethnography. Within certain areas of emphasis its depth of comprehension and completeness of detail are unparalleled. But given its rather unusual focus, the extreme nature of some of its claims, and the crucial, problematic role of the Dogon themselves as active agents in the long ethnographic process, Griaule's work has been subjected to sharp criticism from a variety of standpoints. Some have noted its idealistic bias and its lack of historical dynamism (Balandier 1960; Sarevskaja 1964). British social anthropologists have raised skeptical questions about Griaule's fieldwork, notably his lifelong reliance on translators and on a few privileged informants attuned to his interests (whose initiatory knowledge might not be readily generalizable to the rest of society). Followers of Malinowski or Evans-Pritchard have missed in Griaule's work any sustained attention to daily existence or politics as actually lived, and in general they are wary of a too perfectly ordered vision of Dogon reality (Richards 1967; Douglas 1967; Goody 1967).

Rereading the Dogon corpus closely, other critics have begun, on the basis of internal contradictions, to unravel the equilibrium of Dogon mythology and to question the processes by which an "absolute subject" (here a unified construct called "the Dogon") is constituted in ethnographic interpretation (Lettens 1971; Michel-Jones 1978). In the wake of colonialism, Griaule has been taken to task for his consistent preference for an African past over a modernizing present. Africans have criticized him for essentializing traditional cultural patterns and repressing the role of individual invention in the elaboration of Dogon myth (Hountondji 1976). After 1950 Griaule's work resonated strongly with the Negritude Movement, particularly with Senghor's evocation of an African essence. But as Senghor's brand of negritude has yielded to Césaire's—a more syncretic, impure, inventive conception of cultural identity—Griaule's African metaphysic begins to seem an ahistorical, idealized alter-ego to a totalizing Occidental humanism.

It is impossible here to evaluate many of the specific criticisms levelled at Griaule, especially in the absence of detailed restudy of the Dogon. A few methodological warnings are necessary, however, when approaching such a contested oeuvre. The historian of fieldwork is hampered by limited and foreshortened evidence; it is always difficult, if not impossible, to know what happened in an ethnographic encounter. (This is at least partly responsible for the fact that the history of anthropology has tended to be a history of theory, even though the modern discipline has defined itself by reference to its distinct "method.") Usually, as in Griaule's case, one must rely heavily on the ethnographer's own ex post facto narrations, accounts which serve to confirm his authority. One can also draw on his methodological prescriptions, and those of collaborators; but these also tend to be overly systematic rationalizations composed after the fact. A scattering of relevant journals and memoirs can help somewhat (Leiris 1934; Rouch 1978b; Paulme 1977), as can a critical reading of published ethnographies and fieldnotes—where available (and comprehensible).[2] But direct evidence of the interpersonal dynamics and politics of research is largely absent. Moreover, there is an enormous gap in all histories of fieldwork: the indigenous "side" of the story. How was the research process understood and influenced by informants, by tribal authorities, by those who did and did not cooperate? (cf. Lewis 1973). Griaule's story has the merit of making this part of the encounter inescapable. But our knowledge of Dogon influences on the ethnographic process remains fragmentary.

It is simplistic to tax Griaule with projecting onto the Dogon a subjective vision, with developing a research method for eliciting essentially what he was looking for (Lettens 1971:397, passim). And even the more credible claim that Griaule overstressed certain parts of Dogon reality at the expense of others assumes the existence of a natural entity called Dogon culture apart from its ethnographic inventions. Even if it is true that key informants became "Griaulized," that Griaule himself was "Dogonized," that Ogotemmêli's wisdom was that of an individual "theologian" and the "secret," initiatory nature of the revealed knowledge was systematically exaggerated; even if other priorities and methods would certainly have produced a different ethnography, it does not follow that Griaule's version of the Dogon is false. His writings, and those of his associates, express a Dogon truth, a complex, negotiated, historically contingent truth specific to certain relations of textual production. The historian asks *what kind of truth* Griaule and the Dogon he worked with produced, in what dialogical conditions, within what political limits, in what historical climate.

Masterpieces like *Le Renard pâle* and *Ethnologie et langage* are elaborate inventions authored by a variety of subjects—European and African. These compendia do not represent the way "the Dogon" think: both their enormous complexity and the absence of female informants cast doubt on any such totalizing claim. Nor is their "deep" knowledge an interpretive key to Dogon reality for anyone beyond the ethnographer and a small number of native

---

2. Anyone who has tried to reinterpret fieldnotes will know it is a problematic enterprise. They may be gnomic, shorthand, heteroglot notes to oneself, or the sorts of "fieldnotes" often quoted in published ethnographies—formulated summaries of events, observations, conversations, etc., recomposed after the fact. It is well-nigh impossible to disentangle the interpretive processes at work as fieldnotes move from one level of textualization to the next. Griaule's 173 richly detailed "fiches de terrain" for the crucial interviews with Ogotemmêli (Griaule 1946) are clearly the product of at least one rewriting, eliminating specific linguistic problems, the presence of the translator Kogem, etc.

"intellectuals." But to say that these Dogon truths are specific inventions (rather than parts or distortions of "Dogon culture") is to take them seriously as textual constructions, avoiding both celebration and polemic.

The Griaule tradition offers one of the few fully elaborated alternatives to the Anglo-American model of intensive participant-observation. For this reason alone it is important for the history of twentieth-century ethnography—particularly with the recent rediscovery in America of "long-term field research" (Foster et al. 1979). Griaule's writings are also important (and here we must separate the man from his "school") for their unusual directness in portraying research as inherently agonistic, theatrical, and fraught with power. His work belongs, manifestly, to the colonial period. And thanks to Griaule's dramatic flair and fondness for overstatement, we can perceive clearly certain key assumptions, roles, and systems of metaphors that empowered ethnography during the thirties and forties.

MANUEL D'ETHNOGRAPHIE

One cannot speak of a French "tradition" of fieldwork, as one refers (perhaps too easily) to British or American schools. Nonetheless, if only by contrast, Griaule's ethnography does appear to be peculiarly French. We can suggest this rather elusive quality by evoking briefly two influential precursors. In Paris the most important advocates of fieldwork during the 1920s were Marcel Mauss and Maurice Delafosse—who collaborated with Lévy-Bruhl and Rivet to found the Institut d'Ethnologie. Here, after 1925, a generation of "Africanist" ethnographers was trained.

In the first three decades of the century Black Africa was coming into focus, separated from the "oriental" Maghreb. By 1931, when the *Journal de la Société des Africanistes* was founded, it had become possible to speak of a field called "Africanism" (modeled on the older synthetic discipline of Orientalism). The fashionable vogue for *L'art nègre* and black music contributed to the formation of a cultural object, a *civilisation* about which synthetic statements could be made. Delafosse's *Les Noirs de l'Afrique* and *L'Ame noir* contributed to this development along with the translated writings of Frobenius. Griaule's work unfolded within the Africanist paradigm, moving associatively from specific studies of particular populations to generalizations about *l'homme noire*, African civilization, and metaphysics (Griaule 1951, 1953).

At the Institut d'Ethnologie a regular stream of colonial officers studied ethnographic method as part of their training at the Ecole Coloniale, where Delafosse was a popular teacher before his death in 1926. As a veteran of

Marcel Griaule developing photographic plates, Sanga, October–November 1931. Courtesy Mission Dakar-Djibouti, Musée de l'Homme, Paris.

extended duty in West Africa, Delafosse knew African languages and cultures intimately. When his health was undermined by the rigors of constant travel and research, he retired to France, becoming the first professor of Black African languages at the Ecole des Langues Orientales. A scholar of great erudition, he made contributions to African history, ethnography, geography, and linguistics. At the Ecole Coloniale, where Africans had long been considered childlike inferiors, he taught the fundamental equality (though not the similarity) of races. Different milieux produce different civilizations. If Africans are technically and materially backward this is a historical accident; their art, their moral life, their religions, are nonetheless fully developed and worthy of esteem. He urged his students toward ethnography and the mastery of indigenous languages. His authority was concrete experience, his persona that of the *broussard*—man of the back-country, tough-minded, iconoclastic,

humane, impatient with hierarchy and the artifices of polite society (Delafosse 1909; cf. Deschamps 1975:97). For a generation of young, liberally
inclined colonial officers he represented an authentic, concrete way to "know"
Africa and to communicate its fascination.

After Delafosse's death the principal influence on the first generation of
professional fieldworkers in France was exerted by another charismatic teacher,
Marcel Mauss. Though he never undertook fieldwork, Mauss consistently
deplored France's backwardness in this domain (Mauss 1913). At the Institut
d'Ethnologie he taught a yearly course (*Ethnographie descriptive*) specifically
geared to fieldwork methods. Mauss was anything but an abstract, bookish
scholar; anyone who looks at his "Techniques du Corps" (1934) can see for
themselves an acute power of observation, an interest in the concrete and
the experiential (cf. Condominas 1972). Mauss urged all his students toward
ethnography; between 1925 and 1940 the Institut sponsored more than a
hundred field trips (Karady 1981:176). Unlike Rivers, Malinowski, and later
Griaule, whose teaching reflected their own experiences in the field, he did
not propound a distinct research "method." But if he lacked intimate experience, he did not feel compelled to rationalize or justify his own practice.
Versed in the fieldwork traditions of various nations, his course was an inventory, classification, and critique of possible methods. Mauss provided a sense
of the complexity of "total social facts" (Mauss 1924:274), and the different
means by which descriptions, recordings, textual accounts, and collections
of artifacts could be constituted. His wide-ranging *Manuel d'ethnographie* (1947),
a compilation of course notes brought together by Denise Paulme shortly
before his death, makes it clear that the idea of a privileged approach was
quite foreign to him.

Mauss strongly supported the general trend of modern academic fieldwork,
urging "the professional ethnographer" to adopt "the intensive method"
(1947:13). Serious comparative work depended on the completion of full
local descriptions. But although the *Manuel's* recommendations reflect a close
knowledge of American and British techniques, there is no emphasis on individual participant-observation. Mauss endorses team research; overall, his
approach is documentary rather than experiential and hermeneutic.

This documentary concern would be reflected in the introduction of Griaule's
first major field monograph: "This work presents documents relative to the
Masks of the Dogon, collected during research trips among the cliffs of Ban-
diagara. . . ." (Griaule 1938:vii). It is hard to imagine an account in the
Malinowskian tradition beginning in this way. Although Griaule does considerably more in *Masques Dogons* than simply display collected documents,
the metaphor reveals a particular empirical style (cf. Leenhardt 1932; Clifford 1982a:138–141). For Mauss, who accepted an older division of labor
between the man in the field and the theorist at home, description should

never be governed by explanatory concerns (Mauss 1947:389). To provide the kind of information useful to a comparative sociology, the ethnographer should avoid building too much implicit explanation into ethnographic data in the process of its constitution. Mauss gave no special status to the idea that a synthetic portrait of a culture (something, for him, massively overdetermined) could be produced through the research experience of an individual subject, or built around the analysis of a typical or central institution. His limiting notion of "total social facts" led him rather to recommend the deployment of multiple documentary methods by a variety of specialized observers. Working at a higher level of abstraction, the sociologist could perhaps "glimpse, measure, and hold in equilibrium" (1924:279) the different strata of "total" facts—technological, aesthetic, geographical, demographic, economic, juridical, linguistic, religious, historical, and intercultural. But the ethnographer's task, whether alone or in a research team, was to amass as complete a corpus as possible: texts, artifacts, maps, photographs, and so forth—"documents" precisely localized and covering a broad range of cultural phenomena. Fieldworkers should construct "series and not panoplies" (21). Mauss used old terms precisely: a panoply is a complete complement of arms, a suit of armor with all its accoutrements. The term suggests a functional integration of parts deployed and displayed around a coherent, effective body. Mauss did not see society or culture this way. One should be wary of reducing his concept of total social facts (reminiscent of Freud's "overdetermination") to a functionalist notion of the interrelation of parts.

Mauss' elusive concept nevertheless articulated a fundamental predicament for twentieth-century ethnographers. If every "fact" is susceptible to multiple encoding, making sense in diverse contexts and implicating in its comprehension the "total" ensemble of relations that constitutes the society under study, then this assumption can serve as encouragement to grasp the ensemble by focussing on one of its parts. Indeed, this is what fieldworkers have always done, building up social wholes ("cultures" in the American tradition) through a concentration on significant elements. Many different approaches have emerged: the focus on key "institutions" (Malinowski's Trobriand Kula, Evans-Pritchard's Azande witchcraft); the bringing to the foreground of "totalizing cultural performances" (Spencer and Gillen's Arunta initiation, Bateson's Iatmul Naven, Geertz's Balinese cockfight); the identification of privileged armatures to which the whole of culture could be related (Rivers' "genealogical method" and Radcliffe-Brown's "social structure"); or even Griaule's late conception of initiatory knowledge as the key to a unified representation of West African cultures. In different ways the new generation of academic fieldworkers were all looking for what Griaule would recommend, defending his practice of teamwork in the field—a "rapid, sure method" able to grasp synthetically an overdetermined cultural reality

(1933:8). Thus Mauss' belief that the totality of society is implicit in its parts or organizing structures may appear as a kind of enabling charter for a broad range of fieldwork tactics (approaches to social representation in the rhetorical mode of synecdoche), without which, relatively short-term professional fieldwork would be questionable—particularly research aiming at portrayals of whole cultures. Since one cannot study everything at once, one must be able to highlight parts or attack specific problems in the confidence that they evoke a wider context.

But there is another side to total social facts: the idea is ambiguous, and finally troubling. If it legitimates partial cultural descriptions, it offers no guidance as to which code, key, or luminous example is to be preferred. Like Nietzsche's vision of infinite interpretations, Mauss' idea sees social reality and the moral world as constructed in many possible ways, none of which may be privileged. Modern ethnography took shape in a shattered world haunted by nihilism, and Mauss' own portrayals of the constitution of collective order were acutely aware of the possibility of disorder. *The Gift* is an allegory of reconciliation and reciprocity in the wake of the First World War. As is well known, the war had a devastating impact on Mauss; its sequel in 1940 would deprive him of the will to work and think. With the breakdown of evolutionist master-narratives, the relativist science of culture worked to rethink the world as a dispersed whole, composed of distinct, functioning, and interrelated cultures. It reconstituted social and moral wholeness, plurally. If synecdochic ethnography argued, in effect, that "cultures" hold together, it did so in response to a pervasive modern feeling, linking the Irishman Yeats to the Nigerian Achebe, that "things fall apart."

For a committed socialist like Mauss, the study of society was a refusal of nihilism; its constructions of social wholeness served moral and political as well as scientific ends. But he was too clear-sighted and knowledgeable to espouse any sovereign method for the constitution of totalities. He contented himself with a kind of gay science—generous, rather than, like Nietzsche, sardonic. He presented a generation of ethnographers with an astonishing repertoire of objects for study and ways to put the world together: ethnography was a dipping of different nets in the teeming ocean, each catching its own sort of fish. Schooled in Cushing's work, he knew that the task of representing a culture was potentially endless. "You say you have spent two and a half years with one tribe," he remarked to Meyer Fortes, "poor man, it will take you twenty years to write it up" (Fortes 1973:284).

Mauss' *Manuel* was not a *méthode*, but an enormous checklist; thus one cannot speak of a "Maussian," as one can of a "Malinowskian" or a "Boasian," ethnography. (This fact may explain, in part, why French fieldwork has never assumed a distinct identity and has, in effect, been invisible to anthropologists of other traditions.) His students diverged markedly. Alfred Métraux pursued a distinguished career of American-style participant-observation. Michel Leiris, while making original contributions to Dogon and Ethiopian ethnography, never stopped questioning the subjective conflicts and political constraints of cross-cultural study as such. Maurice Leenhardt, whose late entry into the Paris University was much encouraged by Mauss, represented an older style of research whose authority was rooted in years of missionary work rather than in academic training. Charles LeCoeur, who attended Malinowski's seminar at the London School of Economics, lived among the Teda, learned their language, and formally, at least, conducted fieldwork à l'Anglais. Of Mauss' other students—virtually every major French ethnographer before 1950—only Griaule developed a systematic method and a distinct tradition of research.

DOCUMENTARY VICISSITUDES

Two loose metaphoric structures govern Griaule's conception of fieldwork: a documentary system (governed by images of collection, observation, and interrogation) and an initiatory complex (where dialogical processes of education and exegesis come to the fore). Griaule himself presented the two approaches as complementary, each requiring and building on the other. But one can discern a shift from the documentary to the initiatory as his career progressed and as his personal involvement with Dogon modes of thought and belief deepened. For the sake of analytic clarity, we consider them separately. It should be understood, however, that both are attempts to account for a complicated, evolving ethnographic experience—an experience traversed by influences, historical and intersubjective, beyond the control of Griaule's metaphors.

The notion that ethnography was a process of collection dominated the Mission Dakar-Djibouti, with its museographical emphasis. The ethnographic object—be it a tool, statue, or mask—was understood to be a peculiarly reliable "witness" to the truth of an alien society. The Maussian rationale is evident in a set of "Instructions for Collectors" distributed by the mission.

> Because of the need that has always driven men to imprint the traces of their activity on matter, nearly all phenomena of collective life are capable of expression in given objects. A collection of objects systematically gathered is thus a rich gathering of admissable evidence [pièces à conviction]. Their collection creates archives more revealing and sure than written archives, since these

are authentic, autonomous objects which cannot have been fabricated for the needs of the case [les besoins de la cause], and which thus characterize types of civilizations better than anything else.

(Mauss 1931:6–7)

"Dead," decontextualized objects, the brochure went on to argue, can be restored to "life" by a surrounding "documentation" (descriptions, drawings, photos). The links tying any object or institution to the "ensemble of society" can thus be reconstituted and the truth of the whole elicited scientifically from any one of its parts.

The recurring juridical metaphors (pièces à conviction, besoins de la cause) are revealing; if all the parts of a culture can in principle be made to yield the whole, what justifies an ethnographer's particular selection of revealing "evidence"? Some "witnesses" must be more reliable than others. A corollary of the value placed on objects as "authentic and autonomous," not "fabricated for the needs of the case," is the assumption that other forms of evidence, the "archives" composed on the basis of personal observation, description, and interpretation, are less pure, more infected with the contingent ethnographic encounter, its clash of interests and partial truths. For Griaule, fieldwork was a perpetual struggle for control (in the political and scientific senses) of this encounter.

Griaule assumed that the opposing interests of ethnographer and native could never be entirely harmonized. Relations sometimes romanticized by the term "rapport" were really negotiated settlements, outcomes of a continuous push and pull determining what could and could not be known of the society under study. The outsider was always in danger of losing the initiative, of acquiescing in a superficial modus vivendi. What was systematically hidden in a culture could not be learned simply by becoming a temporary member of a common moral community. It could only be revealed by a kind of violence: the ethnographer must keep up the pressure (Griaule 1957:14). Griaule may have had no choice: in Sudanese societies, with their long processes of initiation, one had either to force the revelation of occult traditions or to be on the scene for decades.

Of all the possible avenues to hidden truths, the least reliable was speech—what informants actually said in response to questions. This was due not merely to conscious lying and resistance to inquiry; it followed from dramatistic assumptions that were a leitmotif of his work. For Griaule, every informant's self-presentation (along with that of the ethnographer) was a dramatization, a putting forward of certain truths and a holding back of others. In penetrating these conscious or unconscious disguises, the fieldworker had to exploit whatever advantages, whatever sources of power, whatever knowledge not based on interlocution he or she could acquire (Griaule 1957:92).

Marcel Griaule photographing from cliff-top near Sanga, October–November 1931. André Schaeffner holds him by the ankles. Courtesy Mission Dakar-Djibouti, Musée de l'Homme Paris.

Griaule looked initially to visual observation as a source of information that could be obtained without depending on uncertain oral collaboration, and could provide the edge needed to provoke, control, and verify confessional discourses. Accustomed to actually looking down on things (his first job in the Air Force had been that of an aerial spotter and navigator), Griaule was particularly conscious of the advantages of overview, of the precise mapping of habitats and their surrounding terrain. This visual preoccupation, apparent in all his methodological works, emerges with disconcerting clarity in *Les Saô légendaires,* his popular account of ethnographic and archeological work in Tchad (1943:53–76).

Perhaps it's a quirk acquired in military aircraft, but I always resent having to explore an unknown terrain on foot. Seen from high in the air, a district holds few secrets. Property is delineated as if in India ink; paths converge on critical points; interior courtyards yield themselves up; the inhabited jumble comes clear. With an aerial photograph the components of institutions fall into place as a series of things disassembled, and yielding. Man is silly: he suspects his neighbor, never the sky; inside the four walls, palisades, fences, or hedges of an enclosed space he thinks all is permitted. But all his great and small intentions, his sanctuaries, his garbage, his careless repairs, his ambitions for growth appear on an aerial photograph. In a village I know in the French Sudan, I recall having discovered four important sanctuaries at the cost of much hard land travel, along with platitudes, flattery, payoffs, and unredeemable promises. Seventeen sanctuaries appeared on an aerial photo thanks to the millet pulp spread out on their domes. All at once the openness of my informants increased to an unbelievable degree. With an airplane, one fixes the underlying structure both of topography and of minds.

(Griaule 1943:61–62)

It is not clear whether this passage should be read as enthusiastic publicity for a new scientific method (Griaule 1937), or as a somewhat disturbing fantasy of observational power. Griaule seldom had an airplane at his disposal in the field, but he adopted its panoptic viewpoint as a habit, and a tactic.

The simple fact of drawing up a map could give overview, an initial mastery of the culture inscribed on the land. Recounting the excavation of ancient funeral remains against the wishes of local inhabitants who considered the graves to be ancestral, Griaule provides an extraordinary phenomenology of the white outsider's struggle to maintain an edge in dealings with the native council of elders. Because their oral tradition is a key source of information for where exactly to dig, they must be induced to talk (1943:58). Griaule is alive to all manner of signs, in behavior and especially in the terrain, that may eventually serve as entrees into the hidden world of custom. His questions aim to provoke and confuse, to elicit unguarded responses. Having arduously mapped the landholdings and habitations of the region he is able to pose unexpectedly acute queries about incongruous sites that are in fact sacred—altars, a strange door in a wall, a curious topographic feature— traces of secrets written on the surface of the habitat. The map-making outsider holds a disconcerting authority: he seems already to know where everything is. Revelations follow. New sites are excavated.

For Griaule a map is not only a plan of work, but "a base for combat," where "every inscribed position is a conquered position" (1943:66). Throughout his account he is conscious of the aggressive, disruptive power of the gaze. Investigation, looking into something, is never neutral. The researchers feel themselves under surveillance: "hundreds of eyes follow us. We're in full view of the village; in every crack in the wall, behind every granary, an eye is attentive" (64). In opposition stands their scientific observation: "To dig a hole is to commit an indiscretion, to open an eye onto the past" (68). Every inquest is "a siege to be organized" (60). This particular war of gazes ends with a nominal truce, a compromise permitting the collection of certain artifacts, while a few especially sacred ones are spared (76). But the theatrical tug-of-war actually ends with an arrangement entirely to the advantage of the outsiders, who are able to complete their excavation, remove numerous relics, and establish ground-rules for later intensive ethnography.

For Griaule, the exhaustive documentation of a culture was a precondition for plumbing its "secrets" through long-term, controlled interrogation of informants. He did not, of course, believe that complete description was possible; but often—especially when defending his practice of teamwork against the Anglo-American model of individual participant-observation—he would betray panoptical aspirations. His favorite example was the problem of describing a Dogon funeral ceremony, a spectacle involving hundreds of participants. An individual participant-observer would be lost in the melee, jotting down more or less arbitrary impressions, and with little grasp of the whole.

Griaule argues that the only way adequately to document such an event is to deploy a team of observers. He offers, characteristically, a map of the performance site and a set of tactics for its coverage—proceeding rather in the manner of a modern television crew reporting on an American political convention (1933:11; 1957:47–52). Observer number one will be stationed atop a cliff not far from the village square, with the job of photographing and noting the large-scale movements of the rite; number two is among the menstruating women to one side; three mixes with a band of young torch-bearers; four observes the group of musicians; five is on the rooftops, "charged with surveillance in the wings with their thousand indiscretions, and going frequently, along with number six, to the dead man's house in search of the latest news." Number seven observes the reactions of the women and children to the masked dances and ritual combats taking place at center stage. All observers note the exact times of their observations, so that a synthetic portrait of the ritual can be constructed.

This only begins the task of adequate documentation. The synoptic outline thus constructed will later be augmented and corrected by processes of "verification" and "commentary." Witnesses must be asked for their explanations of obscure gestures. "Holes" in the fabric will be filled in, including those due to contingencies of a specific performance—the absence or presence of particular groups or individuals, the forgetfulness of the actors, or any divergences from the rite's "ideal harmony" (50). Slowly, over a number of years, building on repeat performances if possible, an ideal type of the rite will be laboriously constructed. But this enormous "dossier" spills out in many directions, and "each part of the observation becomes the core of an enquiry which sooner or later will furnish a vast network of information" (51).

Griaule's *Méthode de l'ethnographie*, from which the above account is drawn, provides a rationalized version of his own research practice. It is often unclear whether the methods propounded are those Griaule actually used, or ideal recommendations based on a rather more messy experience. But the *Méthode* gives a good sense of the overall assumptions and parameters of his fieldwork. In Sanga the Mission Dakar-Djibouti had, in fact, encountered a Dogon funeral, a dramatic, confusing rite featuring spectacular performances by masked dancers. Griaule set about its documentation: his subsequent work would center on the secret society of masks, and various of his co-workers contributed related studies (Leiris 1948; De Ganay 1941; Dieterlen 1941). By dint of repeated visits and intensive collaborative work, an organized corpus of "documents" was built up.

Griaule's focus on the institution of masks did not involve a synecdochic representation of culture as a whole in the functionalist tradition (using the mask society as either an ideal-typical "institution" or its rituals as "totalizing cultural performances"). Rather, working out from this dense cluster of total social facts he and his associates constructed a "vast network of information" as a context and control for what natives themselves said about their culture. Initially, in his "documentary" phase, Griaule used the explications of informants as commentaries on observed behavior and collected artifacts. But this attitude would change, especially after Ogotemmêli: once properly tested and qualified, informants could be trusted with research tasks. With proper control, they could become regular auxiliaries and, in effect, members of the team. The network of observation and documentation could thus be dramatically extended (Griaule 1957:61–64). Teamwork was an efficient way to deal with total social facts, to produce a full documentation on a multiplicity of subjects treated in diverse manners.

As conceived by Griaule, the team was much more than a makeshift collaboration of individuals. It embodied the principle underlying all modern inquiry: specialization and the division of labor. Because social reality was too complex for the single researcher, he must "rely on other specialists and try to form with them a thinking group, an element of combat, a tactical unit of research in which each person, while holding to his own personal qualities, knows he is an intelligent cog of a machine in which he is indispensable, but without which he is nothing" (1957:26). Some of Griaule's early co-workers, like Leiris, Schaeffner, and Paulme, did not find enduring places within this productive mechanism—Leiris' scandalous *L'Afrique fantôme* (1934) was a clear breach of discipline. But others (De Ganay, Dieterlen, Lebeuf, and Calame-Griaule), if not precisely "intelligent cogs," worked freely within the developing paradigm. Griaule spoke of his ideal team in terms of organic solidarity and a quasi-military esprit de corps, and the works of the school do suggest an efficient collaborative enterprise. But as a productive mechanism, the "team" could never be tightly controlled. And when one includes as active agents the Dogon informants, translators, and tribal authorities—whose influence on the content and timing of the knowledge gained was crucial—it becomes apparent that the collaborative documentary experience initiated by Griaule in 1932 had, by the fifties, undergone a metamorphosis.

How, before Ogotemmêli, did Griaule "choose," "identify," "interrogate," and "utilize" informants? (1952c:542–47; 1957:54–61) His methodological strictures are particularly revealing since, as his respect for African oral tradition grew, he came increasingly to center his research on close work with a limited number of *collaborateurs indigènes*. The informant must first be carefully identified and located in a specific group or set of groups within the social fabric. In this way one can allow for exaggerators, and for omissions related to group loyalty, taboos, etc. He or she—in fact Griaule's informants, as he regretfully noted, were almost entirely men (1957:15)—has to be qualified to pronounce on particular subjects, whether technological, historical, legal, or religious. His "moral qualities" are to be assessed: sincerity, good faith, memory. Although many of his informants were significantly influenced by "outside" perspectives (Lettens 1971:520–35), Griaule weighed heavily the attachment to tradition, mistrusting Christians, Muslims, and individuals with too much prior contact with whites (1957:57).

Every informant, Griaule assumes, enunciates a different kind of truth, and the ethnographer must be constantly alive to its limitations, strengths, and weaknesses. In his *Méthode* he discusses different kinds of "liars." Indeed, throughout his work he is preoccupied with lies—although not as simple untruths. Each informant, even the most sincere, experiences an "instinctive need to dissimulate particularly delicate points. He will gladly take advantage of the slightest chance to escape the subject and dwell on another" (1957:58). Native collaborators "lie" in jest, by venality, by desire to please, or in fear of neighbors and the gods (56). Forgetful informants or Europeanized informants are particularly dangerous types of "liars." In an ethnographic "strategic operation" (59), the investigator must break through initial defenses and dissimulations. Often an individual informant must be isolated for intensive questioning, so as to remove inhibiting social pressures (60). When their testimony is confronted with differing versions gained from other interviews, hard-pressed informants enunciate truths they had not intended to reveal. On one occasion Griaule permits himself to dream of an "ideal" situation: "an infinity of separated informants" (1943:62). On the other hand, it may sometimes be profitable to pursue inquiries in public, especially over delicate problems like land tenure, where the researcher can provoke revealing disputes with their inevitable indiscretions (1943:66–68; 1957:60).

Griaule's tactics are varied; but they have in common an active, aggressive posture not unlike the judicial process of "interrogation" (1952:542, 547):

"The role of the person sniffing out social facts is often comparable to that of a detective or examining magistrate. The fact is the crime, the interlocutor the guilty party; all the society's members are accomplices" (1957:59). He is fascinated by the tactics of oral inquiry, the play of truth and falsehood that can lead into "labyrinths" that are "organized." Like a psychoanalyst, he begins to see patterns of resistance, forgetfulness, and omission not as mere obstacles, but as signs of a deeper structuring of the truth:

> The informant, on first contact, seldom offers much resistance. He lets himself be backed into positions he has been able to organize in the course of feeling out the situation, observing the quirks, skills, and awkwardnesses of his interlocutor. The value of these positions depends on what he can make of them; he resists as best he can. And if they are taken by force? After other similar resistances, he will retreat to a final position which depends neither on himself nor his "adversary" but on the system of prohibitions of custom.
>
> (1952c:59–60)

For Griaule, the deep structure of resistances is not specific to an inter-subjective encounter, but derives from a general source, the rules of "custom." This hypostatized entity is the last bastion to be stormed. But as we shall see, it cannot be conquered by frontal assault, by the tactical processes of observation, documentation, or interrogation. A different "initiatory" process will come into play.

Designed for beginning fieldworkers, Griaule's treatises on ethnographic technique remain largely within the "documentary" paradigm. Moreover, Griaule probably did not have time fully to digest the methodological consequences of Ogotemmêli's revelations or of the gathering critique of colonial knowledge in the decade before the *Méthode* was published. It is probably best to read this rather mechanistic compendium of techniques as a less than successful attempt to control an unruly research process, in Georges Devereux's terms (1967), a passage from anxiety to method. Griaule's ultimate complex reciprocal involvement with the Dogon is hardly captured in section titles like "The detection and observation of human facts," or in the portrayal of ethnographers and indigenous collaborators as builders of information networks, collectors of "documents," compilers of "dossiers." Ethnography, in Griaule's juridical language, is still here akin to the process of *instruction*—in French law, the preliminary establishment of the facts of a case, before the *jugement* proper (1957:51). Working among interested parties the ethnographer uses the far-reaching powers of the *juge d'instruction* (one of Griaule's favorite metaphors), to smoke out the truth (cf. Ehrmann 1976). Generally respecting the division of labor laid down by Mauss, and suspicious of abstractions and systematic cross-cultural comparison, Griaule leaves matters of theory and explanation to others outside the fray. The *juge d'instruc-*

tion, having collected enough reliable documents, and having cross-checked his witnesses' versions of the facts, has in his possession everything he needs to determine the truth.

But by 1950, these attitudes toward observation and interrogation were becoming generally suspect, and Griaule's early documentary metaphor was no longer adequate to a research process that was taking on a life of its own. Gradually, Griaule's understanding of the Dogon was becoming indistinguishable from their own increasingly elaborate explications. The originality of the ethnographic activity he set in motion was that it uncovered—and to an undetermined extent provoked—a sophisticated interpretation of their culture by a group of influential Dogon.

IRONIES

Before considering the second phase of Griaule's work, it is worth stepping back for a moment from his research styles and tactics to suggest their relation to the colonial situation. Griaule provides us with a kind of dramaturgy of ethnographic experience before the fifties. In an extraordinary passage— included in both early and late discussions of methodology—he evokes the gamut of power-laden roles adopted by an ethnographer eliciting information from an informant. *"Ethnographie active,"* he writes, is "the art of being a midwife and an examining magistrate":

> By turns an affable comrade of the person put to cross-examination, a distant friend, a severe stranger, compassionate father, a concerned patron; a trader paying for revelations one by one, a listener affecting distraction before the open gates of the most dangerous mysteries, an obliging friend showing lively interest for the most insipid family stories—the ethnographer parades across his face as pretty a collection of masks as that possessed by any museum.
> (Griaule 1933:10; 1952c:547; 1957:59)

The passage evokes a theme infusing all Griaule's work—that ethnography is a theatrical undertaking. His dramaturgy does not, however, include a role popular among fieldworkers in the Anglo-American tradition: the persona of the earnest learner, often cast as a child in the process of acquiring, of being taught, adult knowledge. Perhaps this persona did not occur to Griaule because, seconded by interpreters and European co-workers, he never actually experienced the position of being a stammerer, helpless in an alien culture. It was only after 1950, late in his career, that he began to adopt the standpoint of a student with respect to Dogon culture. But this role was always mixed with the less vulnerable authority of initiate, spokesman, and exegete.

At least in his writings, Griaule never abandoned a basic confidence, a sense of ultimate control over the research and its products. But maintaining control was always a battle, at best a joking relation. Griaule never presented fieldwork as an innocent attainment of rapport analogous to friendship. Nor did he naturalize the process as an experience of education or growth (child or adolescent becoming adult), or as acceptance into an extended family (a kinship role given to the ethnographer). Rather, his accounts assumed a recurring conflict of interests, an agonistic drama, resulting in mutual respect, complicity in a productive balance of power.

Griaule's writings are unusual in their sharp awareness of a structural power differential and a substratum of violence underlying all relations between whites and blacks in a colonial situation. For example, in *Les Flambeurs d'hommes*, an adventure story Griaule called "an objective description of certain episodes from my first trip to Abyssinia" (1953:vi), he coolly notes a "given" of colonial life: the members of his caravan having shown themselves reluctant to attempt a tricky fording of the Nile, "there followed blows, given by the White Man and not returned; for a White is always a man of the government, and if you touch him complications ensue" (7–8). A revealing stylistic device is deployed here, as elsewhere in Griaule's accounts of fieldwork (1948a): a use of the passive voice and of generic terms for himself— "the White Man," "the European," "the Traveller," "the Nazarite," "the Foreigner." The story of the beatings suggests an automatic series of events, to which all parties acquiesce. A European in Africa cannot, should not, avoid the parts reserved for him. Griaule does not think of eluding the privileges, and constraints, of his ascribed status—a dream that obsesses, and to a degree paralyzes, Michel Leiris, his colleague of the Mission Dakar-Djibouti. Leiris' field journal (1934) and his later writings, both ethnological and literary, portray a slow reconciliation with a theatrical conception of the self. But his acceptance is always ambivalent, in creative conflict with a desire for immediate contact and participation (Clifford 1982b). Griaule, by contrast, harbors no qualms about his own theatricality. Once this is clear, puzzling aspects of his practice become clearer—for example, his ideal "coverage" of the Dogon funeral.

Griaule's elaborate panoptic plan will raise the hackles of any ethnographer schooled in participant-observation. The crew he envisages must necessarily disturb and perhaps orient the course of the ceremony, but this does not seem to concern Griaule. Does he naively imagine that seven observers will not exert a considerable influence? The question is beside the point, for Griaule never thought of being an unobtrusive participant. His research was manifestly an intrusion; he made no pretense that it be otherwise. Thus, to an important degree, the truth he recorded was a truth provoked by ethnography. One is tempted to speak of an "*ethnographie vérité*" analogous to the *cinéma vérité* pioneered by Griaule's later associate Jean Rouch—not a reality objectively recorded by the camera, but one provoked by its active presence (Rouch 1978).

One suspects that Griaule saw culture itself, like personality, as a performance or spectacle. In the years following the Dakar-Djibouti mission Griaule and his teams turned up every year or so at Sanga. The arrival of these increasingly familiar outsiders was a dramatic event. Time was of the essence; informants were mobilized, rituals acted for the cameras, and as much Dogon life as possible recorded. In fact, Griaule's early research tended to concentrate on aspects of cultural life susceptible to demonstration and performance: masks, public rituals, and games. It is significant in this regard that Sanga, the Dogon community most accustomed to ethnography, is today the region's principal tourist center, routinely performing its dances for outsiders (Imperato 1978:7–32).

Griaule's penchant for the dramatic infuses his work; and for the historian this poses problems of interpretation. For example, a heightened but characteristic passage in *Les Saô légendaires* exults in a breakthrough. Having maneuvered native interlocutors into giving up information they had not intended to divulge, Griaule contemplates the promise of future work in the area:

> We would be able to make asses of the old hesitators, to confound the traitors, abominate the silent. We were going to see mysteries leap like reptiles from the mouths of the neatly caught liars. We would play with the victim; we would rub his nose in his words. We'd make him smile, spit up the truth, and we'd turn out of his pockets the last secret polished by the centuries, a secret to make he who has spoken it blanch with fear.
>
> (Griaule 1943:74)

How is one to read such a passage? Griaule always liked to provoke: a passage written to shock in 1943 is still shocking, and puzzling. In the narrative to which it is a kind of climax, one watches with discomfort and with growing anger as the ethnographer bullies, cajoles, manipulates those whose resistance interferes with his inquiry, natives who do not wish to see their ancestral remains collected in the interests of a foreign science. But Griaule will not permit us to dismiss him out of hand. If we now perceive such attitudes and acts as an embarrassment, it is thanks to Griaule that we see them so clearly. He rubs our nose in them.

Because Griaule played colonial roles with gusto and with a certain irony, the words quoted above cannot be placed neatly in their historical context and dismissed as attitudes unfortunately possible in the colonial period. It was more typical of the period to hide such violence than to bring it to the fore. Yet if the violence is, in some sense, Griaule's point, nowhere does he suggest a criticism of forced confessions in ethnography. On the contrary, his methodological writings give instructions on how to provoke them. Griaule does not express serious second thoughts about establishing dominance, finding and exploiting the weakness, disunity, and confusion of his native hosts. Thus an historical reading of such awkward passages cannot understand Griaule as either a typical participant or a self-conscious critic within the colonial situation. His position is more complex.

One is tempted to ascribe such passages to Griaule's "style"—his penchant for banter, for charged metaphors, for provocation. But this merely raises the question of how a style functions as part of a research activity, and how it plays against an ideological milieu. Griaule's style is not merely, as some have assumed, a *faiblesse*, a distracting and unfortunate deviation from the scientific business at hand (Lettens 1971:12, 491). It is rather a meaningful response to a predicament, a set of roles and discursive possibilities that may be called *ethnographic liberalism*. A complex, contentious recent debate on anthropology and empire has largely established that ethnographers before the 1950s acquiesced in colonial regimes (Leiris 1950; Asad 1973; Copans 1974). White rule or cultural dominance was a given context for their work, and they adopted a range of liberal positions within it. Seldom "colonialists" in any direct, instrumental sense, ethnographers accepted certain constraints while, in varying degrees, questioning them. This ambivalent predicament imposed certain roles.

Griaule's style of ethnographic liberalism may be understood both as a dramatic performance and as a mode of irony. The most acute observers of the colonial situation, Orwell and Conrad for example, have portrayed it as a power-laden, ambiguous world of discontinuous, clashing realities. Like the young district officer who unwillingly shoots an elephant to avoid being laughed at by a crowd of Burmese, and like all the characters in *Heart of Darkness*, displaced Europeans must labor to maintain their cultural identities, however artificial these may appear. Both colonial and ethnographic situations provoke the unnerving feeling of being on stage, observed and out of place. Participants in such milieux are caught in roles they cannot choose. We have seen Griaule's heightened awareness of the masks worn as part of fieldwork's clash of wills, wits, bluffs, and strategies. He is not unique in stressing the importance of theatricality and impression management in ethnography, the sense that research relationships develop "behind many masks" (Berreman 1962). And most ethnographers, like him, have rejected the pretense of going native, of being able to shed a fundamental Europeanness. But only a few have portrayed so clearly the tactical dissimulations and irreducible violence of ethnographic work (Rabinow 1977:129–30).

Unlike a Conrad, Orwell, or Leiris, Griaule seems not oppressed by his role-playing. But although he is not critical, he is ironic. If he compares ethnography to a theatre of war or a judicial proceeding, one need not assume that in the field he acted consistently as a company commander or an ex-amining magistrate. To take Griaule's metaphors at face value is to miss their implicit analytical function. And it is also to push aside his other personae: his charm, his temper, his playful banter, his growing sympathy, even love, for the Dogon.

Ethnographic liberals, of which there are many sorts, have tended to be ironic participators. They have sought ways to stand out, or apart, from the imperial roles reserved for them as Whites. There have been frequent varia-tions on Delafosse's *broussard*. Many have, in one way or another, publicly identified themselves with exotic modes of life and thought or cultivated an image of marginality. Griaule's exaggeration is another response. Ethno-graphic liberalism is an array of ironic positions, roles both within, and at a certain remove from, the colonial situation. Its complete dramaturgy remains to be written.

The political and ethical tensions visible in Griaule's writings have only recently become explicit subjects of analysis. A penetrating paragraph writ-ten in 1968 by Clifford Geertz reflects the beginning of the end of innocence in fieldwork:

> Usually the sense of being members, however temporarily, insecurely and in-completely, of a single moral community, can be maintained even in the face of the wider social realities which press in at almost every moment to deny it. It is this fiction—fiction, not falsehood—that lies at the very heart of success-ful anthropological field research; and, because it is never completely convinc-ing for any of the participants, it renders such research, considered as a form of conduct, continuously ironic.
>
> (1968:154)

By the late sixties the romantic mythology of fieldwork rapport had begun publicly to dissolve. Since then a growing reflexivity in ethnographic thought and practice has deepened the recognition of its ironic structure, its reliance on improvised, historically contingent fictions. This new awareness makes possible a reading of Griaule that sees a theatrical, ironic stance as central to his ethnographic work.

INITIATION

Although Griaule's sense of the moral tension and violence inherent in field-work was unusually acute, he developed nonetheless an enabling fiction of reciprocal encounter with the Dogon. This fiction, not falsehood, is most

clearly embodied in the work after Ogotemmêli. In Griaule's ongoing research (closely linked with that of Dieterlen) one sees the overlay of an
ethnographic fiction (Dogon initiatory knowledge) by a fiction of ethnography (fieldwork as initiation). To account for this doubling we may return to
Geertz's ironic fiction of moral community, which he sees as dissipating, temporarily at least, the ethical tensions inherent in fieldwork. Geertz under-
mines the myth of ethnographic rapport before reinstating it in an ironic
mode. Like Griaule he seems to accept that all parties to the encounter recognize its elements of insincerity, hypocrisy, and self-deception. He sees this
recognition as a precondition for a lived fiction (a drama, in Griaule's terms)
that is in some very guarded, but real, sense genuine. Just how this productive complicity is actually enacted is always difficult to know. But if, as Geertz
suggests, such lived fictions are central to successful ethnographic research,
then we may expect to find them reflected in the texts that organize, narrate,
and generally account for the truths learned in fieldwork. In fact, many ethnographies include some partial account of fieldwork as part of their representation of a cultural reality. But whether or not an explicit or implicit
fieldwork narrative appears in the ethnography, its very shape—the definition of its topic, the horizon of what it can represent—is a textual expression
of the performed fiction of community that has enabled the research. Thus,
and with varying degrees of explicitness, ethnographies are fictions both of
another cultural reality and of their own mode of production. This is unusually clear in the late work of Griaule and Dieterlen, where "initiation"
provides the common organizing metaphor.

To say that ethnography is *like* initiation is not to recommend that the
researcher should actually undergo the processes by which a native attains
the wisdom of the group. Griaule has little use for such a *"comédie"* (1952c:549).
The metaphor of initiation evokes, rather, the deepening of understanding
that accrues to long-term field research with repeated visits throughout the
anthropologist's career. It evokes, too, a qualitative change in ethnographic
relationships occurring as a culmination of the long, persistent documentary
process. Initiation finally gives access to a privileged stratum of native understanding, something Griaule claimed was "a demonstration, summary but
complete, of the functioning of a society." The ethnographer, rather than
trying to blend into the society under study, "plays his stranger's role." A
friendly but determined outsider, pressing constantly against customary in-
terdictions, the ethnographer comes to be seen as someone who, precisely
because of his or her exteriority with respect to native institutions, is unlikely
to falsify them. "If he is to receive instructions and revelations that are the
equivalent, and even superior to those enjoyed by initiates, the researcher
must remain himself. He will be careful not to try to gain time by telescoping

Marcel Griaule and Michel Leiris prepare to sacrifice chickens before the Kono altar at Kemeni, September 6, 1931, as a condition of entry to the sanctuary. Courtesy Mission Dakar-Djibouti, Musée de l'Homme, Paris.

the information; rather he will follow steps parallel to those of initiation as it is practiced by the men of the society" (548).

The narrative of "parallel" (or specifically *ethnographic*) initiation appears prominently in *Le Renard pâle* and *Conversations with Ogotemmêli*. The first decade of documentary work at Sanga had unfolded at the lowest of four stages of Dogon initiatory knowledge. All the early questions of the Griaule team were answered at a level of instruction offered by elders to beginners—the *parole de face*. But the ethnographers returned repeatedly. They proved their good faith: Griaule, for example, used his aerial photography to advise the Dogon on crucial questions of water management. Gradually the persis-

tent researchers approached deeper, secret levels of cultural knowledge. Then—
"The Dogon made a decision" (Griaule & Dieterlen 1965:54). The local
patriarchs met and decided to instruct Griaule in *la parole claire*—the highest,
most complete stage of initiatory knowledge. Ogotemmêli would begin the
task. Others continued when he died shortly after his famous conversations
with Griaule.

Taken as a whole this narrative is certainly too neat, and patently self-
justificatory.[3] But whether or not the "decision" by "the Dogon" was motivated in just this way, and whatever the exact status of Ogotemmêli's discourse (individual speculation or cultural knowledge), the overall initiatory
paradigm does raise important questions about short and long-term ethnography. There can be no doubt that Griaule's repeated visits resulted in a
progressive, qualitative deepening of his understanding. Open-ended, long-
term study may well yield results that differ importantly from those of intensive sojourns of a year or two, followed perhaps by a later return visit to
measure "change" (Foster et al. 1979). The aging of both fieldworkers and
informants, the accumulated experience of cooperative work over decades,
produce at least the effect of a deepening knowledge. To conceive of this
experience as an initiation has the merit of including indigenous "teachers"
as central subjects in the process. Dogon instruction of Griaule in *la parole
claire* is also an implicit criticism of the earlier "documentaries" research;
indeed, one wonders if most ethnographies generated over a relatively narrow
time span may not be *paroles de face*. The narrative of initiation sharply questions approaches that do not strive for a certain level of complexity in representing "the native point of view." Ogotemmêli's initiative need not be
portrayed as a completion (in Griaule's words a *couronnement*) of the earlier
research. It can also be seen as a comment on it, and a shifting of its epistemological basis. And here the Dogon "side" of the story remains problematic:
direct evidence is lacking, and the initiatory narrative with its assumed tel-
eology—a progress toward the most complete possible knowledge—ceases to
be helpful.

Ogotemmêli's intervention was clearly a crucial turn in the research process. It revealed the extent of Dogon control over the kind of information
accessible to the ethnographers. It announced a new style of research in
which the authority of informants was more explicitly recognized. No longer
untrustworthy witnesses subjected to cross-examination, the Dogon "doctors," Ogotemmêli and his successors, were now learned interlocutors. During

3. We need not go as far as Lettens (1971:509), who suggests that the entire initiatory logic
of progressively revealed secrets was an invention of Griaule to cover up the failures of his first
phase of research, in the light of Ogotemmêli's revelations. Lettens' extreme skepticism is largely
unsubstantiated and unconvincing, given widespread evidence for Sudanese initiatory systems,
and given his rather rigid and literalist conception of initiatory processes.

the "documentary" phase of the research the ethnographer had been an aggressive collector of observations, artifacts and texts. Now he or she was a
transcriber of formulated lore, a translator, exegete, and commentator. In
Griaule's account of their meetings, Ogotemmêli is not interrogated in the
manner outlined in the *Méthode de l'ethnographie*. "*Le blanc,*" "the Nazarite,"
as Griaule now sometimes calls himself, has become a student; the secret is
communicated freely, not confessed.

However, the documentary and initiatory paradigms are linked by important underlying assumptions. To see ethnography either as extracting confessions or undergoing initiation, one must assume the existence and importance of secrets. Cultural truth is structured, in both cases, as something to
be revealed (Griaule's frequent word is *decelé:* disclosed, divulged, detected,
uncovered). Moreover, the new paradigm incorporates the theatrical conception of fieldwork. In a "parallel" initiation the ethnographer plays the part of
an initiate, the informant an instructor. A dramatic relationship, recognized
as such by both parties, becomes the enabling fiction of encounter. Indeed,
if all performances are controlled revelations presupposing a "back region"
hidden from view where the performance is prepared and to which access is
limited (Goffman 1959:238; Berreman 1962:xxxii), then a theatrical model
of relationships necessarily presupposes secrets. Thus an underlying logic of
the secret unites the two phases of Griaule's career.[4] Whether the ethnographer is a relentless "judge" or helping "midwife" the truth must always *emerge,*
be brought to light. And as an initiate, the researcher receives and interprets
revelations.

This view of the emergence of truth may be contrasted with a conception
of ethnography as a dialogical enterprise in which both researchers and natives are active creators, or, to stretch a term, authors of cultural representations. In fact, Griaule's experience with the Dogon may be better ac-
counted for in this second perspective. But to say this presupposes a critique
of initiatory authority. Dialogical, constructivist paradigms tend to disperse,
or share out ethnographic authority, while narratives of initiation confirm
the researcher's special competence. Initiation assumes an experience of progressive, connected revelations, of getting behind half-truths and taboos, of
being instructed by authentically qualified members of a community. This
experience of a deepening "education" empowers the ethnographer to speak

4. Jamin (1982:88–89) discusses this aspect of Griaule's work. And for a stimulating treatment of the social functions of secrets see his *Les lois du silence* (1977). Secrets are part of the
mise en scène sociale, generators of group identities and of cultural meanings which, not goals to
be finally attained, are "endlessly deferred and dissimulated" (104). My discussion, below, of the
exegetical function of *la parole claire* draws on this general perspective, as well as on Kermode
(1980). For a trenchant critique of the "cryptological" assumptions underlying Griaule's and
many "symbolic anthropologists'" practice see Sperber (1975:17–50).

as an insider, on behalf of the community's truth or reality. Though all cultural learning includes an initiatory dimension, Griaule presses its logic to the limit: "proceeding by means of successive investigations among more and more knowledgeable strata of the society it is possible to considerably reduce a population's area of esoteric knowledge, the only one, to tell the truth, that is important, since it constitutes the native key to the system of thought and action" (1952c:545).

This "native key" began to emerge for Griaule and his co-workers in the late forties. The landmark books announcing its discovery were *Dieu d'eau* (*Conversations with Ogotemmêli*) and Dieterlen's *Essai sur la religion Bambara* (1951). The two works revealed a "deep thought among the blacks," "an intricate network of representations" (Dieterlen 1951:227). The "innumerable correspondences" of the Bambara and Dogon emerged as a "coherent tableau," a "metaphysic" (Griaule 1951:ix). Once Ogotemmêli had, in thirty-three days of meandering talk, enunciated the basic outlines of Dogon cosmogonic myth, an enormous work of elucidation remained. As recorded in Griaule's day-by-day account, his discourse was riddled with gaps and contradictions. The cultural master-script he sketched would require elaborate exegesis, cross-checking against other versions of myths, and attention to the script's enactment in virtually every domain of collective life.

This work was to occupy Griaule and his co-workers for decades. It would also occupy their small group of key informants, drawn from the estimated 5 percent of "completely instructed" Dogon in the Sanga region, as well as from the 15 percent of the population who possessed a fair portion of the secret knowledge (Griaule 1952a:32). There is disagreement about the precise nature of the Dogon "revelations" produced in this collaboration. Some have seen them as theological speculations by individual Dogon, or as mythopoeic inventions (Goody 1969:241; Lewis 1973:16; Copans 1973:156). Griaule and Dieterlen, however, strongly reject the notion that the knowledge they report is in any significant sense the original creation of specific Dogon. In their view, the uniformity of custom and the widespread behavioral articulation of the esoteric knowledge makes it unlikely that any individual could do more than slightly inflect the enduring mythic structures. But to pose the issue as a debate between personal originality and cultural typicality (cf. Hountondji 1976:79–101) is probably fruitless, given our ignorance about key informants. It is based also on a false dichotomy: all authors, whether African or European, are original only within limited symbolic resources, and in restricted relations of textual production.

It is tempting to portray the late works of the Griaule school, in the words of Pierre Alexandre, as "second level ethnography—the ethnography of Dogon ethnography" (1973:4). But the notion of "levels" is misleading, and does not do justice to the way Griaule's version of custom and the versions enunciated by Dogon informants are dialogically implicated one in the other. It is difficult, if not impossible, to separate clearly Dogon ethnography from Griaule's ethnography. They form a common project: the textualization and exegesis of a traditional system of knowledge. The cultural "text" does not exist prior to its interpretation; it is not dictated by fully instructed informants and then explicated and contextualized at a second "level" by European ethnographers. Griaule and Dieterlen give evidence that there can, in fact, be no complete version of the Dogon "metaphysic." If, in Griaule's telling metaphor, it is "written" throughout the culture—in the habitat, in gestures, in the system of graphic signs—these traces are of the order of a mnemonicon rather than of a complete inscription. In fact, a "fully instructed" Dogon will spend a lifetime mastering *la parole claire*. To grasp the full range of its symbolic correspondences, signs, myths, rites, and everyday gestures, requires a continuous process of concrete poesis. The mythic "word" is endlessly materialized, exchanged, interpreted. And because stable order is relentlessly disrupted by the forces of disorder, incarnate in the mythic fox, cosmos and society are constantly reinscribed.

The ethnographic encounter is one of the occasions of this reinscription, but with a significant difference. Now the Dogon dialectic of order and disorder takes place on a world stage, leading to the inscription of a new kind of totality, a Dogon essence or culture. In *Le Renard pâle* we see an attempt to establish a cultural base line, to separate off, for example, "commentaries" by informants from the recorded myths and variants. But it is unclear how rigorously such a separation can be made, for as Dieterlen says, these glosses demonstrate the Dogon propensity to "speculate on the history of creation," illustrating "the native development of thought on the basis of mythic facts" (Griaule & Dieterlen 1965:56). The development of mythic thought, as of any thought, is both structured and open-ended. But the activity of exegesis depends on the positing of a restricted set of symbols by the hermeneutical imagination. There must, in principle, be a stable corpus for interpretation. Griaule's "full" initiatory knowledge—which can never be expressed in its entirety—functions in this canonical manner. It provides a stopping point for the process of cultural representation. On the basis of this original master-script, a potentially endless exegetical discourse can be generated. *La parole claire*, like any primal text or ground of authority, acts to structure and empower interpretation.

Griaule's paradigm of initiation functioned to transform the ethnographer's role from observer and documenter of Dogon culture to exegete and interpreter. It preserved and reformulated, however, the dominant themes of his earlier practice: the logic of the secret, an aspiration to exhaustive knowledge, a vision of fieldwork as role-playing. It expressed also the sense one has throughout Griaule's career of his Dogon counterparts as powerful agents in the ethnographic process: initially clever tacticians and willful resisters, later teachers and colleagues. By attaining *la parole claire* and working like any initiate to grasp the "word's" incarnation in the experiential world, Griaule becomes (always in his parallel, "ethnographic" position) one of a restricted group of "doctors" or "metaphysicians" who control and interpret Dogon knowledge. Griaule is an insider, but with a difference. For it is as though the Dogon had recognized the need for a kind of cultural ambassador, a qualified representative who would dramatize and defend their culture in the colonial world, and beyond. Griaule, in any case, acted as if this were his role.

The stance of the ethnographer who speaks as an insider on behalf of his or her people is a familiar one—it is a stock role of the ethnographic liberal. Griaule adopted this standpoint in the early fifties, with confidence and authority. An active advocate and mediator in the colonial politics of the Sanga region, he effected a reconciliation between traditional Dogon authorities and the new chiefs installed by the government (Ogona d'Arou 1956:9). In a variety of forums, from the pages of *Présence Africaine* to UNESCO international gatherings, to the Assembly of the Union Française (where he served as President of the Commission on Cultural Affairs), he urged respect for the traditions of Africa. Fortified by Ogotemmêli's revelations, he portrayed in elaborate detail a mode of knowledge to rival, or surpass, the Occidental legacy of the Greeks. Speaking personally, in the voice of an initiate, he could report that "with them, everything seems truer, more noble, that is to say more classical. This may not be the impression you have from the outside, but as for me, each day I seem to be discovering something more beautiful, more shaped, more solid" (1951:166). One senses in the work of Griaule and among his co-workers—especially Germaine Dieterlen—a profound, sometimes mystical engagement with the Dogon *sophie* (Rouch 1978b:11–17). But whereas Dieterlen has tended to efface her own authority behind that of the Dogon, Griaule, who lived to see only the beginnings of "decolonization," spoke in frankly paternalist accents as an advocate for African traditional cultures.

His late generalizations are governed by a familiar chain of synecdoches. Ogotemmêli and Sanga stand for the Dogon, the Dogon for the traditional Sudan, the Sudan for Black Africa, Africa for "*l'homme noir.*" Griaule moves freely from level to level, constructing an elemental civilization strikingly different from that of Europe. But difference is established only to be dissolved in a totalizing humanism (1952b:24). Once traditional African essence is characterized and sympathetically defended, it is then portrayed, in the last instance, as a response to "the same great principle, to the same great human uncertainties" that Western science and philosophy have engaged (1951:166). The ethnographer speaks as a participant in two civilizations, which by means of his initiatory experience and special knowledge can be brought together at a "human" level.

In the early fifties, Griaule presents himself as someone who *knows* Africa; and he knows, too, what is good for Africa. Ethnographic understanding is critical in a changing colonial context: it permits one to "select those moral values which are of merit and should be preserved," to "decide what institutions and what systems of thought should be preserved and propagated in Black Africa" (1953:372). Tradition must be well understood so that change can be properly guided. "It is a question of taking what's theirs that is rich, and transposing it into our own situation, or into the situation we wish to make for them (1951:163). Griaule's "we" belongs to 1951 and the colonial *Union Française*, of which he was a Councilor.

The cultural riches that will somehow be preserved or transposed are always located in the domain of tradition or "authentic" custom—an area more or less free of European or Islamic influences. But the ethnographic liberal who represents the essence of a culture against impure "outside" forces encounters sooner or later a contradiction built into all such discourses that resist, or try to stand outside, historical invention. The most persistent critics of Griaule's defense of Africa were educated Africans, "*évolués,*" who rejected any reification of their cultural past, however sympathetic. Griaule tended to explain away these resistances as unfortunate consequences of an unbalanced education: "You can't be simultaneously at school and in the sacred grove" (1951:164; Malroux 1957:15). The black intellectuals who objected to his eloquent portrayals of their traditions were no longer authentically African, but victims of "that kind of 'leading astray of minors' which all colonial powers have indulged in" (1953:376).

Such statements no longer carry the authority Griaule was able to impart to them in the early fifties and were in fact challenged on the occasion of their enunciation (Griaule 1951, discussion:147–66). More congenial today are the views expressed at the same moment by Griaule's early colleague, Michel Leiris. A brief final contrast will evoke the changing ideological situation in the years before Griaule's death, a situation in which ethnography is still enmeshed.

Leiris was perhaps the first ethnographer to confront squarely the political and epistemological constraints of colonialism on fieldwork (Leiris 1950). He viewed the ethnographer as a natural advocate for exploited peoples, and he warned against definitions of authenticity that excluded *évolués* and the impurities of cultural syncretism. Both Leiris and Griaule contributed essays in 1953 to a UNESCO collection entitled *Interrelations of Cultures*. The differences in their approaches are still instructive today. Griaule's "The Problem of Negro Culture" argues that "traditional religions, as well as the social and legal structure and technical crafts of the black races emanate from a single, rigid system of thought—a system that provides an interpretation of the universe, as well as a philosophy enabling the tribe to carry on and the individual to lead a balanced life" (1953:361). Dogon and Bambara examples are elicited to illustrate this "metaphysical substratum," which Griaule presents throughout as characteristic of "the Negro," or of "negro culture" (362).

Leiris, in approaching his topic, "The African Negroes and the Arts of Carving and Sculpture," evokes a historically specific problem of intercultural translation. He begins by tracing the discovery of "*art nègre*" among the avant-garde in the early century, Europeans inventing an African aesthetics for their own artistic purposes. He then throws doubt on his own undertaking by pointing out the absurdity of an African attempting in a short essay to deal with the whole of "European sculpture." He proceeds to base his generalizations about "African" art, not on any presumption of a common essence, but on a contingent perspective. He writes as a Westerner perceiving similarities among the diverse sculptures of Africa and even presenting them as expressions of a "civilization," while understanding these ensembles to be, in a sense, optical illusions. The apparent unity of black art forms inheres only in a perception of the common ways they *differ* from those to which a European is accustomed. This refusal to represent an exotic essence—an important issue of epistemological tact—is based (in part at least) on the ways Leiris' ethnographic career diverged from that of his co-worker on the Mission Dakar-Djibouti. Leiris never underwent any "initiation" into an exotic form of life or belief. Indeed, his work (especially *L'Afrique fantôme*) is a relentless critique of the paradigm of initiation. His literary work, largely devoted to a heterodox, endless autobiography, reinforces the ethnographic point. How could Leiris presume to represent another culture, when he had trouble enough representing himself? Such an attitude made sustained field-work impossible.

Griaule's energetic confidence in cultural representation could not be farther from Leiris' tortured, lucid uncertainty. The two positions mark off the predicament of a post-colonial ethnography. Some authorizing fiction of "authentic encounter," in Geertz's phrase, seems a prerequisite for intensive research. But initiatory claims to speak as a knowledgeable insider revealing essential cultural truths are no longer credible. Fieldwork cannot appear primarily as a cumulative process of gathering "experience," or of cultural "learning" by an autonomous subject. It must rather be seen as a historically contingent, unruly, dialogical encounter involving, to some degree, both conflict and collaboration in the production of texts. Ethnographers seem to be condemned to strive for true encounter, while simultaneously recognizing the political, ethical, and personal cross-purposes that undermine any transmission of intercultural knowledge. Poised between Griaule's enactment and Leiris' refusal of this ironic predicament, and working at the now-blurred boundaries of ethnographic liberalism, fieldworkers struggle to improvise new modes of authority.

They may perhaps find some retrospective encouragement in the Griaule tradition of ethnographic cultural invention. For the story contains elements that point beyond initiatory authority and the neo-colonial context. To date, the most illuminating account of how research proceeded in the wake of Ogotemmêli is Geneviève Calame-Griaule's preface to *Ethnologie et langage: La parole chez les Dogon* (1965). She tells how "the extremely precise views" she gathered from her interlocutors led to the elaboration of "a veritable Dogon 'theory' of speech" (11). She introduces her four key collaborators, giving hints of their personal styles and preoccupations. We learn that one of them, Manda, was the Dogon equivalent of a "theologian," and that he guided the ethnographer toward the relations of speech and the person that became the book's organizing principle. Even the book's descriptions and interpretations of everyday behavior were the work of both ethnographer and informants, many of the latter possessing extraordinary "finesse in observation" (14). While Calame-Griaule still makes a guarded claim to represent an overall Dogon "cultural orientation," her preface goes a long way toward casting the ethnographic process in specific dialogical terms. The theory of speech that Calame-Griaule has brilliantly compiled is inescapably a collaborative work, continuing her father's productive encounter with the inhabitants of Sanga. And it is an authentic creation of "Dogon thought's need in expressing itself for dialectic, for an exchange of questions and answers that interpenetrate and weave themselves together" (17).

REFERENCES CITED

Alexandre, P. 1971. De l'ignorance de l'Afrique et de son bon usage: Notule autobiocritique. *Cahiers d'Etudes Africaines* 43:448–54.

Alexandre, P., ed. 1973. *French perspectives in African studies.* London.

Balandier, G. 1960. Tendances de l'ethnologie françaises. *Cahiers Internationaux de Sociologie* 27:11–22.

Asad, T., ed. 1973. *Anthropology and the colonial encounter.* London.

Berreman, G. 1962. Behind many masks: Impression management in a Himalayan village. In *Hindus of the Himalayas,* xvii–lvii. Berkeley (1972).

Calame-Griaule, G. 1965. *Ethnologie et langage: La parole chez les Dogon.* Paris.

Clifford, J. 1981. On ethnographic surrealism. *Compar. Stud. Soc. & Hist.* 23:539–64.

————. 1982a. *Person and myth: Maurice Leenhardt in the Melanesian world.* Berkeley.

————. 1982b. Feuilles volantes. In *Collections passion,* ed. J. Hainard, 101–13. Neuchâtel.

Cohen, M. 1962. Sur l'ethnologie en France. *La Pensée* 105:85–96.

Condominas, G. 1972. Marcel Mauss et l'homme de terrain. *L'Arc* 48:3–7.

Copans, J. 1973. Comment lire Marcel Griaule? A propos de l'interprétation de Dirk Lettens. *Cahiers d'Etudes Africaines* 49:154–57.

————. 1974. *Critiques et politiques de l'anthropologie.* Paris.

De Ganay, S. 1941. *Les devises des Dogon.* Paris.

Delafosse, L. 1976. *Maurice Delafosse: Le berrichon conquis par l'Afrique.* Paris.

Delafosse, M. 1909. *Broussard: Les états d'âme d'un colonial.* Paris.

Demarle, M., ed. 1957. *Marcel Griaule, Conseiller de l'Union française.* Paris.

Deschamps, H. 1975. *Roi de la brousse: Mémoires d'autres mondes.* Paris.

Devereux, G. 1967. *From anxiety to method in the behavioral sciences.* The Hague.

Dieterlen, G. 1941. *Les âmes des Dogon.* Paris.

————. 1951. *Essai sur la religion Bambara.* Paris.

————. 1955. Mythe et organisation sociale en Soudan français. *Journal de la Société des Africanistes* 25:119–38.

————. 1957. Les resultats des Missions Griaule au Soudan français (1931–1956). *Archives de Sociologie des Religions* (Jan.–June):137–42.

Douglas, M. 1967. If the Dogon. *Cahiers d'Etudes Africaines* 28:659–72.

Ehrmann, H. 1976. *Comparative legal cultures.* Englewood Cliffs, N.J.

Fortes, M. 1973. On the concept of the person among the Tallensi. *La notion de personne en Afrique Noire,* no editor. Paris.

Foster, G., et al., eds. 1979. *Long-term field research in social anthropology.* New York.

Geertz, C. 1968. Thinking as a moral act: Ethical dimensions of anthropological fieldwork in the new states. *Antioch Rev.* 28:139–58.

Goffman, E. 1959. *The presentation of self in everyday life.* Garden City, N.Y.

Goody, J. 1967. Review of *Conversations with Ogotemmêli,* by M. Griaule. *Am. Anth.* 69:239–41.

Griaule, M. 1933. Introduction méthodologique. *Minotaure* 2:7–12.

————. 1934. *Les Flambeurs d'hommes.* Paris.

————. 1937. L'Emploi de la photographie aérienne et la recherche scientifique. *L'anthropologie* 47:469–71.

————. 1938. *Masques Dogons.* Paris (1963).

————. 1943. *Les Saô légendaires.* Paris.

————. 1946. Notes de terrain, Dogon, Ogotemmêli, 1946. (11 microfiches.) Paris (1974).

————. 1948a. *Dieu d'Eau: Entretiens avec Ogotemmêli.* Paris. Translated as *Conversations with Ogotemmêli.* London (1965).

————. 1948b. L'Action sociologique en Afrique Noire. *Présence Africaine* (March–April):388–91.

————. 1948c. *Les grandes explorateurs.* Paris.

————. 1951. Préface. In *Essai sur la religion Bambara,* by G. Dieterlen, vii–x. Paris.

————. 1952a. Le savoir des Dogon. *Journal de la Société des Africanistes* 22:27–42.

————. 1952b. Connaissance de l'homme noir. In *La Connaissance de l'homme au*

XXe siècle, 11–24. Neuchâtel.

———. 1952c. L'Enquête orale en ethnologie. *Revue Philosophique* (Oct.–Dec.):537–53.

———. 1953. The problem of Negro culture. In *Interrelations of cultures*, 352–78. Westport, Conn., UNESCO.

———. 1957. *Méthode de l'ethnographie.* Paris.

Griaule, M., & G. Dieterlen. 1965. *Le Renard pâle.* Vol. 1. Paris.

Hountondji, P. 1976. *Sur la "philosophie" africaine.* Paris.

Imperato, P. 1978. *Dogon cliff dwellers: The art of Mali's mountain people.* New York.

Jamin, J. 1977. *Les lois du silence: Essai sur la fonction sociale du secret.* Paris.

———. 1982. Objets trouvés des paradis perdus: À propos de la Mission Dakar-Djibouti. In *Collections passion*, ed. J. Hainard, 69–100. Neuchâtel.

Karady, V. 1981. French ethnology and the Durkheimian breakthrough. *J. Anth. Soc. Oxford* 12:165–76.

Kermode, F. 1980. *The genesis of secrecy: The interpretation of narrative.* Cambridge, Mass.

Lebeuf, J. 1975. Review of *Mystagogie et mystification*, by D. A. Lettens. *Journal de la Société des Africanistes* 45:230–32.

Leenhardt, M. 1932. *Documents néo-calédoniens.* Paris.

Leiris, M. 1934. *L'Afrique fantôme.* Paris (1981).

———. 1948. *La langue secrete des Dogons de Sanga.* Paris.

———. 1950. L'Ethnographe devant le colonialisme. In *Brisées*, 125–45. Paris (1966).

———. 1953. The African Negroes and the arts of carving and sculpture. *Interrelations of cultures*, 316–51. Westport, Conn., UNESCO.

Lettens, D. A. 1971. *Mystagogie et mystification: Évaluation de l'oeuvre de Marcel Griaule.* Bujumbura (Burundi).

Lewis, I. 1973. *The anthropologist's muse.* London.

Malroux, P. 1957. Marcel Griaule. In *Marcel Griaule, Conseiller de l'Union française*, ed. M. Demarle, 13–16. Paris.

Mauss, M. 1913. L'Ethnographie en France et à l'étranger. *Oeuvres* 3:395–434.

———. 1924. Essai sur le don. In *Sociologie et anthropologie*, 145–279. Paris (1950). Trans. I. Cunnison, *The Gift.* New York (1967).

———. 1931. *Instructions sommaires pour les collecteurs d'objets ethnographiques.* Paris.

———. 1934. Les techniques du corps. In *Sociologie et Anthropologie*, 365–86. Paris (1950). Trans. B. Brewster, *Sociology and psychology: Essays.* London.

———. 1947. *Manuel d'ethnographie.* Paris (1967).

Michel-Jones, F. 1978. *Retour au Dogon: Figures du double et ambivalence.* Paris.

Ogono d'Arou. 1956. Allocution prononcée au cours des funérailles de Marcel Griaule à Sanga. *Journal de la Société des Africanistes* 26:8–10.

Paulme, D. 1977. Sanga 1935. *Cahiers d'Etudes Africaines* 65:7–12.

Rabinow, P. 1977. *Reflections on fieldwork in Morocco.* Berkeley.

Richards, A. I. 1967. African systems of thought: An Anglo-French dialogue. *Man* 2:286–98.

Rivet, P., & G. H. Rivière. 1933. Mission ethnographique et linguistique Dakar-Djibouti. *Minotaure* 2:3–5.

Rouch, J. 1978a. Ciné Transe. *Film Quart.* (Spring):2–11.

————. 1978b. Le Renard fou et le maître pâle. In *Système des signes: Textes réunis en hommage à Germaine Dieterlen*, 3–24. Paris.

Sarevskaja, B. 1963. La *Méthode de l'ethnographie* de Marcel Griaule et les questions de méthodologie dans l'ethnographie française contemporaine. *Cahiers d'Etudes Africaines* 16:590–602.

Sperber, D. 1975. *Rethinking symbolism.* Cambridge, England.

LEARNING ABOUT CULTURE

Reconstruction, Participation, Administration, 1934–1954

HOMER G. BARNETT

RECONSTRUCTION

My ethnographic fieldwork began in the summer of 1934 under the guidance of A. L. Kroeber, my teacher and curriculum advisor at the University of California in Berkeley. The project was financed by a grant awarded to a visiting Polish professor, Stanislaw Klimek, who proposed the use of mathematical formulas for a more precise estimate of the number and range of native culture areas along the southern Oregon coast to the extent that they could be determined by interviewing survivors of a decimated population, most of whom were clustered on the Siletz reservation. Among those who were completely dispossessed in the middle of the last century, these Indians retained only a few relics of their indigenous culture. Although they were able on the basis of ancestral traditions to describe with some accuracy cultural features they had never actually witnessed, acculturation and the hybridization of originally unique complexes had reduced to a minimum the value of direct observations of an informant.

The fieldwork procedure for this program was developed in 1933 by Klimek and E. W. Gifford of the Berkeley staff (cf. Golbeck 1980). It began

---

Homer G. Barnett was born in Bisbee, Arizona, in 1906, and after receiving his B.A. from Stanford, spent five years "knocking about the world" as a merchant seaman. Undertaking graduate study at the University of California, Berkeley, in 1932, with the intention of becoming a high school teacher, he was attracted to anthropology and received his Ph.D. in 1938 under A. L. Kroeber. The following year he became a member of the faculty at the University of Oregon, where he is now Professor Emeritus of Anthropology.

with a review of all available documents on Oregon tribal groups to establish an inventory of their similar and distinctive features, which were designated traits or culture elements. Tentative lists were assembled under relevant captions, such as DRESS and HUNTING, with space provided for the response of each informant in a recognized ethnic group. Every trait and its variations were numbered and their local presence (+) or absence (−) recorded as in this example:

	Tolowa	Chetco	Sixes River	Alsea
266. Moccasins	+	+	+	+
267. Women	+	−	+	+
268. Deerskin	+	+	+	+
269. Laced	+	−	?	?
270. Painted	+	−	−	+

Using a mental record of the trait list as a guide, available informants were asked in a casual and impromptu manner questions about their knowledge of the particular custom being explored. Differences in opinion about traits were not mentioned and leading questions were avoided. An informant would be asked, for example, how his people made canoes, and if the name of a native craftsman could be elicited, that was used as a guide and reference to substantiate vague generalizations. It was emphasized that no detail should be neglected, and manual demonstrations and gestures were encouraged. Peripheral questions were asked to clarify uncertainties that seemed significant; and, finally, if these efforts failed, direct questioning began. When clearly and confidently given, volunteered information was valued above doubtful answers obtained by rapid-fire questioning. The procedure was adhered to consistently, except when salient features indicated that a more direct approach would not alter the facts.

Although irrelevant items were gradually dropped from the original trait list, the list was also increased in several ways. Most of the additions were volunteered by informants through substitutions, denials, or by the refinement of an original trait. Frequently the elaboration consisted of an enumeration of attributes; sometimes it outlined a process in a precise manner; in other instances it developed through a consideration of conceptual opposites or alternatives, or by attention to problems of greater importance. In every case a feature was listed as a separate element when nothing of critical importance or differential value could be gained by further subdivision.

The purpose of this research design was twofold. The initial phase re-

quired the specification of the components of a culture area, with indicators
of their contexts and their relationships to each other. Since a simple statement of the presence or absence of a trait was meaningless without reference
to a more inclusive or collateral associate, contextualization was provided by
recording the features of a belief or behavior as they were expressed by an
informant. The result was not only a catalogue of elements, but a presentation of the matrix that contributed to their meaning. The relationship between traits was also essential to an understanding of processes and patterns.

In the second phase of the project, carried out under the direction of
Klimek, the numerical results of the first phase were used to calculate degrees
of cultural similarity between the nine tribal areas under investigation. Using
a mathematical formula known as Yule's Q2, a "coefficient of similarity" could
be established between any two selected tribes or areas:

$$C \text{ of } S = \frac{(ad - bc)}{(ad + bc)}$$

—where "a" represents the dual presence of a trait, "d" its dual absence, "b"
its presence for one group and absence for the second, and "c" its presence
for the second and absence for the first. Based upon a total of 1,832 elements
the coefficients in this survey varied from .07 to .86, depending upon geography and intercultural awareness.

Although there was never a possibility that the mathematical treatment
of field data would not be included in my final report, I could not ignore the
implications of precision inherent in the coefficient of similarity formula.
Something had been lost and something added by the translation of informants' words and gestures into numbers. When I mentioned this to Kroeber
during one of our conversations he reminded me that all of us were in search
of a more scientific expression of our conviction than "American and English
lifestyles are different, but they have more in common than either has with
the Japanese." Then, without committing himself, he encouraged me to include this paragraph in my report:

> The translation of diffuse, vaguely comprehended culture complexes into pre-
> cise mathematical terms which can be readily manipulated has its attractions,
> but it also leaves much to be desired. For one thing, the fundamental units are
> not truly so, but are frequently somewhat variable and of unequal significance.
> A "plus" may be, and often is, qualified by some additional statement; there
> are emphatic, undeniable occurrences and occurrences in moderation or even
> some of questionable certainty. Again, the arts and crafts give little difficulty,
> being tangible and rigidly definable, whereas the recording of the social aspects
> of any culture immediately introduces the interpretative element and inevi-
> tably embarrasses the objective quality of the testimony.
>
> (Barnett 1937:158)

IN RETROSPECT: OREGON

Accepting my status as a student, and fieldwork as an essential requirement
for an anthropological career, I welcomed Kroeber's offer to continue the
element survey among the Gulf of Georgia Salish of Canada during the summer months of 1935 and 1936. I was grateful for the opportunity to expand
my experience, not only as a personal asset, but to provide the basis for a
more professional evaluation of Yule's coefficient, in the hope of dispelling
my earlier misgivings about a mathematical treatment of informants' responses. My second field trip convinced me, however, that a manipulation
of numbers can not explain the behavior of people.

A comparison of cultures by matching their traits is an acceptable technique for determining degrees of similarity. But those traits cannot be pro-
cessed by mathematical formula without distorting their significance. Matching is not measuring, and the subordinate features in a cluster of traits are
not the numerical equivalents of their foundation. Shoelaces and shoes are
not equivalent units; and laces and soles do not make a shoe. The truth is
that mathematics applies to nothing except the features of its own abstract
design. That design varies with different sets of independent and non-
contradictory axioms with only one restriction: regardless of its postulates
and their possible reference to objects, every system must be logically consistent. As the mathematical philosopher Bertrand Russell defined it, mathematics is "the subject in which we never know what we are talking about,
nor whether what we are saying is true." While this need not concern math-
ematicians, it raises a fundamental issue in the application of their designs to
empirical data. The issue is a question: How do we *count* our experiences?

Since mathematics does not derive from observation, its creators have
established their own conceptual units and the relations between them. Every
unit in that domain, symbolized by "1," is identical with every other "1," and
invariably "$1 + 1 = 2$." Whether that system is useful to an anthropologist,
or even relevant, depends upon whether concerned colleagues can agree upon
the definition of a unit. What is a marriage? What is creativity? Beyond that,
the essential question in the application of Yule's formula is not whether
members of both tribe A and tribe B wear moccasins, but whether moccasins
are the numerical equivalent of a victory celebration or the practice of sha-
manism. Recording an invariant plus for all "elements" does not reflect the
interests or interpretations of the people surveyed. Nor does Yule's formula
permit a recording of numerical difference between a whole and its subordinate features, such as a moccasin and its artistic elaborations. All are listed
as equivalent units, though patently the features are contingent and cannot
exist independent of their foundations. Invariably coefficients and other numerical translations of thought and behavior transcend the realm of experi-

ence and distort sensory reality in their passage through a formula. As another expert on the subject, Albert Einstein, remarked: "So far as theorems of mathematics are about reality, they are not certain; so far as they are certain, they are not about reality." Q.E.D.

PARTICIPATION

My hope of participating in the lifestyle of a small community was not realized until 1947–48, when Al Murphy, a graduate student, and I lived for nine months in the village of Ulimang in the Palau Islands. We were escorted to the community by its district chief, who authorized our entry but soon returned to Koror, the island capital established by the U.S. Navy in accordance with a recently imposed civilian code of law. The chief's departure left us without a translator or a guide among neighbors as perplexed as we were about what to do or say when we met on a public path or on the beach. We had been given no grammar or ethnographic report, only an English-Palauan word-list and brief descriptions of the pre-European cultures of Micronesia prior to the Japanese invasion of the region.

Although our introduction by the chief was essential, it had the adverse effect of elevating my status to that of a dignitary, and thus delayed our hope of being accepted without prejudice or authority. Some people avoided me, others saluted. Men bowed slightly, women glanced in another direction or pretended to be preoccupied with something in their hands. Children were taught to be especially considerate. When I approached their schoolgrounds they faced me, stiffened their arms at their sides, bowed, and, regardless of the time of day, said "Good morning, Sir." Practically everyone who passed our house attempted to peek, and that happened often because we lived on the path from the school to a bathing pond—where I was twice surprised by two school boys seeking a more intimate understanding of the "Sir" to whom they were obliged to bow their heads. My most disconcerting experience as a stranger began when two elderly men knocked on our door and beckoned me to follow them. They were agitated and would say no more than "Come help, come help." I reached for Murphy's hand and followed them to a dilapidated house where they pointed to an old woman lying motionless on a couch. I touched her hand, but withdrew immediately. My suspicion of the men continued until I learned that I had been rechristened in transit to Ulimang. Prior to our arrival a rumor circulated to the effect that the district chief would be accompanied by "Doctor Somebody" on his next visit to Ulimang.

That misfortune was my first lesson on the subject of being a Palauan;

namely, that friendship and confidence were crucial to its realization. There-with I decided to develop a more personal relationship with Kai, the owner of the house in which Murphy and I lived. Kai agreed, but cautioned that he would not be available for conversations—which he called "Yuk"—at any time he was engaged in contract labor for carpentry and the manufacture of copra and coconut oil. When I emphasized that understanding his language was a basic requirement for friendship, he volunteered to introduce me to Mekur, a young schoolteacher who became another good friend. In order to promote that relationship, and to prevent interruptions by children or their parents, we agreed that he should join me for language study in my home at his convenience. Beginning in the late afternoon, or after dinner, our meet-ings often continued until ten o'clock. During these late night sessions, I learned not only the Palauan language, but something about their illegal activities—which need not be specified.

Mekur owned a Japanese-English dictionary, which had been useful as a part of his education while the Japanese controlled the school system, and with the arrival of the Americans he became an English teacher. Although his hope to improve his social status by serving as a language teacher failed with the transfer of authority, he accepted this without resentment or distrust of Americans. He was an ambitious but not an unusual Palauan.

I soon discovered that the presence of Japanese men in Ulimang had af-fected the lifestyle of practically everyone. Then came the Americans with another display of attractive novelties. By 1947 that model dominated the scene to the extent permitted by a limited income and a mail-order cata-logue. Workshop tools and kitchen utensils were no longer novelties, but the opportunity to parade new fashions on Sundays and other American holidays was welcome, and often inspired rivalry among those who could afford it. Grass skirts and breech cloths had been forbidden by the Japanese, and were no longer an issue. Ordinarily men wore khaki shorts, but on festive occa-sions they covered their bodies as much as possible with long pants, shirts, colored glasses, military caps, and shoes ranging from tennis oxfords to slip-pers, depending upon status and pretension. Size was a secondary considera-tion, because that required an understanding of mail-order catalogue codes. Young women dressed more gracefully. All-white ensembles consisting of shoes, socks, and gown were the most stylish, especially with colored streamers fas-tened in rosettes on the chest like a delegate's badge. Lipstick and rouge were fairly common, but most husbands objected to face powder because of its arresting effect. High-heeled shoes were appealing, but most women who could afford them preferred the balance of carrying one in each hand. Their most consistent purpose, like that of their boy friends, was to resemble an

American, by choice or accident. The struggle was evident when officials from Koror were invited to a celebration: after their departure everyone hurried home "to get into something comfortable."

The only traditional Palauan song-dance to survive the Anglo-Japanese invasion was performed by older women. Standing in two lines and facing each other, the participants lifted one heel at a time and lowered it while pivoting their bodies through a right angle with a rolling motion of their hips. Their song was low and mournful, its words relating the historic event to be solemnized by the dance. The more popular song-dances derived from a variety of sources. Some body movements—hip slapping and head turning—could have been Palauan, but others were alleged to be fox trots, tangos, and waltzes with stilted posturing taken from Japanese drama. It was genuine entertainment to witness the Palauan imitation of a Japanese imitating an American interpreting "China Town" or "Mexicali Rose."

Soon after his self-styled "summer vacation" (a retreat for study in October), Mekur invited me to attend a meeting of his class, no doubt to exhibit our friendship, but expressed as an appeal to assist him in the pronunciation of English words. When I entered the classroom the students stood at attention, saluted me, and sang what was intended as "The Star Spangled Banner." The assignment for the day was to learn the English translation of a Palauan adage, which Mekur presented to the class in its traditional rhythmic style:

> Chief say, men do
> Man say, women do
> Women say, child do.

That particular lesson lost nothing in translation. It was in fact a reliable guide to the traditional status structure based upon wealth and sex, with restricted degrees of authority vested in each domain. A chief discussed problems with and issued orders to men only, while a husband, having paid a bride price for his wife, assumed control of their internal and external affairs, with the understanding that children were the responsibility of women until sons reached maturity, when that obligation was transferred to fathers.

Palauans lived in a man's world for which they gave women credit. The foundation for this salute to motherhood was the traditional requirement that all inherited privileges and responsibilities were transmitted through maternal lineages. These privileges included not only wealth but domains of action. Two levels of leadership and two classes of titles were conferred on men accepted as chiefs. One class acknowledged authority only within a clan, the other within a community, whether that domain consisted of a village, a district, or a regional combination of districts. Only leaders with regional

qualifications were accorded the title of *rupak* in recognition of their distinction as political leaders and as judges of the conduct of their subordinates.

Prior to their constraint by foreign authorities, *rupaks* had assumed complete responsibility and dictatorial power, including the right to requisition
food, to impose fines on members of their village or district, to declare rules
of conduct and personally judge offenders, and to conscript service for their
own benefit and that of the community. Because they were priests as well as
secular leaders, *rupaks* assumed supernatural power to sanction their preemp-
tory decrees. They expected to be informed of any unusual event within their
jurisdiction, and did not hesitate to summon a person to give an account of
his intentions or behavior. They were present at all public and important
family affairs, acting as advisors and recorders. In addition to the powers
accorded to *rupaks,* titled men of all degrees were granted gestures of respect.
No common person would confront them. Their inferiors stepped off a trail
and bowed as they passed, addressing them in a subdued tone. Although all
these acknowledgments of high rank were repressed by foreign intervention,
an entitled chief in 1947 still evoked respect, because titles themselves were
venerated. Their acquisition was an inspiration and often initiated a remarkable transformation in the behavior of men who inherited them.

When Mekur explained to his class the meaning of "Man say, women do"
he did not mention the relationship conveyed by the common expression
"Women are strong, men are weak." His neglect was deliberate, because that
lyric was a tribute often used by husbands to excuse their mistakes and encourage compassion by their wives. Men were generous in their acknowledgment of a woman's importance, to the extent that it did not alter the fundamental reality of male dominance. They claimed for their wives, and allowed
them to claim for themselves, important privileges within the limits of female
moderation. With that understanding their magnanimity was genuine. They
wanted to believe what they said about women, and encouraged their wives
to concur, especially when praising them in the presence of an American.
Men and women accepted their difference in status, but their display of mutual support has at times misled sympathetic but unwary foreigners into be-
lieving that the Palauans lived in a matriarchal system administered by re-
spected, kindly, elderly women.

Mekur was even more circumspect when he taught members of his class
to repeat "Women say, child do," because his efforts as a teacher could be
misunderstood as a violation of that rule. Actually, this expression was also
more of a tribute to a matrilineal heritage than a statement of fact, though it
did influence the training of children from infancy to adolescence. Traditionally, not only mothers but any female surrogate nourished and disciplined
boys as well as girls in a household. They provided all of the necessary care

and protection, and were also expected to punish their wards by any suitable means, from neglect, to fright, to a slap on the face.

Men financed their children's physical needs and thereby maintained control over their future; but except for that investment, child care for them was a pastime, not an obligation. They monitored toddlers while wives worked in taro patches when no older sister was available, or during that part of the day when girls were in school. But none of this was man's work. Feeding, bathing, pacifying, loving—these were for women. The male attitude resembled that of a zoo visitor: although a young animal evokes yearning and compassion, it is not the spectator's responsibility.

My knowledge of family affairs derived from both planned and casual contacts with neighbors. Accepting the reciprocal roles of guest and host provided the opportunity to witness behaviors that were seldom described. The following examples have been abstracted from my informal journal of daily events.

> *December 25.* Kai arrived for dinner earlier than expected. He was all dressed up with his hair plastered to his head with coconut oil. He had promised to make noodles, another proud accomplishment which he had learned from the Japanese. Instead, Rdor, his brother-in-law from across the path, brought his style of noodles. Kai and I killed and plucked a chicken; Rdor cleaned it. The three of us sat on the floor inventing jokes of any kind that we could think of while Murphy prepared our dinner. We were ready to eat by 3:00, but Kai's wife Emei had not appeared. When I asked about her he replied that she was working in her taro field. Even with that signal it did not occur to me that she was not to eat with us until I remembered my unexpected visit last Saturday when I wanted to ask Kai a question and arrived before dinner. I was invited to join him, and when I nodded in acceptance Emei and their two children left us and ate in another room. I knew that families do not eat together when a guest is present, but I thought that after four months of daily "hellos" we were friends.

> *January 1.* Kai and Rdor prepared dinner for Murphy and me, then brought it to our house. When we sat down they threw up a coconut leaf screen to hide all of us from the view of passers-by, the reason for the secrecy being, I guessed, that they did not want to be seen eating with us—until they began pouring drinks of rum to celebrate the occasion. After joking for 30 minutes Rdor made gestures urging me to eat. I saluted Murphy and we ate our dinner; but they did not. They left immediately. I was disconcerted, then disgusted when I learned that they lost no time eating the remains of the food which they took with them to Kai's house. There was nothing hostile in their behavior, and I learned another lesson: record and forget it!

> (cf. Barnett 1970a:17–18)

In March Murphy and I were invited to attend a three-day celebration, a *kledaol,* on another island to honor and encourage its rehabilitation after a severe storm. Accompanied by the local chief we witnessed displays of Palauan talent in skits which they called *shibais* in imitation of the Japanese. Both men and women staged them but not in a mixed company. Mostly satires lampooning a well-known person or ridiculing a custom, these pantomimes were accompanied by songs and exaggerated posturing, with the ubiquitous hip wiggle slipped into the plot. In-character dress was not an ideal; oddity of fit or combination attracted more attention. Actors portraying Palauan men wore shorts with loin cloths stretched over them; men playing the part of women exaggerated sexual characteristics; those cast as Japanese soldiers wore every available kind and combination of uniform, with wood saws cast as swords and bamboo poles as guns.

An episode in the life of a peeping tom induced the most raucous laughter. The girl's role was portrayed by a boy wearing a padded blouse and a cloth over his head. Skipping "her" way to a bathing pool with soiled clothes over her arm, "she" was followed by a man who concealed his face behind a few leaves while she washed the clothes and herself, wiggling her hips as she hummed a tune. When she detected the man behind the leaves she screamed, and the culprit was taken to an American police sergeant. The result was a caricature of American law in action. The few words of English known to the stern-faced sergeant emerged from an otherwise unintelligible mumble, punctuated by peremptory gestures. Confusion and mistaken accusations dominated the scene for five minutes; but finally the case was closed with a ten-year jail sentence.

That was the end of the *kledaol* and of our odyssey. The chief who escorted us was friendly and responsive to our suggestions. He also introduced us to local leaders and attempted to promote conversations with them. No doubt one of the reasons for his cordiality was the hope that it would be mentioned in our comments to other chiefs and to American officials in Koror. It also occurred to me that he regarded us as an exhibit of the degree to which itinerant Americans can be naturalized.

IN RETROSPECT: PALAU

My Palauan experience shifted my fieldwork interest from the North American Indians to indigenous populations in the Pacific area. It also revived a latent interest in culture change, with a concern for innovative processes rather than the histories of their products. That interest was immediately aroused by the Palauan reception of Japanese and American custom. Their imitations of dress style, songs, and dances were more than copies of foreign

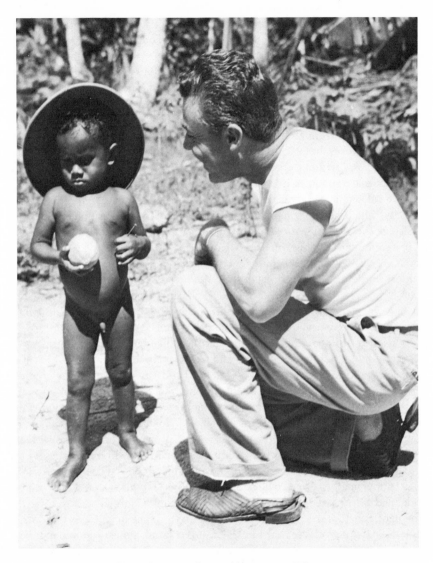

Homer Barnett with a neighbor's son, on Palau.

models, and many re-creational deviations were deliberately innovative. So were their push carts for carrying supplies and trash, old rubber tires for protecting row boats at landing piers, and the coconut oil machine which Kai assembled from the remains of a gasoline engine. In fact, by 1947 the acceptance of the odds and ends of foreign technology and discipline had altered the daily and weekly rhythm of work and play in Ulimang, but it did not suppress local ingenuity upon any occasion. My friendship with Kai and other creative individuals encouraged curiosity about how a cultural change is initiated. For a culture historian, such as Kroeber, who wrote and lectured extensively on "culture growth," it was sufficient to describe the features of a specified period, such as the Industrial Revolution, and trace their local or foreign origins and consequences. My interest in cultural change, activated by observing Palauan responses to alien influences, concentrated upon the processes (such as analysis and recombination) whereby change is accomplished. The psychological and individualized approach that I adopted in *Innovation* was without question inspired in part by my familiarity with the antics of *shibai* and peeping tom celebrities (Barnett 1953; cf 1940, 1942).

My Palauan experience also corrected the textbook image of a "primitive" society, which had to some extent been sustained by my Oregon work. My Palauan friends and critics were much more than clusters of culture traits. They were human beings, neither vicious nor dangerous, retarded nor sullen, no more or no less perfect than Americans. Their children were admonished to follow the models of honesty and generosity established by paragons in a heroic age. Despite that training, my Palauan friends frequently revealed their own genre of American selfishness, deception, and obsequious pretense—all with the familiar exoneration that "nobody is perfect."

I also learned about Palauan humor, which, like our own, was both stratified and brutal. Children bantered and teased their mothers, but that indulgence was short, and they were soon slapped and ordered to join play groups that enforced their own rules of behavior. Men joked with each other, using expressions that were vulgar and not suitable in the presence of women and children, who were an everlasting source of manufactured stupidity created by men in private competition. Wives reciprocated more quietly and with a pretense of being ladies. Although I never joined them, I often witnessed a group of two or three women laughing while one mimicked the swagger of a pretentious man or the scowl of an irate father. Children and adults alike ridiculed physical defects and ineptitude. A young man named Alsat was a frequent target for their jesting. Appearing on the scene in blue shorts, boots, and a junior navy officer's cap the day Murphy and I arrived in Ulimang, he asked in an authoritative manner what our luggage contained. The boy who carried our suitcase laughed and offered him the job. Alsat refused and snarled at me when I smiled. Our other helpers laughed when one of them said "He crazy." After persistently annoying us for several weeks, he marched directly to me one day while we were seated on a bench in the schoolgrounds. He grabbed my feet, abruptly looked at the soles of my shoes, then shouted, accusing me of doing something wrong, which he did not specify. We laughed as he marched to the school building to inform the attendant of my "crime."

Later the attendant joined us to apologize, explaining that the man's conception of himself as an officer was due to the stress of privation during the war. The loss of relatives and the shock of bombs and gunfire had apparently disturbed his contact with reality. He developed a mild megalomania and periodically imagined that he was a Japanese security officer. That resolved my dilemma about how to confront the "Crazy One." Recalling that I had seen many Americans laughing at misery and injustice, I never laughed at him again for the sake of being a Palauan (Barnett 1970b:93–94, 103–4).

This perspective is not a plea for compassion, but an illustration of my conviction that fieldwork is one of the most effective means of understanding one's self. Sharing a different lifestyle has a mirror effect, providing glimpses of an observer's foibles as well as his dignity. I am grateful to the Palauan people for their contribution to my professional career.

ADMINISTRATION

I have chosen to submit the report that follows for two reasons. It differs from RECONSTRUCTION and PARTICIPATION in that I monitored the fieldwork of other anthropologists; and the project that it delineates raised fundamental questions about the future of anthropology as a science of human behavior.

The program began in 1951 with the employment of anthropologists to assist in the administration of Micronesians who were under the jurisdiction of the United States (see Barnett 1956:86–101 for background details). At that time seven anthropologists held civil service positions with the governing agency, the Trust Territory of the Pacific Islands, one being associated with each of the six regional divisions of the area and myself with the Headquarters Staff of the Commissioner of the Territory. All of us had been employed in accordance with a so-called job description—an anonymously authored document serving as our professional charter. It permitted an extensive freedom of activity with respect to our research, advice, and program evaluation. Positively phrased, it was so inclusive in its implications that no generally understood boundary existed between the duties of the anthropologists and other personnel concerned with the same problems. A more objectionable feature of the situation, as it was viewed in 1951, was the anthropologist's involvement in policy formation at both Headquarters and District levels. That often resulted in differences of opinion as to what was desirable for the Micronesians, with the views of the anthropologist—avowedly the specialist on human behavior—in jeopardy.

In order to eliminate that source of confusion, as well as to designate an arena for the anthropologist's scientific contribution, it was decided by the Headquarters Staff to restrict the anthropologist's participation in policy decisions to the submission of information for which he could provide evidence, and to relieve him of any obligation to implement a decision. He was to be treated not as an administrative officer, but as a technical specialist who accepted research assignments and referred decisions to his executive associates. His own efforts were to be confined to social, economic, and other analyses that would enable them to assess the consequences of their previous decisions for future action.

This generalized statement of the anthropologist's role was particularized, and a rationale offered for its premises and safeguards, in a memorandum approved by the seven anthropologists and issued by the commissioner in 1952. The following is a concise summation of that document:

1. Since anthropologists will be involved with the collection of information about, and maintaining an intimate knowledge of, the indigenous cultures of the area, they should be in a position to contribute to effective administration in three respects:
   a) Advising on the implementation of educational, economic, judicial, and other departmental projects, and on the solution of problems arising from such implementation;
   b) Evaluating the success of specified programs with reference to their objectives;
   c) Independently formulating and implementing research of theoretical interest to the anthropological profession and/or of practical importance to the administration.
2. An anthropologist must maintain, insofar as possible, a neutral position with respect to administrative policy and action. Anything which tends to identify him as a governmental official invested with the power to enforce his convictions detracts from his usefulness as a source of unbiased information, because it jeopardizes confidential relationships with his informants and frequently involves him in factional struggles.
3. It is desirable that anthropologists be accorded the freedom and the facilities to interview informants under the most favorable conditions. It is expected that at times information will be given in confidence; and allowance should be made for this possibility in local housing and office arrangements whenever possible.
4. It is evident that an anthropologist's familiarity with, and his acceptance by, the Micronesians of this District provide him with information not otherwise obtainable. From both an ethical and a practical standpoint, he is obligated to preserve confidence.

(Barnett 1956:102)

While the announced purpose of this plan was to promote more effective cooperation between administrators and anthropologists, its significance was more comprehensive. Based upon the conviction that anthropology was or could become an applied science, it entailed the premise that a science could demonstrate means but could not specify ends. The anthropologist must therefore confine himself to statements of fact and probability, referring to the administrator the responsibility for making policy decisions based upon those facts and probabilities.

These determinants of the role of anthropology in administration, which were not widely accepted as guides to action by anthropologists or other social scientists, were derived by analogy from the characteristics of the applied physical sciences. Since the validity of the analogy may be debatable, and could raise questions of truth or necessity, it may be well to elaborate upon them. With reference to the possibility of a scientific application of anthropological data, it must be admitted that the research and constructs of academic anthropology are rather sterile for this purpose. Theoretical science of any kind can rarely be translated directly into practice. It must be adapted, and in many instances modified to accommodate empirically derived concepts. Beyond that, applied science must develop its own insights and methods. This is especially true of applied social science, because its primary concern is with change, whereas theoretical sociology and anthropology deal with structures that are inherently static—even though one structure is supposed to flow into or become another. Serious attention to the results of empirical studies of change cannot fail to reveal that much has been learned, or can be learned, about dynamic regularities in human behavior. It is not pretentious to assert that we are often in a position to predict and control such changes, granted the ordinary limitations imposed upon an applied science: namely, the demands for rigor in analysis, attention to specificity, stipulation of conditions, and conclusions stated as probabilities.

There is another reason for the valid objection that traditional anthropology offers little insight into practical problems, and it is intimately related to the first. Despite an expressed appreciation of psychology and psychiatry, anthropology has not incorporated their insights into its contribution to the study of man. It satisfies itself with abstract forms and hypostatized forces rather than with human beings and their motivations. Presumably, academic anthropology can operate with this separation of man from his incentives; but my Palauan experience taught me that the student of change, observing people creating and reacting to novelties, cannot rest satisfied with the separation. Human behavior is a socio-psychological phenomenon, to the understanding of which psychology has quite as much to offer as does anthropology. A conjunction of these disciplines, and others, to form a *social* instead of a *departmental* science, offers considerable promise for the future.

There seems to be no reason in principle for assuming that a human being is more difficult to understand or control than is an atom. In all science, including that of all "things" social, it is the prediction of causes, not effects, that is precarious. Under natural conditions—that is, conditions not externally manipulated—the conjunction of events necessary and sufficient to produce another event has such a complex of antecedents that it is rarely possible to do more than state that it is likely to occur. For this reason, in anthropology, as in physics, a prediction is properly phrased in the conditional tense: if A happens, then B will probably follow.

Anthropological forecasting in the Trust Territory was not pretentious, and when not required as a written record it was offered as a guess or a supposition. It was offered with the conviction that any rational guide to action was better than one based upon ignorance or preconception. It was replete with qualifications: a particular sequence *could* occur or *might* occur; it is more or less likely, possible, or expectable. The reasoning that produced such projections was by analogy with what was known to have happened elsewhere, or at another time among the same people, under comparable conditions. Sometimes the result was nothing more than an objectively organized compilation of common sense; but even that can be valuable in an emotionally charged atmosphere.

IN RETROSPECT: MICRONESIA

Like any other human endeavor, scientific activity is governed by a set of values. Personally, a scientist is supposed to be open-minded, cautious, and detached. Whether he is right is less important than whether his methodology is appropriate to its purpose; that is, whether it answers the questions asked in a manner which can be verified by others. Adherence to such values is the result of choice. It is opposed, for example, to reliance upon doctrine or intuition; and it is a preference that cannot be supported by a resort to scientific methods. It is true that values can be studied scientifically; so can science itself. In either case, however, the method operates under the dictates of a supraordinate value system representing ends which can be accepted or rejected—by appeal to other values—but which cannot be exhibited as true or false.

The purpose of any science is arbitrary, and cannot be the subject of its inquiry. Neither can it justify other goals or procedures except by granting the values that direct them. It may rate, grade, and evaluate alternatives and preferences, accepting the ends they seek as given; but it cannot evaluate those ends except by reference to other goals accepted as given. In brief, science is concerned with means and not ends; but neither ends nor means are absolutes. That which is an end in one value context may become a means or an instrument in another. There are scientific means to save human lives, but no scientific justification for doing so—unless we can demonstrate that they are the means to some other granted purpose, such as happiness, which may in turn be demonstrated to be a means to achieve social unity or another unquestioned value. Just as the suitability of means to relative ends can therefore be demonstrated, so can the wisdom of choice between alternative means; but again, only under the jurisdiction of an extrinsic criterion operating as a value. There are extravagant as well as inexpensive means to save a life, healthful as well as unhealthy avenues to happiness.

In brief, science can ascertain properties but it cannot discover or adjudicate their virtues. It can rate values in terms of stated criteria, not in terms of their desirability. Its discoveries and creations cannot be translated into good and evil. Translation requires the imposition of a scale of moral values, the validity of which may be debated, but without proof. In Kant's terms, science deals with hypothetical, not categorical, imperatives.

The allocation of policy to the Trust Territory adminstrator was part of the decision not only to establish effective collaboration with anthropologists, but to ensure a division of function based upon competence and acknowledged responsibility. The administrator, by the terms of his employment, was expected to render decisions concerning Micronesian welfare, and to assume responsibility for their consequences. Since there could be no scientific determination of the ends to be accomplished, it followed that the anthropologist, acting as a scientist, was not professionally qualified to define the purposes of the United States government. It may be argued that the administrator was not qualified either, but that is a matter of opinion, and cannot be demonstrated except, again, on certain value assumptions. In any event, the argument would not qualify an anthropologist, because it does not follow that those who know a people best know what is best for them.

This division of function did not preclude expressions of opinion or value judgments by Trust Territory anthropologists. In fact, I was often urged to state my opinion, and probably should have referred questions to my associates more often than I did (e.g., when they involved economic policy). In any event, all of us at Staff Headquarters were expected to state when and why we were expressing a prejudice or a preference. Contrary to the contention sometimes voiced by social scientists, this obligation did not require a schizophrenic personality, any more than does the pressure on a man to behave as both a father and a physicist, or both a biologist and a Democrat. It does ask that men claim no more distinction for their preferences than they are entitled to as social philosophers.

This leads to a more serious question that will not have escaped the reader: namely, do we want a rigorous science of human behavior? And if so, are we prepared to deal with its consequences? We share this dilemma with the physicists, but are more deeply involved; for we propose to understand and thereby to provide a basis for the human direction of human affairs. That decision weighs heavily because science, any science, and its applications are neutral instruments; and they can operate for the good or ill of mankind, depending upon the value system of the man who assumes that responsibility.

REFERENCES CITED

Barnett, H. 1937. Cultural element distributions: VII. Oregon coast. *U. Cal. Anth. Records* 1:117–32.

———. 1940. Cultural processes. *Am. Anth.* 42:38–42.

———. 1942. Invention and cultural change. *Am. Anth.* 44:14–30.

———. 1953. *Innovation: The basis of cultural change.* New York.

———. 1956. *Anthropology in administration.* Evanston.

———. 1970a. Palauan journal. In *Being an anthropologist: Fieldwork in eleven cultures,* ed. G. Spindler, 1–31. New York.

———. 1970b. *Being a Palauan* (Fieldwork Edition). New York.

Golbeck, A. 1980. Quantification in ethnology and its appearance in regional culture trait distribution studies (1888 to 1939). *J. Hist. Behav. Scis.* 16:228–40.

FOLLOWING DEACON

The Problem of Ethnographic Reanalysis, 1926–1981

JOAN LARCOM

While not familiar to many anthropologists, Bernard Deacon (1903–27) is better known to those interested in kinship studies. Just before his tragic death in the New Hebrides (Vanuatu), where he was completing over a year of productive field research, Deacon made his most memorable anthropological contribution, the discovery of a six-class marriage system on the island of Ambrym. Deciphering this marriage system was hailed as a brilliant achievement, ample testimony to the promise of an exceptional fieldworker; it occupies a prominent place in a recent review of W. H. R. Rivers and the growth of the "Cambridge School" in British anthropology (Langham 1981). Deacon's work on Ambrym has been subjected to reanalysis, and its significance is still being debated (Lane 1958; Patterson 1976; Scheffler 1970). This paper, however, offers a different assessment of his work from the singular perspective of an ethnographer who succeeded him in his field site. Through a series of unforeseen circumstances, I found myself following Deacon to South West Bay, Malekula, in the New Hebrides. Working in a place where he had also worked brought home to me the central and ambiguous role of precursors in the practice of ethnography.

This paper, then, is a reflection on predecessors, those anthropological ghosts or living beings that have preceded us to our field sites, our "ancestors" in a particular ethnographic sense. Their numbers are many: Malinowski's

Joan Larcom is Assistant Professor in the Department of Sociology and Anthropology, Mount Holyoke College. Her doctoral dissertation (Stanford University, 1980) was based on field research among the Mewun of Malekula, Vanuatu. She currently has a grant to return to Vanuatu to work on the interplay of localism and nationalism.

voice influences the several that have followed him to the Trobriands, and no one who has worked in the New Guinea Sepik can ignore the shadow of Gregory Bateson. In the 1920s and 1930s anthropologists could think of themselves as explorers, moving into virgin territory. This is no longer the case. The days have passed when professors were able to cordon off unworked and potentially excellent research locales for their favored students.[1] The ethnographic field has become crowded, with few sites left for unprecedented study. Most ethnographers find themselves with precursors in the field; it is this overlap—the dilemmas and opportunities it creates—that has shaped this paper. A small tribute to a gifted ethnographer, my reflections are offered from the standpoint of a successor and reinterpreter of Deacon, for whom his legacy has come to appear as a complex element in a continuing work.

"A. B. DEACON, ANTHROPOLOGIST"

Deacon was trained in anthropology at Cambridge just after the death of W. H. R. Rivers in 1922, before the reorienting influence of Malinowski and Radcliffe-Brown had been strongly felt in British anthropology. For him, the most pertinent anthropological influences were still those of Rivers' followers, who were then divided into two theoretical camps. Proponents of kinship studies, including Deacon's Cambridge mentor W. E. Armstrong, were concerned with social organization approached through the "genealogical method." In contrast, the "hyper-diffusionists" (Grafton Elliot Smith and William Perry) pushed Rivers' "historical" interests to far-fetched extremes, interpreting all human history in terms of the transmission of ancient Egyptian culture to other parts of the world (Langham 1981:passim). Each of these intellectual factions was to claim Deacon as their scion.

Deacon's own combination of social structural and historical interests, however, was characteristically Riversian. In a letter to A. C. Haddon written from the field, he affirmed himself "a disciple of Rivers (early Rivers) more than of any other ethnologist in so far as I have any theories at all"

---

1. This professorial power was evident at the time of Deacon's fieldwork in a letter Radcliffe-Brown wrote to Haddon shortly after Deacon's death: "I am grateful for the information you gave me about Firth and Fortune. It is singular that you should feel exactly as I feel about Fortune's desire to work in Tikopia. The Australian National Research Council has provisionally agreed to give him a grant for a year's work, but I have told them that it seems desirable for me that Fortune should work not in Tikopia, but in some other region, and it is left in my power to settle this. . . . Since Hogbin has gone to Rennell Island I feel that it might perhaps be a good thing to let Firth have Tikopia, if he likes, since this is one of the best fields for anthropological work still left in the Pacific. . . . (ACHP: ARB/ACH 1927).

(ACHP: ABD/ACH n.d.). Like Rivers, he considered social structure fundamental to ethnological analysis (Deacon 1934:698). In this he reflected the influence of Armstrong, whose lectures and evening conversation classes seem to have had great impact. Deacon praised Armstrong as a "confirmed logician" (Deacon 1934:xiv), and he, too, was absorbed by the fascinating logic of kinship systems. In his field notes, he frequently used Armstrong's idiosyncratic circular notation system for recording social organization, and corresponded regularly with his tutor about his social organizational discoveries.

But like the Rivers of the *History of Melanesian Society* (1914), Deacon also saw the study of kinship systems, their historical roots, and the processes of their transformation as the means to work out a grand diffusionist scheme of Pacific cultures. As an undergraduate, Deacon had written a paper correlating ghost societies and initiation cults of New Guinea with one another and with those of the Kakihan of Ceram in Indonesia. This earned him the attention of Elliot Smith, who avowed high hopes for Deacon's future in anthropology, and who later found his fieldwork "a wonderful corroboration of our recent [diffusionist] work" (Langham 1981:240).

Yet Deacon himself was never a diffusionist extremist. Later, considering an expansion of his Kakihan paper, he puzzled over the occurrence of similar ghost cults and initiation rites found in widely separated places. The difficulties of hyper-diffusionism continued to disturb him during his long voyage to the New Hebrides in the fall of 1925. Taking as an example the instance of ghost societies in Tierra del Fuego and their resemblance to those he had already described, he worried the explanatory issues of evolution and transmission (diffusion) in a letter posted from Colombo to Armstrong:

> What do you make of the whole thing? It seems to me to be remarkably similar to the sort of thing that goes on in parts of New Guinea. . . . What does it mean? Ought the psychoanalysts to tackle it? I wish I could make up my mind about "convergences" of this kind. Are you to leave things to the "comfortable doctrine" of evolution? Transmission and evolution seem equally difficult.
> (Langham 1981:216)

Deacon remained sharply critical of the diffusionist methodology, at the same time that he remained loyal to diffusionism's historical approach (ABDP: ABD/MG n.d.). While on Malekula, he wrote that one of his goals was to contribute to a compendium of cultural distributions—a collected "cyclopedia of distributions" that could be used to check theories such as those of Elliot Smith and Perry, which tended to "slur over gaps" and thus "distort the actual complexity" (ABDP: ABD/MG n.d.). He saw himself, in short, as a man between the "two extremes" of "Malinowski and Smith-Perry" (ACHP: ABD/ACH n.d.).

After spending his days on shipboard studying Biblical texts written in the South West Bay dialects, Deacon arrived in Malekula in mid-January 1926. His subsequent stay was divided between three different locations—South West Bay, Lambumbu, and Ambrym (an island off the northeast coast of Malekula)—trying to discern the precise connections and paths of diffusion for various cultural phenomena. His linguistic talents (he had grown up in Russia) enabled him to learn all three dialects well enough to do most of his research through them. A skilled and tactful fieldworker who cross-checked the veracity of his informants thoroughly, he managed to assimilate a tremendous amount of information during his five months at South West Bay. His fieldwork garnered not only detailed descriptions of several kinship systems, but also careful records about varieties of ceremonial life, magic, vernacular texts, and photographs. In a milieu where tensions between pagan and mission, Melanesian and colonist, English and French, Catholic and Protestant, were high, Deacon won the affection and respect of both Melanesians and European settlers.

After fourteen months in the New Hebrides, Deacon packed up his artifacts and notes and was about to depart for Australia, where his already bruited discovery of the six-class marriage system on Ambrym had smoothed the way for him to take up a lectureship at the University of Sydney during the temporary absence of Radcliffe-Brown. In Haddon's words, "[Deacon] was just entering into the life for which he was so well prepared and for which his friends confidently anticipated a brilliant success . . . " (Deacon 1934:xxvii). But on the eve of his departure in early March 1927, Deacon took ill with blackwater fever (or malignant malaria). He died within a week, two months after his twenty-fourth birthday.

The very day I arrived in South West Bay, nearly fifty years after Deacon's death, a group of people took me up to a hillside overlooking the Pacific. There, alongside a colorfully leaved croton bush, was a concrete memorial slab inscribed with the words, "A. B. Deacon, Anthropologist."

THE ANXIETY OF INFLUENCE

Deacon's presence in my field site was to have a strong effect on my own ethnographic writing. But at first I was dismayed to find him there. My disappointment may be explained by certain assumptions about originality that influenced me before I had to confront the problem of ethnographic reanalysis.

My college background had been in literary criticism, an interest I abandoned for anthropology. What had offended me about my concentration in

English was not the concern with literary works themselves but a growing emphasis, as I advanced toward graduation, on literary criticism. Original literary creations seemed smothered by massive accumulations of second-hand commentaries. One could never start fresh. I was, moreover, oppressed by a problem more recently addressed by Walter Jackson Bate in *The Burden of the Past and the English Poet*. Writing on the part earlier writers played in the work of eighteenth- and nineteenth-century authors, Bate quotes Samuel Johnson on his predecessors: "It is, indeed, always dangerous to be placed in a state of unavoidable comparison with excellence, and the danger is still greater when that excellence is consecrated by death . . . " (Bate 1970:3). Jeopardy of comparison has led many, then, to an "anxiety of influence" (Bloom 1973), a fear of the predecessor. Comparison and anxiety in turn rest on the question, essential for the neoclassical and romantic writers and now increasingly significant for anthropologists: "What is there left to do?" (Bate 1970:3). The apparent virginity of anthropological research attracted me— the possibility of being one's own authority, of moving into really new material. With hopes for exotic freshness, I went on to graduate school prepared for the pristine.

I brought there with me an old interest in the Chamula Indians, Tzotzil-speaking Maya residents in the Chiapas highlands of Mexico. This attraction carried me through a summer of fieldwork in Chamula under the auspices of Stanford's fieldwork program, part of preparation for the master's degree. When I wrote my master's thesis on this Indian *municipio*, I was able to skirt several earlier papers by students working in the highlands with the Harvard Chiapas program. Thus the problem of predecessors did not emerge again until I was preparing my Ph.D. research proposal. My qualifying exams, oriented towards Mesoamerica, were successfully completed, and I turned my attention to the literature on Chamula. Finding myself wading through volumes of material by Mexican and, in particular, Harvard researchers, I began to reconsider my plans. I did not relish tiptoeing through a field already mined by many other anthropologists, each a potential detonator for my own proposal.

Consulting a well-travelled fellow student, I asked him, half joking, if he knew of an area untouched by anthropologists. He replied that he did indeed know of one—the southern highlands of Malekula—and added that it was unstudied for a very good reason: it was the worst field site he had ever seen. Malekula's rainy season, lasting about half the year, makes its steep mountainous interior particularly inaccessible. The generally sultry climate and a surfeit of insect-born diseases add to the difficulties of ethnographic work.

Beginning to research this Melanesian area immediately, I found that several researchers had done some work on the coasts, most of it completed over fifty years before. But there was a group living in the southern Malekulan highlands, still wearing grass skirts and penis wrappers, who were as yet little

Joan Larcom with informants in Southwest Bay, Malekula, Vanuatu. Courtesy Ann Skinner-Jones.

studied anthropologically (Muller 1972). It was perfect, although a bit intimidating. I was particularly interested in a south Malekulan women's ranked society known as the *nimangi*, and I prepared to study this political group to learn its ramifications in women's status among themselves and also in relation to men. Six months after I first read about the women's *nimangi*, I was in the Malekulan highlands, after fording innumerable streams on the uphill climb.

As I perhaps should have anticipated, the site proved unworkable for me. I had my young daughter with me on the trip, and the highlands site seemed too formidable; when the rains began in earnest shortly after my arrival, the fords of streams and rivers became impassable rushing torrents. The prospect of both of us being totally isolated there for a much longer period than I had expected, with health and other hazards, persuaded me to relocate in a more accessible area on the Malekulan coast of South West Bay in an area known as Mewun.

The five hundred or so residents of Mewun now live in four coastal villages, easily reached by government and church personnel, as well as trade ships that purchase cash crops. This demographic pattern, though, represents a steady relocation over the past eighty years, as Mewun have left smaller hilltop villages further inland and moved to coastal mission villages. This migration, which was synonymous with conversion to Presbyterianism, began in the late nineteenth century and was finally completed in 1972, when the last "pagan" bachelor joined the church and a mission village. Although missionized Mewun retains certain aspects of its traditional economy (its strong agricultural basis, and its tangential relation to cash cropping), social life appears to have been very much altered by mission influence. For example, formerly important institutions such as the men's club houses, bridewealth, and polygyny—as well as the *nimangi*—are forbidden in mission villages. Once in South West Bay, I changed the focus of my research to explore the effects of missionization on Mewun people.

But with my arrival there, the problem of the predecessor loomed again. As I stood ambivalent before Deacon's grave on my first day there, I reshouldered the "burden of the anthropological past." I was following somebody both excellent and dead.

REINTERPRETATION: PUTTING KINSHIP IN ITS PLACE

How did I use Deacon during the fieldwork period? I had read his book *Malekula* (1934) before going to the New Hebrides. But when I found myself living on his very field site, I had a copy of the book sent to me. To a certain extent, the book directed my questions about the changes wrought by missionaries and other types of contact. But much of Deacon's description seemed outdated, alien, and of little interest. Of what use were magical formulas to cause impotence in an enemy, or detailed rhythmic notations of former drum-signalling, now forgotten?[2]

Because the Mewun I was observing seemed so thoroughly missionized and

2. Since the New Hebrides received its independence from the colonial governments (the United Kingdom and France) on July 31, 1980 (when the name of the new nation was changed to Vanuatu), Mewun interest in drum-signalling has revived, and the signals themselves are now significant markers of group membership (Larcom 1982).

changed, Deacon's book seemed at best useful as an approximate base line record of what had been lost. Its subtitle was, after all, *A Vanishing People in the New Hebrides*. It was only later, while I was drafting some preliminary chapters of my dissertation after reading through many of Deacon's notes and letters in Cambridge and London, that his contribution to my understanding of the Mewun became clear. Gradually, with distance from the immediacies of the field, the similarities between what he perceived and what I saw a half-century later became apparent.

While the behavior that each of us had recorded in fieldnotes was superficially very different (different dress styles, different work patterns, different living arrangements, different religious life), I began to see certain central concerns common to the Mewun, whether his informants in 1926 or mine in 1974. For lack of a more apt word I have called this complex of concerns an ideology. Getting closer to Melanesians' experience, it could perhaps equally well be called a socio-mythic landscape, or a set of persistent, spatialized structural principles. Let me describe this complex very briefly but concretely, using material that the two of us assembled.

In his notes, Deacon recorded details of a ceremony performed in a particularly sacred spot, the central place for a group of Mewun people. This ceremony, called "The Making of Man," was performed periodically to ensure the fertility of the place's inhabitants and to ward off sickness and death for all the Mewun. During it, the elders of the group broke ordinary incest taboos by having sexual intercourse with their closest female relatives. The principle concern of the ceremony, as expressed to Deacon, was the protection and bolstering of fertility.

At the time this ceremony was performed, the Mewun had good reason to be alarmed about fertility. Aside from the shortage of women that may have resulted from their practice of female infanticide, depopulation from introduced disease was a particular threat to the entire place and its inhabitants during the early decades of this century. The concern with fertility expressed by the ceremony Deacon recorded apparently permeated much of the early contact pagan Mewun society, and it remained an important issue for the Mewun during my field stay.

I am not arguing that the concern with fertility was a uniquely Mewun concern. But what did strike me as unusual after my fieldwork, and after reading much of what Deacon had written, was the way fertility was connected with Mewun elders, then and now, and particularly the way fertility was and is a reflection of their concept of "place" as a symbol connecting the living with the dead, and with the ecosystem. In contrast to many other areas where, with education and European cultural influence, elders seem to lose power to the young, the Mewun gerontocracy still retains much of its authority. In Deacon's time older men held sway over young men through their control of pigs, which were necessary bridewealth to obtain a wife and the fertility that accompanied marriage. Today, young men of Mewun are held under the control of the group's elders through the older men's direct control of marriageable women they have claimed through fosterage. Although bridewealth in pigs has been replaced by sister exchange, older men still control these "sisters" today, as they did pigs in earlier times. As long as they control the women, they also have much influence over would-be bride-grooms, eager to attain the status that accompanies marriage and fertility.

In a sense, Mewun would seem to articulate with Rivers' earlier theory of Melanesian gerontocracy, formed on the basis of his Pentecost and Ambrym research—that various anomalous forms of marriage were the consequences of elders' dominance over younger men and their monopoly of younger women. Prevented from marrying women of their own generation, young men even-tually took cast-off wives the older men no longer wanted. Elders would cus-tomarily dispose of their wives to their sons' sons and their sisters' sons. This custom would then make common practices of two forms of marriage Rivers proposed as explanations of certain Melanesian kinship anomalies: marriage with the wife of the father's father or with the wife of the mother's brother (Langham 1981:111). In Deacon's time, the South West Bay area might well have promised, at first glance, to be an ideal location to confirm Rivers' theory of anomalous marriage. But although superficially well-suited to the intensive genealogical research concerns of Deacon's day, South Malekula was to yield little more than confusion to Rivers' and Deacon's views of Mel-anesian history and social organization.

Today, both gerontocratic privilege and control of marriage work through Mewun concern for the preservation of their place. Mewun interest in fertil-ity goes beyond immediate society, status, or demography, into the socio-mythic concept of the place. When I asked why all men were so very intent on marriage now (for marital politics dominate Mewun men in a competitive and intense way) men replied that they were afraid that, if they did not marry, their place would die. Remarks like this meshed with Deacon's previ-ously cryptic descriptions, like that of "The Making of Man"; all of them revolved around an enduring interest in the place.[3] Thus, Deacon's records unlocked for me the depth of the ideology of place as a structure enfolding and extending kinship relations. With his training in the genealogical method, Deacon saw Mewun organization in terms of kinship, but his text itself be-trays his difficulties with this approach. Indeed, it is these difficulties with kinship and social organization as much as his repeated references to the role

3. The interest in "place" may be widespread in Vanuatu: after the country received its independence, its citizens were designated as *woman ples* or *man ples*, which is Bislama pidgin for "woman of the place" or "man of the place."

of place in social life that suggest his emphasis on kinship as the paramount factor in social life was misplaced.

Some of his struggles with kinship, which did much to redirect my attention to locality or place as the focal point of social organization, justify a more detailed discussion. Operating within the Riversian framework, Deacon gathered lists of kinship terms from Mewun and adjacent districts. He proposed that Mewun was divided into kin groups tied to particular villages by origin myths, totems, and property rights. These kinship units he described as "local, patrilineal, exogamous descent groups or clans" (Deacon 1934:52), each tracing descent from a single village or locality.

However, when he sought to define Mewun clans more precisely, in terms of their actual genealogical relationships, he learned there was no Mewun word for the entity he called "clan." The closest approximation to this was words meaning "one village" or "gong-beat." Thus, one would inquire of a man to what clan he belonged by asking, "The name of village one thy?" (Deacon 1934:52). But "one village" could be a misleading gloss. Often a village was seen as a "parent," with "offspring" villages as satellites continuing to recognize the ceremonial and mythic sacred place in the "parent" village. Although they resided elsewhere, those living in the "offspring" villages considered themselves still to belong to the "parent" village; and marriages between the "parent" and the "offspring" villages were usually, but not always, forbidden.

"Gong-beat" (*nambög*) was also problematic as a term for "clan." Deacon's text notes that "all the villages of a single clan are further united in the possession of a distinctive gong-beat . . . , which strangely enough is the only name which the clan possesses" (Deacon 1934:54). This gong-beat would be two or three distinctive rhythms used for drum-signalling the "parent" and "offspring" villages represented by it. But again anomalously, a certain "clan" (as Deacon defined this social unit) might have three gong-beats to itself, permitting intermarriage between certain members of the group. The implications of this anomaly for exogamy or clan rights are not explored in Deacon's notes or book. To add further to the muddle, several of these "gong-beats" were translated to denote "place": "Is it at your place?"; "Is my . . . pig at your place?"; "A man of my place is dead" (Deacon 1934:500–501). The link between gong-beat and place, rather than clan, is certainly at least suggested in Deacon's book.

Thus neither "one village" nor "gong-beat" glossed adequately as Deacon's "local, patrilineal, exogamous descent groups." Both sometimes worked at cross-purposes to the genealogical exogamy Deacon proposed as part of marriage regulation of kinship groups. Loyalty or ceremonial recognition of the centrality of a given sacred *place* known as the *logho* was apparently the *only* residual and consistent basis for determining the exogamous unit that Deacon referred to as clan. People belonging to such a place and observing the rituals for a specific *logho* did not intermarry (for detailed discussion, see Larcom 1980:63–72).

In his fieldnotes Deacon listed his continuing "sources of confusion" in kinship (ABDP: Notebook I), one of which was the frequent marriage between ostensibly prohibited relatives.[4] Like Rivers, in whose program he had been trained, Deacon sought to unravel marriage rules in particular as important bases for the generation of social groups (Schneider 1968:passim; 1982). But after six weeks of research in South West Bay, Deacon wrote to Armstrong about the perplexing marriage rules (DMGP: ABD/WEA 3/1/26): "In theory, so far as I can see, a man can hardly marry at all." The word for classificatory brother and sister was extended very broadly beyond the descent group to all the children of women from a man's mother's clan. Moreover, this rule prohibiting him from marrying into his mother's family also applied to his son and his son's son. Deacon learned, however, that such marriage prohibitions could in practice be easily circumvented. In Mewun and some surrounding districts a man could dissolve the kinship tie with a female relative simply by giving her family a pig. This was called "washing out the name," and paved the way for a permissible marriage with that previously related person (Deacon 1934:137).

Not only were clan relationships rather easily adjusted to other social concerns, but sometimes the concept of clan, as Deacon used it, seemed to have no basis at all in reality. "Because many groups have died out, a village at present may stand on ground not rightly belonging to any inhabitant, and the inhabitants may likely belong to five to six different groups or clans of which they are the only survivors" (ABDP: Notebook F). Deacon's information remained inconclusive and, as the preceding quote suggests, he attributed the unruly fit of "clan" in Mewun to post-contact influences of missionaries, as well as to depopulation from European-introduced diseases.

How far Deacon might have moved toward reordering his kinship notes to revolve more centrally around ties to place (*logho*) rather than those based on genetic ties can only be conjectured. It is important to remember, though, that the editor who prepared Deacon's notes for publication was a student in the same program, and that she came to his notes with the same intellectual

---

4. As two other principal "sources of confusion," Deacon listed "MBW [mother's brother's wife] nomenclature" and "counting through male and female lines" (ABDP: Notebook I). The latter again suggests that Deacon found the flexibility of Melanesian kinship disturbing because of his loyalty to definitive kinship systems as central modes of organization in each society he studied.

training—without, however, the confusing experience of a field situation that defied Riversian interest in coherent kinship systems. In this context, a subtle shift of emphasis between Deacon's field notes and Camilla Wedgwood's final edited rendition is worth noting.

In his notebook, Deacon wrote concerning clan disarray: "Before European influence disintegrated exogamous descent clans (totemic), all male members resided in a descent locality" (ABDP: Notebook K). By the time this statement was elaborated into finished text, its facts were slightly realigned to create some interesting changes in emphasis:

> Descent is patrilineal, and before the disintegrating influence of European contact had disturbed the social life of the people, the male members of a clan all resided in the village or locality in which their fathers, fathers' fathers, and fathers' fathers' fathers had lived before them, while the women of each such group went at marriage to live in the localities of their husbands' clans. Today, however, owing to the very rapid depopulation of the southwestern region, it is not uncommon to find the survivors of several clans living together in the same village.
>
> (Deacon 1934:52–53)

Although both versions assume post-contact "disintegration," the field-note version gave greater relative emphasis to locality. As Deacon actually saw them, one of the most distinctive aspects of clan relationships was in fact locality or place. But in the published version, the genetic aspects of social organization are spelled out as "fathers, fathers' fathers, and fathers' fathers' fathers," to eclipse the significance of locality as focal point of social organization. Thus some of the emphasis on clan and kinship in the final published version of Deacon's research may well reflect Wedgwood's own intellectual commitment to her Cambridge training in the Rivers' tradition.[5]

Deacon's difficulties with the kinship system suggest that what he explained as a disruption of genealogical relations through relocation was not an aberration, but a reflection of the importance of place membership (which could be changed by fosterage, by local endemic warfare, by the "washing out" of names) in contrast to genealogical ties. Rereading Deacon in the light of my own research suggests that while consanguinity may be one viable

---

5. It is relevant to consider here Wedgwood's role in Rivers' program and her reassertion of what Deacon tentatively thought he saw in Malekula: descent localities. A Melanesian researcher for many years, Wedgwood remained committed to a view of Melanesian social organization as a blend of territory and kinship. With I. Hogbin as co-author, she later labeled this blend a "carpel," which was defined as "an exogamous unilineal group which has its social centre within a parish territory" (1953:243). The term "carpel" has not become widely accepted, although it does reflect two concerns with which Deacon struggled, locality and descent.

metaphor for Mewun relationships, it is overshadowed by the relational richness of contiguity—the focal idea of living together in the special sacred
place of one's group. Everyone in Mewun belongs to a place, and is identified
by its name, such as a man of Melpmes or woman of Melaai. But this place
is more than a locale. Myth has it that the original inhabitants of a place
came out of the ground in its sacred central point, marked by a stone. In
turn, these people were and are sustained by this ground through food from
its plants and animals. When a man or woman dies, his plants and animals
become inedible or *tabu* to his neighbors because the deceased *is* that plant
or animal. As Deacon put it, the man *is* his pig (Deacon 1934:539), and
eating his pig is not only a hostile gesture, like cannibalism, but one that
will make any friend of the dead person weep from memory. Mewun see both
the food source and the person as incorporated quite literally by their common ground. "There is a very close spiritual alliance between the people of
a clan, their [sacred place] and all things that live therein taken collectively"
(Deacon 1934:798). When Mewun die, they return to the "dark Paradise" as
underground ancestral spirits. Ancestors from time to time become living
beings again, but not in a sense of reincarnation that suggests rebirth through
time cycles. For Mewun the spirits of the dead are always present; when the
living sleep, their spirits socialize with those of the dead. All plants, animals,
the quick and the dead, are held in relationship with one another through
the centrality of place.

The priority of place over kinship as an organizing construct is supported
also by the significance of fosterage, or the process of feeding someone which
ties that person into the foster parents' place. Food-sharing seems long to
have been the basis of strong personal ties in South Malekula: "Two men who
habitually eat together, sharing a common meal, come to feel that they are
united by a very intense bond, by something that may be described almost as
love" (Deacon 1934:538). Similarly, fosterage is not a debt to be repaid by
the loyalty and adherence of the young fostered person; rather it is a gesture
that incorporates the place itself into the individual who is fostered. By eating the food of the place, persons—even newcomers dislocated from their
birthplaces—are brought into the set of relationships organized around the
socio-mythic place.

Of course, this is an oversimplified statement of the Mewun view of place;
I have written on it in more detail elsewhere (Larcom 1980). But I would
like to stress here that I would never have been aware of its complexity or
persistence had I not had the benefits of Deacon's perceptions, his notes on
the making of man, on food taboos, place names and epithets, and his repeated and unresolved struggles with the inadequacy of kinship as an organizing principle.

FIELDWORK: READING BETWEEN THE LINES . . .

Deacon's faith in the hypotheses he brought with him to Malekula was at least shaken by his fieldwork on that island. From the beginning he was aware of the effect his preconceptions might have on his research success:

> The consciousness of a connexion between two things forms gradually, till it becomes a general hypothesis for the working out of a number of problems. These lead on again, the thing becomes unconsciously modified, and you find everything needs rearranging. . . . Generally you are unconscious that you have been associating things in a certain way till it suddenly becomes necessary to associate them in another. . . . [I]t is ghastly how conventional one is, in thought—I mean in the deepest most analytic or most imaginative thought . . .
>
> (ABDP: ABD/MG n.d.)

Letters home reveal his despair over the incoherence of Malekulan social life and his diminished loyalty to any particular working hypothesis. Well into his fieldwork (possibly from Lambumbu where he worked without the companionship of other Europeans for four months) he wrote: "It is very difficult, in more or less complete isolation, to gain sufficient stimulus for work. I find I have to build it up internally by theorizing. Almost any hypothesis is good enough to get on with. I feel very grey at present about the possibility of making a coherent system of the New Hebrides or Malekula" (ABDP: ABD/MG n.d.). In particular he was disillusioned by Rivers' theory:

> Rivers' theory I begin to find a hindrance. I was brought up on it at Cambridge, and now it cloys me. On every page I want to cry out "But there are so many other things!!" and in lots of it I am very much puzzled to know what Rivers really thought about certain things—whether he was aware of particular difficulties, whether he regarded them as difficulties.
>
> (ABDP: ABD/MG n.d.)

We can only speculate about most of those "certain things" Deacon found hard to fit into Rivers' theory, but surely Deacon's problems as he sought to identify exogamous clans were among the "particular difficulties" he encountered. His struggles with conflicting data, rooted in locality, may well have been another. His notes and book do mention the importance of place, as a ceremonial focal point known as the logho, an identifiable part of gong-beat queries and responses. The significance of Melanesian localism was not lost on Deacon: "The native is essentially a villager and an agriculturist, but he has a wider 'county' or 'district' life which corresponds to our 'national' life— it is higher than our 'county' or 'district' life since it is that of the whole social group, the 'county'" (ABDP: ABD/MG n.d.).

But Deacon's fieldwork method was not suited to a study of stability or consistency derived from localism. As noted earlier, he was interested in comparative genealogical information, a research inquiry well adapted to mobile investigations in successive areas. After six weeks in South West Bay, he wrote to Armstrong: "Most work here is really archaeology, and I am doubtful about the value of remaining the whole time in one place, unless one can spend, say two years out here—then you might get a more profound knowledge, which would be extremely valuable" (DMGP: ABD/WEA 3/1/26). Deacon stayed on there for three and a half more months, during which time he used the genealogical method to decode the social organization of several defunct cultural districts (Wien, Hurtes, Wiliemp), as well as two surviving ones (Mewun and Seniang). He moved to Lambumbu and Lagalag for four months, followed by a month of research in northeast and eastern Malekula. Even his most successful Ambrym investigations, which spanned late November through early February, were interrupted by at least one trip back to Malekula (DMGP: ABD/WEA 12/6/26). Despite the fact that his fieldwork definitely disturbed his initial expectations concerning Malekulan social organization, Deacon's mobility did not encourage him to rework or reconsider his interest in genealogical inquiries. In his view, place membership remained a manifestation of clan membership, rather than something more fundamental that was simply expressed in a kinship idiom.

Just as Deacon's field experience caused him to move away somewhat from his prior commitment to Rivers' theory, so fifty years later did my research in South West Bay also alter preconceptions carried to Mewun. If Deacon's search for a coherent social organizational system was disrupted by Malekulan concerns with place, so in a similar way my initial theoretical view of social change was shaken by the tenacity of native ideology about the same organizing construct—place.

I went to the field with a theory of cultural change, particularly Melanesian, that proved to be ill-founded. Steeped in Melanesian ethnography before I arrived in Malekula, I had been persuaded by other writers, as well as by Deacon's book, that the cultural life of Melanesians was unusually vulnerable to the attractions of Westernization and the temptations of a cash economy (Sorenson 1972). Like Deacon, I carried with me to the field theoretical interests nurtured by my graduate training; finding myself in mission villages on the Malekulan coast, I planned to analyze social change using the processual model propounded by Fredrik Barth (1967) and others. This approach focussed on the assumption that social change occurs as individuals make rational choices to maximize social or economic gains.

Research with the Mewun jeopardized several concepts inherent in Barth's utilitarian model, but the issue of individual maximization as an explanation for social change was, in particular, a dead end. After a half-year in Mewun I began to explore cash cropping as an indication of increased economic changes in families appearing to acculturate quickly. During my first six months of fieldwork the price of copra or dried coconuts, the most common cash crop, had risen from its lowest price in decades to an all time high. Yet I did not notice villagers spending increased amounts of time processing copra. To explain this, and to see if I was missing some important economic shifts, I sought the help of a Tahitian-Chinese store owner who had been purchasing most of the Mewun copra for twenty years. When I asked him which Mewun man or family was selling him the most copra, he made a noise of disgust: "When you see a man take his family and move far away from this place, then I'll show you a man who is interested in money." Within a single sentence, he thus sewed together place and persistence, which had already been connected by many Mewun comments I had continually misread through my incompatible hypothesis.

Arriving in Mewun with the preconception that here was an area acculturating (or de-culturating) quickly to a very Western pattern, I left Malekula with a contrary impression—one of Melanesians as tenacious and persistently recreating what they deemed to be significant parts of their organization, not just socially and economically but also spiritually. This sense of persistence within a superficially changing atmosphere had struck me especially when I read Deacon's letters about fieldwork. His comments on change were statements I could have written myself: "All the natives round S. W. Bay are 'civilized'! Smith-Rewse [British Resident Commissioner in Vila, New Hebrides] says that 'trade' is not much use—the natives have got used to money. . . . Even in the interior the natives know they can buy what they want with silver money, and prefer it to 'trade'" (ACHP: ABD/ACH 1/3/26). If Mewun people were on the road to acculturation when Deacon wrote about them, they did not seem to have travelled along it much further in the fifty years before my arrival. What persisted during those years, however, was not a house type, an enduring ritual, or a style of dress. It was rather a constantly recreated ideological core, focussed on the meaning of place as the locus and organizer of fertility and cultural life.

Under the influence of fieldwork, both Deacon and I moved away from our original hypotheses. While he grew toward a tentative interest in place as a significant part of descent systems, I went in the direction of a fresh appreciation of the tenacity of ideology. Reacting to my own fieldwork in the context of Deacon's writing, I was persuaded to set aside the Barthian individual-focussed, processual model of change, and to move to a view of Mewun culture as one dominated by ideological principles, one of which is the socio-mythic place, constantly being maintained, implemented, and supported by creative but in a sense superficial changes. Rather than an archeological record of what had disappeared in Mewun, Deacon's written work thus proved more valuable to me as a view of what remained. As I put aside my hopes for original authority and explored Deacon's research records in conjunction with my own, new aspects of each of our observations and new relationships between them were highlighted. Thus his notes, his letters, and his book helped me to achieve both a new sense of the meaning of place and an understanding of the ideology persisting behind that concept of locality. But Deacon's most significant contribution to my research was a general lesson—that of the importance of our precursors' texts in our continuing work.

IN PRAISE OF PRECURSORS

This returns us to the broader meaning of predecessors for those who follow them. Ethnographers today are confronted by a double task: the interpretation of a culture, and the interpretation of ethnographic writing about that culture. Anthropologists have long been aware of the first task. They have plumbed their subjects' experience, giving meaning to it, even discovering things about a people that they could not themselves articulate. Fieldworkers have not hesitated to interpret, sometimes quite freely, the behavior of people they observe. They are perhaps less willing to accept that such interpretation is also appropriate to the works of our predecessors—not only ethnographers, but also missionaries, government officials, and travellers. These writings are, in effect, part of the field, and anthropology works increasingly in a literary context.

Literary criticism, with its growing recognition of sociological context, has come part way to meet anthropology since I studied and forsook it. The criticism that drove me into anthropology was the so-called "new criticism," now very old. It viewed its enterprise as a textual decoding of the author's secret meaning. More recent criticism tends to view literature as written by more than an author—by history, by social space, by language and other symbols (Barthes 1977:155–64). Once an author releases a book, its meaning becomes public rather than private, open rather than closed. While the author produces some of a book's meaning, only part of this significance is produced by writing—the rest is created by reading or rereading. Thus a literary work may now be seen as a field of meaning that the reader, at least in part, creates.

While anthropologists have always regarded cultural behavior as a field of signification, they may now begin to see the works of their predecessors as an additional part of the field to be interpreted. Deacon's work, *Malekula*, lends itself particularly well to rereading in this fashion. This is in part due to the posthumous compilation process undertaken by Camilla Wedgwood. The difficulties of her project have been described by her mentor Haddon:

This was a very heavy task as the notes and descriptions were written at various times, often on odd scraps of paper, and usually without any indication of place or date. . . . The methods that Miss Wedgwood had often to adopt were rather in the manner of Sherlock Holmes than those of an ordinary editor. . . . [Deacon's] notes tell very little about the daily life and behaviour of the people, but this would have been supplied had he been spared to put his material into book form. This background of knowledge and his reflection upon what he was told and what he himself observed are irretrievably lost to us, and for this reason the book does not do justice to this highly endowed, painstaking, and thoughtful investigator.

(Deacon 1934:xxviii)

Wedgwood had at hand the debris of the ethnographic process: sketchy, unlocated and undated notes, including rituals, magical spells, kinship terms, etc. Some notes were limited analyses of social organization on Malekula virtually ready for publication, while others were disoriented, with no reference to place, time, or informant. Some of Deacon's papers were in fact lost (those left at South West Bay when he died there), and portions of the rest were certainly disarrayed before they were sent to England.

As I have suggested, I initially found the resulting text to be unwieldy and rather irrelevant. Edited by a hand unfamiliar with the facts recorded, the ethnographic detail in Deacon's book had often been exoticized to the point of incomprehensibility. Since the readily familiar aspects of Malekulan life were exactly what Deacon did *not* record, Wedgwood did not have this crucial interpretive road into the data; her compilation could not reflect the ethnographer's creative interplay between the familiar and the strange.

But there turned out to be a positive side to this style of ethnography. Wedgwood found it impossible to evaluate some of the disconnected notes taken down by Deacon, and this persuaded her to include in the book sizeable chunks of the descriptive texts given him by the Mewun. Wedgwood was aware that her decision to include texts and ritual descriptions as well as untranslated phrases might well overburden *Malekula* with imponderabilia, but she defended their inclusion as salvage for the future: "In view, however, of the fact that the people of Malekula are dwindling in numbers, and that their culture is rapidly dying out, it seemed better to preserve and put on record even what is as yet unexplained in the hope that before it is too late, other workers may elicit the interpretation of these passages" (Deacon 1934:xxxv). Thus, Deacon's book remains an unusually "open" ethnography, with fruitful possibilities for reinterpretation.

That task is facilitated by the fact that *Malekula* was composed of more than fieldnotes and initial analyses. Wedgwood was able also to read many of Deacon's letters to his mentors, to his mother, and to his friends. In contrast to the fieldnotes, whose context was largely stored in Deacon's head and thus lost, the epistolary material was prepared with a view to communicating Deacon's experience and thoughts to the recipient, and was therefore to a certain degree synthesized and comprehensive. True, Deacon revealed different aspects of his ethnographic workshop to each of his correspondents. In tone and content his letters to Haddon and Armstrong differ noticeably from those to his mother and to his close friend Margaret Gardiner. To his professors Deacon wrote summaries of ethnographic patterns and comments on anthropological theory, as well as brief prospectuses on his research plans, on the information he hoped to supplement and eventually include in a full ethnography. In contrast, those to Margaret Gardiner, written to an intellectual equal as well as a confidante, are both speculative and emotional, revealing his considerable discontent about field methodology and even about the ethics and epistemology of the anthropological enterprise:

> [S]ets of facts remain constant but the nature of their relation one to another is changed by every fresh fact, and it is fearfully necessary to go thro' notes and *put in the altered relations,* or otherwise the notes may be quite misleading and almost without value if you died suddenly before "writing up."
>
> (ABDP: ABD/MG n.d.)

Deacon's letters suggest that the more sensitive ethnographers of the early "intensive study" mode were not untouched by the concerns that have preoccupied many of the current ethnographic generation. For present purposes, however, the point is rather that these letters, which facilitated Wedgwood's earlier task of second-hand ethnographic construction, can also, when read today in tandem with *Malekula,* facilitate reconstruction from a different point of view.

As cultures are more and more intensively studied, and as fieldwork enters its second half-century, the history of anthropology will no doubt recognize that ethnographic interpretation is becoming increasingly interwoven with texts such as Deacon's. Aside from what such texts may offer us for better understanding of the history of anthropology, there is also the lesson they offer us for the ongoing practice of fieldwork. Fieldwork itself has already been acknowledged by some as a "reading"—although one of a text that has never been written: "Doing ethnography is like trying to read (in the sense of 'construct a reading of') a manuscript—foreign, faded, full of ellipses, incoherences, suspicious emendations, and tendentious commentaries, but written not in conventionalized graphs of sound but in transient examples of shaped behavior" (Geertz 1973:10). Returning from a field site, the ethnographer carries a "manuscript" no one else has "read." Each fieldworker may be viewed as harvesting a netful of "fresh facts," but as Deacon perceived, the relationship between these facts may change with each new catch. With the increasing number of predecessors' texts, however, a fieldworker can also look to what is past, to the works of precursors, for "old" facts to be used newly, to be related in original ways to those from our own research.

But is ethnography, then, moving rapidly in the direction of literary criticism, with its accretions of "second-hand" commentary? Will ethnographic field research become optional or even obsolete, subsumed by the textual reanalysis of written ethnographies? I think not, because fieldwork provides a context that gives essential and particular meaning to earlier ethnographic writing about a field site. The need for field experience to give significance to the work of our ethnographer-predecessors takes us safely away from the realm of conventional literary criticism.

Deacon was right in assuming that his sets of facts by themselves, without his interpretations, could be almost valueless; I found this to be the case when I first read his posthumous ethnography. But to his successors, with their own context of fieldwork, Deacon's descriptions of South West Bay will remain an essential resource. Through an analysis of the Mewun ideology of place and its continuity, I hope to have suggested at least one possible completion or outcome of his most excellent research; I offer this not as a privileged recension of Deacon but as an addition to the growing field of work to be reread and reinterpreted by our successors, be they other anthropologists or the Mewun themselves.

ACKNOWLEDGMENTS

I wish to thank Carolyn Clark, James T. Clifford, Triloki Pandey, and George W. Stocking for their very helpful editorial and substantive comments on this essay, as well as the librarians of the two repositories in which most of the manuscript materials I have drawn upon are deposited. I am also grateful to Margaret Gardiner for several helpful comments, for permitting me to copy three letters by Deacon to Armstrong that are in her possession, and for allowing me briefly to consult the manuscript of her forthcoming *Memoir of Bernard Deacon*, which is to be published by the Salamander Press of Edinburgh in 1984. My own argument and use of evidence—deriving as they do from the comparison of my fieldwork experience with that of Deacon—have of course been developed entirely independently.

REFERENCES CITED

ABDP. See under Manuscript Sources.
ACHP. See under Manuscript Sources.
Barth, F. 1967. On the study of social change. *Am. Anth.* 69:661–69.

Barthes, R. 1977. *Image-music-text.* New York.

Bate, W. J. 1970. *The burden of the past and the English poet.* New York.

Bloom, H. 1973. *The anxiety of influence: A theory of poetry.* New York.

———. 1975. *A map of misreading.* New York.

Burghart, R. 1981. Review of *W. H. R. Rivers,* by R. Slobodin. *Rain* 46:9–10.

DMGP. See under Manuscript Sources.

Deacon, A. 1934. *Malekula: A vanishing people in the New Hebrides.* London.

Gardiner, M. 1982. Bernard Deacon. *Rain* 49:10–11.

Geertz, C. 1973. *The interpretation of cultures.* New York.

Hogbin, H. I., & C. Wedgwood. 1953. Local groupings in Melanesia. *Oceania,* vol. 23, no. 4, and vol. 24, no. 1.

Lane, R., and B. Lane. 1958. The evolution of Ambrym kinship. *Southwest. J. Anth.* 14:107–35.

Langham, I. 1981. *The building of British social anthropology: W. H. R. Rivers and his Cambridge disciples in the development of kinship studies 1898–1931.* Dordrecht, Holland.

Larcom, J. 1980. Place and the politics of marriage: The Mewun of Malekula, Vanuatu. Unpublished doctoral dissertation, Stanford University.

———. 1982. The invention of convention. *Mankind* 13:330–37.

Layard, J. W. 1928. Degree-taking rites in South West Bay, Malekula. *J. Roy. Anth. Inst.* 58:139–223.

Muller, K. 1972. Field notes on the small nambas. *J. Soc. Oceanistes* 38:153–67.

Patterson, M. 1976. Kinship, marriage and ritual in North Ambrym. Unpublished doctoral dissertation, University of Sydney.

Rivers, W. H. R. 1914. *The history of Melanesian society.* New York (1968).

———. 1922. *Essays on the depopulation of Melanesia.* Cambridge, England.

Scheffler, H. W. 1970. Ambrym revisited: A preliminary report. *Southwest. J. Anth.* 26:52–66.

Schneider, D. M. 1968. Rivers and Kroeber in the study of Kinship. In *Kinship and social organization,* by W. H. R. Rivers, 7–16. London.

———. 1982. Biological and social paternity. *Rain* 48:17–19.

Sorenson, E. R. 1972. Socio-ecological change among the Fore of New Guinea. *Cur. Anth.* 13:349–83.

MANUSCRIPT SOURCES

The manuscript materials consulted in writing this essay include the papers of A. Bernard Deacon in the possession of Ms. Margaret Gardiner of London (cited as DMGP), those in the Royal Anthropological Institute Library, London (cited as ABDP), and the papers of A. C. Haddon in the University Library, Cambridge (cited as ACHP).

"FACTS ARE A WORD OF GOD"

An *Essay Review of James Clifford's*
Person and Myth: Maurice Leenhardt
in the Melanesian World*

PAUL RABINOW

This is an important book. It is well-crafted, affording us a sensitive and intelligent presentation of complex issues by an acute and learned observer. It does its historical and biographical job of restoring to his proper station an important figure in modern anthropology; a sort of historical justice is accomplished. And it poses an open-ended challenge, an invitation, to rethink our received understandings of twentieth-century anthropology. Clifford violates a number of taboos, *idées reçues*, and thereby opens in a constructive fashion a range of issues and possible future developments.

There are a number of points in the book about which serious debate is possible. It hesitates. But it is exactly at those points of hesitation that important and unresolved questions are posed. The book hovers between an excellent, but rather standard biographical form, and a post-structuralist intercalation of mixed genres of texts and voices, between a successful standard historical approach and a more dangerous post-modern one whose claims to

*Berkeley: University of California Press, 1982.

Paul Rabinow is Associate Professor of Anthropology, University of California, Berkeley. His works include *Reflections on Fieldwork in Morocco* and (with Hubert Dreyfus) *Michel Foucault: Beyond Structuralism and Hermeneutics*. His current research is on urban planning, social science, and political strategies in the French colonies, focussing on the career of Lyautey in Vietnam, Madagascar, and Morocco.

traditional standards are less secure, but whose claims to creativity are stronger. The tension is not fully resolved; the book's ethos is in the second camp and its form and most of its content are in the first. A certain tentativeness, however, is certainly preferable to a false closure.

Maurice Leenhardt, Clifford's protagonist, was born in 1878 into a devout provincial Protestant family headed by a pastor-cum-geologist. His youth parallels that of the Third Republic, although the conflicts of religion and science, local affinities and national consolidation, colonial expansion and internal implantation and reform which racked the Republic were characteristically muted by the Leenhardt family. These seemingly polar opposites were turned from antagonistic, negating alternatives, into complexes of mutually invigorating relations through which character was shaped and an unequivocally public persona forged. The universalism of science and the particularities of locale, the universalism of an ethical calling and the need to accept the particularities of individual conscience, were both highly formative, mutually supporting, contrasts in Leenhardt's youth. He saw them, however, not as strict separations, but as a field of differences to grow in. Leenhardt never rebelled directly against his father's synthesis. But he did reinterpret these imperatives in his own fashion, emphasizing and developing different dimensions of the relational oppositions that characterized his milieu. In this Protestant family, character formation was a central duty.

This is not to say that Leenhardt's youth was without conflict. Living up to his father's scientific and ethical standards was not easy. Leenhardt failed his *baccalauréat* twice, obviously a shock and source of shame for a member of a bourgeois family. His father, with some reluctance, sent the young man away to Paris to a Protestant preparatory school, fearing the boy would be tempted by the worldly aestheticism of the capital. He wasn't. But he did hate the austerity of the school and its dry, pedantic exercises. Rather than rejecting them, however, he was led to a search for more redeeming features within the Protestant institutional world. He discovered these in the Maison des Missions, home of the Société des Missions Evangeliques, a non-denominational and multinational society devoted to converting the heathen. Like many other young people Leenhardt was fascinated by the reports and displays of exotic cultures he encountered at the Maison, which opened for him a model of missionary activity and a career based on "the primary role of native Christian pastors and laity and a commitment to linguistic sophistication and translation" (23). After a meeting with two articulate and dignified Malagasy ministers, he felt that he had found a form in which his own sensibilities and talents could flourish.

After passing his *bac* in 1898, Leenhardt applied for a position in New Caledonia. Because of his inexperience, he was accepted only with reluctance by the missionary hierarchy. There had been no other applicants. At his ordination ceremony, Leenhardt pronounced a farewell speech that was in some ways a definition of his ethical and scientific task: "The Christian church seems nowhere so pure as in missions, where it finds itself liberated from the dogmatic political debris with which history has burdened it. . . . It is the young churches in pagan lands who will provide us with the fresh blood needed for the vitalization of our tired milieux" (29). Leenhardt would struggle with the contradiction of respect and change throughout his entire career, gradually moving, through his ethnographic work, to an appreciation of the maturity and fullness of Melanesian culture, but never fully transcending his commitment to conversion, and hence to the alteration of these other people's culture. At the time of the ordination speech, however, only a germ of this existential dilemma is present.

Protestant missionaries were encouraged to marry; Leenhardt did to an unusually intelligent and steady woman of his class. Shortly thereafter the Leenhardts boarded a steamer for the six-week voyage to New Caledonia and a new life. They were greeted at Noumea, a shoddy colonial capital, by a mayor who asked why they had come, since there would soon be no natives left for them to missionize. Although the French colony was not entirely monolithic, and Leenhardt would later learn adroitly to exploit its fissures, Noumea was marked by insularity, racism, and a pathetically thin mimicking of remembered "French life." New Caledonia was atypical of French colonialism, however, in that it had been used by the Second Empire as a dumping ground for criminals. After a forced-labor construction of Noumea itself, many of these deportees were given plots of land expropriated from the native inhabitants in the hinterlands. This led to a bloody uprising and repression in 1878–79, to increased fear of the "savages," and to the establishment of a reservation system in poor agricultural land high in remote mountains. This trend was only reinforced in 1894 by the arrival of a staunch Republican governor, who sought to stop the flow of criminal deportees and launched an aggressive campaign to attract stable families of French settlers in order to construct a rural democracy of small, independent landholders. As in other French colonies, a drive to register and "regularize" land titles led to a further confiscation of native land holdings, because of the lack of formal titles, distrust of the authorities and refusal to comply, or simply a *post festum* validation of the already widespread theft of native lands.

Reservations were established and strictly controlled; native movement required written permission usually granted only for purposes of labor gangs; gendarme posts dotted the countryside. Bucolic rural democracy was not the result. Leenhardt, who was never a categorical anti-colonialist, described the system of labor contracts as one of "slavery." In sum, at the time of Leenhardt's arrival in New Caledonia,

The plight of the island's Melanesians was indeed desperate. An ever-increasing European presence—penitentiary, mines, colonization—had shaken their culture to its roots. Leenhardt was already familiar with the litany of disaster: military conquest, disease, alcoholism, uprooting, the relocation of reservations on inferior lands. In two terrible decades just preceding his arrival (according to the best modern estimates) the indigenous population had fallen by fully thirty-three percent.

(35)

Leenhardt's consistent stand towards colonialism and the colonial administration was one of loyal opposition. Although he was sorely tested by its abuses, and his naiveté about the *mission civilatrice* of the French soon lost its sheen, he never turned against the colonial mission of France per se. The complexity of his understanding deepened over the years, but never to the point of a radical alteration of perspective. Leenhardt opposed the exploitative aspects of the colonial system, but in fact spent his life working within its purview. If change was inevitable, Leenhardt held, it was best that as much as possible of the indigenous culture be preserved—through conversion.

Leenhardt's early experience of colonial administration is meshed with what he called "government anthropology." As needs for labor power increased, the government pushed for a tighter "tribal" organization—one they could control, catalogue, and observe directly. While Leenhardt opposed these abuses, he also opposed colonialist administrators who sought to freeze local customs into a timeless mold of supposed tradition. Leenhardt believed both in the inevitability and the preferability of change in New Caledonia—he could hardly have been a missionary and believed otherwise—but he was optimistic about the potential for cultural change as an authentic evolution that did not rip asunder all links to the past. Leenhardt saw, somewhat paradoxically, that the government's position of relativism was a tool for preventing the Melanesians from developing means of self-defense. If the Melanesians were to survive with any cultural authenticity at all, they would have to develop ways of coping with the coming world, meaningfully. Although Leenhardt was one of the great ethnographic explorers of "archaic consciousness," he still believed that it was archaic, and that progress was inevitable.

Clifford makes a compelling comparison between Leenhardt and Michel Leiris, whose classic essay of 1950, "L'ethnographe devant le colonialisme," is still the most lucid and uncompromising condemnation of colonialism and anthropological complicity to have been written. Unlike Leiris, Leenhardt never abandoned what can only be called his blind faith in the *rayonnement de la culture française:* despite all his years of bitter experience of the racism, exploitation, and lack of cross-cultural communication on New Caledonia, he clung to a belief in the universal possibility and necessity for progress, democracy, citizenship, and Christianization under the French flag. And yet the programs of Leiris and of Leenhardt for anthropology in the face of colonialism are rather similar. Leiris called for a political advocacy of native culture, but distinguished between "safe-guarding small cultures and preserving them—as objects of study and aesthetic appreciation" (197). He called for offering the possibility of education, preferably bilingual and bicultural, that emphasized local custom and history. Leenhardt would not only have agreed with this type of program—he spent his life instituting it.

Both Leenhardt and Leiris agreed that in this encounter between colonized and colonizer, Western culture had the most to learn spiritually. The distortions—sexual, aesthetic, corporal—that had eroded French culture could perhaps be redirected, softened, and ameliorated by an open and patient contact with these other peoples. The final task was not to resist change, but a more hermeneutic one: the necessity to study the other so as to return, changed, to oneself. This difficult journey was indeed one that Leenhardt and Leiris both accomplished in differing but exemplary fashions. Leenhardt's naiveté was to think that the *petit colon* government officials, or the directors of the nickel mining company, or the head of the Missionary Society, were interested in pursuing such a quest.

At the time of Leenhardt's arrival, about one-third of the native population had been converted to Catholicism, and an active and successful campaign of Protestant conversion was being waged by native missionaries from the nearby Loyalty Islands under the direction of a French missionary, Philadelphe Delord. "The early evangelists' message was simple: learn to read, learn to count, give up drinking, and attend prayer meetings. Among the surrounding colonists, however, such a message was construed as an encouragement to insurrection" (43–44). In this delicate and dangerous situation Leenhardt undertook two different types of activity, often in tension if not outright contradiction. The organizational task of consolidating and expanding the mission's position put Leenhardt constantly in conflict with the colonial administration. Leenhardt, the "participant," saw the necessity for defending his flock and their basic human rights against a predatory colonial environment. Over time, he developed a set of tactics for exploiting the innumerable petty differences, rivalries, and factions within the colonial hierarchy. This entailed a painful self-control, a delay of protest: an imitation of a native mask of acquiescence. Clifford's account of Leenhardt's patience and progress—and the subsequent loss of many of the gains by his less sophisticated or less talented replacements—suggests how much such a strategy depended on Leenhardt's unique skills, and how little generalizable as a method they proved to be.

Leenhardt the "observer" faced an even more difficult task. Gradually he came to see that ethnographic understanding was a linchpin both for his own mission and for the survival in a healthy form of the "Canaques" (the French colloquial appellation for the native Melanesians). The task of the missionary/ ethnographer was to gain an understanding of local culture that would enable him to change it without "violating" its life-sustaining form. The missionary, as opposed to the anthropologist with his "easy relativism," could never be a mere observer. His observation was always observation for change. "As a veteran, Leenhardt would pose a rule of conduct for novice evangelists: they should never forbid any native custom that they had not first thoroughly understood" (62). To those of us not imbued with the missionary calling such a credo is chilling. And yet, Clifford shows how this stance led Leenhardt (and other exceptional and honest missionaries) to a sustained inquiry about other cultures often surpassing that achieved by more scientifically oriented ethnographic colleagues. Leenhardt spent decades, not months, in the field; he truly mastered the local dialects; he *believed* in the sacred, as did those he studied. In a changing world, the missionary contributed to change; but the best missionaries, Clifford suggests, directed that change in a hermeneutic fashion: one that would deepen their own spirituality while helping the native culture both to preserve something of the power of tradition and to develop means of making sense of rapid and often brutal changes. But as Clifford makes clear, sustaining such a hermeneutic was complex and problematic, even for Leenhardt. Few in Leenhardt's missionary headquarters, or among his successors, really followed such a route—a failure that was to be a constant source of doubt and pain for him.

Another dialectic was also at work. Clifford shows us that Leenhardt became increasingly suspicious of his own successes. Protestantism was expanding, Leenhardt was ostensibly getting the job done; but doubts persisted for him about the depth of these conversions. In this context, Leenhardt became preoccupied in the 1920s with the importance of ethnography as a tool for comprehending Canaque culture. He had been introduced to the work of the Durkheimians and Lévy-Bruhl before the war; and although he rejected their conclusions as too schematic and general, too removed from on-the-ground complexities, his work was increasingly informed by their questions. In good ethnographic fashion, he saw the Melanesian synthesis not as "prelogical" but as a fully valuable, cohesive, and autonomous synthesis of elements of tradition, locale, and myth. And yet, inherent in missionary work was a push to situate his understanding of the worth of primitive culture in an evolutionary context that would provide a justification for conversion. Conversion for Leenhardt entailed a move "from concrete towards abstract modes of thought and expression, from a diffuse, participatory consciousness toward self-consciousness, from the affective domain of myth toward detached observation and analysis. The process must not, however, be accomplished in simple imitation of whites, but rather as an independent invention. It must develop as 'some kind of appropriate civilization, affirming itself gradually' " (78). The problem was how to accomplish this conversion without totally destroying the earlier cultural synthesis.

Leenhardt's answer was to develop a dialectic of understanding and change based on a concept of "translation." Clifford shows, with a great deal of sympathy and originality, how Leenhardt's conception of translation of cultural texts was conceived as a back and forth appropriation and re-translation of the key symbols of Canaque culture to the Bible and then back again. Broadening the French Protestant conception of God, he sought to create a more androgynous, less transcendent, more local one. It is in Clifford's descriptions of this process that Leenhardt's reply to a Parisian questioner as to how many people he had converted on New Caledonia—one!—can be appreciated.

Clifford opens the second half of his book with a hortatory admonition for the need to rethink and recast anthropology. "Anthropology, a science and an aesthetic that functioned rather comfortably within the imperial context, can no longer ignore that its 'data'—the human objects of its study and affection—have often been exploited, sometimes dying, individuals and cultures. As a response to this unhappy circumstance, a tone of elegiac regret is no longer sufficient" (124–25). But this is in fact the tone of Clifford's book! I hesitated to write that sentence until I understood that one of Clifford's strengths is exactly that his "deconstruction" of anthropological texts does not exempt his own from the process; even better, Clifford supplies all the tools to do the job. But he does not quite finish the task.

Clifford rightly indicates the refusal to thematize the colonial context in anthropology has produced a series of systematic aberrations. The political field in which anthropologists worked has been supposedly erased by "scientific" methods of inquiry and description. But, clearly, this approach has yielded neither a science nor an adequate description of the processes of change that "primitive society" was undergoing during this century. Both of these points are by now almost commonplace. There is another position, however, which is more controversial: a religious position which holds that the destruction and alteration of primitive culture are somehow transformed by the process of conversion and thereby transcended. Leenhardt was committed to this path. But is Clifford? At key junctures he poses this problem as a series of questions and contradictions, thereby avoiding judgment, and thereby producing the tone of elegiac regret. Clifford keeps all the right balls in the air, but at times he is perhaps a little too adroit for his own good.

The aestheticization of culture that we find in Leenhardt (grounded in a religious world view), and in Clifford (grounded in a textualist stance), is perhaps indication of a refusal to push the implications of the political and existential realities of "conversion" to their endpoints. The problem may well be more acute for Clifford than it was for Leenhardt. For, after all, Leenhardt was a missionary. Clifford provides us the materials for constructing a critique of Leenhardt's choices, but stops short of using them.

Clifford proposed to switch our analytic attention from an exclusive emphasis on the Other to a more vulnerable, dialectic and plural analysis of the research process itself. Although both of Clifford's admonitions are welcome reminders, they are hardly the pathbreaking suggestions they would have been in Leenhardt's time. In the last ten years there has been an increasing volume of literature on the historical and political circumstances of the practices of anthropology. Clifford and Jean Jamin are currently writing what promises to be a major work in this vein on anthropology and surrealism between the wars in France. There have also been a fair number of attempts to describe the anthropological process itself (Crapanzano 1980; Favret-Saada 1977; Rabinow 1977). That there is much that remains unsaid is clear. I think, however, that Clifford is also hinting at something yet more radical.

Clifford's thesis is that there was no unspannable gulf between Leenhardt the Ethnologist and Leenhardt the Missionary; only a field of tensions in which Leenhardt forged his life. Clifford quotes Merleau-Ponty on the healthy man: one who uses the contradictions in his life in a creative way. Rejecting, however, recourse to such *demodé* categories as a "life," Clifford "applied to Leenhardt his own theory of the Melanesian person, a person seen as decentered, 'outside' itself, continually rising to occasions. The notion of an 'inner' life is probably best understood as a fiction of fairly recent, and far from universal, application—even in the West" (6). Later, Clifford relates this conception of the person, in passing, to Lacan's notion of the decentered subject (185). Whatever the abuses such a conception might engender, it can also open up a method for writing a biography in which the person, his time, and unresolved contradictions are seen not as antagonistic but as fused. The result can be, as in this case, a provocative challenge to rethink our own experiences and our own modes of inquiry. Although hesitating between structuralist depersonalization and a hermeneutic flood of signification, this contribution is surely one of the most original of Clifford's book.

We come back, however, to ethnography. Leenhardt worked "mainly" with the converted. His central concern as a missionary was not to eradicate the pre-Christian culture of the Canaques, but to find ways to translate what was living in that culture, and compatible with Christianity, into a new synthesis. Leenhardt was well suited to carrying this delicate task to fruition because in his family piety and science had gone hand in hand. His father's motto, after all, was "Facts are a word of God." But natives are not rocks, and the divine order his father saw in geologic formations is not of the same order as claiming to find a divine order, however sensitively and nervously relativized, among groups of human beings who conceived of themselves in other terms. Leen-hardt was "far from the sort of missionary who attempted to forbid or forcibly disrupt the practices of the unconverted. He did, however, claim moral au-thority over Protestants, those who, in theory at least, had made a break with tradition" (135)—that is to say, Leenhardt's informants. I think Clifford hesitates here. He is presenting Leenhardt's ethnography as being, to an ex-tent, exemplary; the emphasis on change, on text, on multivocality, Clifford is telling us, is the way to go. But surely he cannot mean that these elements are exemplary for us, as anthropologists, in the way Leenhardt fused them—ethnography and conversion. As Clifford says at such junctures in his book: questions, questions.

This ambiguity and perhaps ambivalence is made clearer by examining Clifford's presentation of Leenhardt's method of "intertextuality." Clifford juxtaposes Leenhardt's emphasis on the collection of vernacular texts with that of Boas and of Malinowski. The constitution of an indigenous record preserves something of a once living culture for posterity; one thinks of Geertz's "record of humanity" as a repository of textual sources available for reinter-pretation. This sort of record was at the heart of Leenhardt's procedures. His best informants were trained rigorously and patiently in the transcription of their own culture's texts. By so doing, Clifford claims, a co-authored text, one beyond a single "interpretive authority," was produced. Leenhardt's early works, *Notes d'ethnologie néo-calédonienne* (1930), *Documents néo-calédoniennes* (1932), *Vocabulaire et grammaire de la langue Houailou* (1935), are all products of this method. Ethnography became an informed transcription hovering close to the ground, to use another Geertzian phrase, never soaring far above the text. Leenhardt typically presents a page of Houailou vernacular, accompan-ied by a strict literal transcription and juxtaposed to a free rendering in French. Leenhardt trained a small battalion of Canaque Protestants in transcription and set them loose to write their own texts: fifteen different *transcripteurs* are listed on one title page. Clifford emphasizes that the ethnographer was not present to direct (distort) the content of the text. Even if this were true, it is not clear why this is important—the texts in such a post-structuralist pro-jection cannot claim any authenticity, or be somehow "truer" expressions of Canaque culture. Rather—and I think this is or should be what Clifford is claiming—they represent an ethically superior product of joint work and mutual recuperation. They have gained a poetic superiority. A new hybrid is thereby created: categories violated, genres blurred, worlds fused.

Again Clifford gives us the tools with which we could deconstruct this position if we wanted to. He tells us that the texts were obviously divorced from the immediate contexts of ritual performance in which they arose and to which they were meaningfully related. Surely the informants lost richness by practicing an art of transcription they had not fully mastered, and which paled alongside their own verbal eloquence. Finally, the mere fact of writing "implied a considerable degree of self-conscious distance from the customs described and thus could inject an element of abstraction and overintellectualization into the primary ethnographic evidence" (140). There is also an obvious element of self-censorship. The reader of these transcriptions was Leenhardt; his informants had been carefully trained as to what was Christian and what was not. Leenhardt's informants' livelihood and even safety depended on their ongoing relationship with him. Thus co-authoring is not without its context. The juxtaposing of a certain Foucaultian imagery of the anthropologist as dossier collector, scientist, and jurist with a certain Derridean imagery of the missionary/ethnographer and flock tracing inter-textual productions is not totally convincing. As I indicated earlier, however, one of the consistent strengths of Clifford's book is its resolute honesty and its opening up of important questions that rarely have pat answers. All the evidence is there; the counter-interpretations one might produce are opened up by the text itself. After some thought, I decided that Clifford is very wise in sustaining a certain ambiguity in his work. However, the line between ambiguity and complicity presumably must be drawn somewhere. At times Clifford seems to equate the patience and good sentiments Leenhardt displayed with his informants with a post-structuralist method of co-authorship. But surely the point of post-structuralist, post-authorial writing is not conversion? Nonetheless, many interesting paths are suggested for our future exploration. If fieldwork and anthropology are interpersonal, cross-cultural processes, Clifford is correct in reminding us that "the 'authorship' of its initial written data is plural and not easily specified" (144).

In 1926 Leenhardt returned to Paris to face an uncertain future. He was on bad terms with the directors of the Missionary Society, who disapproved of his unorthodox methods. He accepted some teaching at the mission headquarters in Paris, but clearly was not welcomed there. He and his wife worked in the Paris Mission Populaire de la Bienvenue as urban missionaries; until 1938 he was the secretary of the Ligue de la Moralité Publique. He never turned on the church; he stoically accepted its "rules"; he was not a rebel.

It was the newly forming anthropological world in Paris that would give Leenhardt a place, a context within which he could grow for the rest of his life. The two most important actors were Lucien Lévy-Bruhl and Marcel Mauss. He found in them a combination of erudition and political humanism which, although profoundly different from his own, was nonetheless highly compatible. Leenhardt thrived in a field of differences that allowed, nay produced, dialogue. The differences between these men in age, religion, class, status, and theoretical opinion proved mutually enriching. Lévy-Bruhl in particular turned to this professor of "Canaque humanities" to test, and ulti-

mately to modify profoundly, his own theories of prelogical mentality. Mauss,
a freer personality than the somewhat austere Lévy-Bruhl, joined the older
man in protecting Leenhardt and ultimately finding a place for him at the
Ecole Pratique des Hautes Etudes, where Leenhardt eventually succeeded
Mauss in the chair of "non-civilized peoples."

In this context, it seems clear that Clifford is proposing a major recasting
of the history of French anthropology. The Durkheim/Mauss/Lévi-Strauss
lineage constructed by Lévi-Strauss is being gently put in question. I think it
is important to end with a brief exploration of this rereading. The simplest
contrast between Lévi-Strauss and Leenhardt concerns the interpretation of
myth. Both men labored to understand the centrality of myth in primitive
life. Both men saw myth as arising out of a concrete environment, where
culture and nature commingled and from which pieces and shreds were patched
together into a larger integrative whole. But from there their paths diverge.
Lévi-Strauss pursues "intellect" and Leenhardt "affect." Both have clearly articulated views. Impulses and emotions, Lévi-Strauss argues, explain nothing: "they are always results, either of the power of the body or the importance of the mind" (177). The "cerebral savage" lives between the biochemical
and the logical, with few, if any, important mediations. This is a position
Lévi-Strauss has defended for years. For him a vast range of human experiences (passions, history, politics, ambiguity, consciousness, action) are epi-
phenomenal. But it is exactly these themes (with the exception of politics),
as Clifford has so eloquently demonstrated, that are at the heart of Leenhardt's work. "Leenhardt refused to reduce emotion to physiological impulse,
nor would he assimilate its conscious expressive modes to rationality. The
heart had its reasons, or perhaps its rhythms. Its structure of articulation was
not, properly speaking, a classification or logic, a metaphysics or theology,
but a given experiential landscape" (177). Here Clifford displays his interpretive skills, his fine writing, his complex vision. These are the themes that
have been submerged or cast out of French anthropology—to its detriment,
in my opinion—by Lévi-Strauss. Leenhardt along with Clifford's other
wellspring, Michel Leiris—Leenhardt's first student—constitute a counter
tradition. Why deny it?

The two camps are not compatible. For Lévi-Strauss "it is not important
[at this level], that the mythic processes take place in a Melanesian valley or
in a study at the Collège de France" (181). The universal human mind, with
its endlessly repetitive operations, is everywhere the same. But the radical
dissatisfaction with the West and the difficult journey out to other fundamentally different human experiences can not be bridged so easily. Surely for
Michel Leiris or for Maurice Leenhardt it is precisely the differences between
life in a Melanesian valley and life in the offices and lecture halls of the
Collège de France that make anthropology worth doing. The historical pro-

cess of subsuming the first mode under the discourse and institutions of the second surely must be criticized, thematized, and understood as an irreducible mediating level that can not be simply skipped over by thought experiments. Perhaps this historical process is ineluctable. And yet, it is that added edge of resistance, found implicitly on almost every page of Clifford's book, that— had it been heightened—might have enabled him to go beyond that tone of elegaic regret of which he rightly is wary. Nonetheless, James Clifford has given us much to think and feel about in *Person and Myth*. We look forward, with great anticipation, to his future writings.

ACKNOWLEDGMENTS

I would like to thank Burton Benedict and Stephen Foster for their help.

REFERENCES CITED

Crapanzano, V. 1980. *Tuhami: Portrait of a Moroccan.* Chicago.
Favret-Saada, J. 1977. *Deadly words: Witchcraft in the Bocage.* Cambridge, England.
Rabinow, P. 1977. *Reflections on fieldwork in Morocco.* Berkeley.

THE DAINTY AND THE HUNGRY MAN

Literature and Anthropology in the Work of Edward Sapir

RICHARD HANDLER

"We lived, in a sense, lives in which the arts and the sciences fought uneven battles for pre-eminence." So wrote Margaret Mead of her student days in the early 1920s at Columbia University (1959:xviii). Mead's "we" refers to a community of anthropologists that included Franz Boas, Edward Sapir, and Ruth Benedict. That Boas was privately a pianist and the others more publicly poets is well known; that they developed a science of anthropology centered on the concept of culture and that some of them came to see culture as the art of living—as lifeways at once "satisfactory and gracious" (Mead 1928:12)—is also well understood. But the connection between the *practice* of art and the development of anthropology has been less thoroughly explored. This paper explores that connection in the work of the person for whom art was perhaps most important—Edward Sapir, Boas' most brilliant student and a key figure in the development of Boasian anthropology. For Sapir, art became a medium in which to work out an approach to questions of culture. What he came to understand in the practice of poetry, music, and criticism became central to his understanding of culture.

Sapir's contribution to "Boasian anthropology" must be understood in the context of the tensions and ambiguities in Boas' work, as well as Sapir's approach to their resolution. Two tendencies with respect to the study of cul-

---

Richard Handler is Assistant Professor in the Department of Sociology and Anthropology, Lake Forest College. His doctoral dissertation (University of Chicago, 1979) concerned the relationship of social scientific theory and nationalist ideology in Quebec. He is currently working on a book on the anthropology of Jane Austen's novels.

ture were implicit in Boas (Stocking 1968:214). On the one hand, he saw culture as "an accidental accretion of individual elements." At the same time, he recognized that culture could be understood as an organizing spirit or "genius" continually assimilating these atomistic elements, integrating them in a "spiritual totality" that must be appreciated as a unique, historical whole. Beneath this seemingly simple opposition lie a host of epistemological difficulties, stemming, at least in part, from Boas' "peculiar position within and between two traditions in German thought," those of "monistic materialism" and "romantic idealism" (Stocking 1974a:8–9). Thus, for example, Boas recognized the validity of two types of science, the physical and the historical, and claimed that each originates in a fundamental disposition of the human mind. Physical science stems from an "aesthetic" impulse which requires order and systematicity; it seeks general laws that transcend individual facts. Historical science depends on an "affective" impulse, "the personal feeling of man towards the world" (Boas 1887:644); it seeks to understand phenomena in their own terms rather than as exemplifications of general laws. Boas believed that both types of science aimed for "the eternal truth" (643), but at the same time he feared that the search for true scientific laws meant an imposition of conceptual schemes onto raw facts. On the other hand, Boas understood the objects of historical science (cultural wholes and the *Geisten* that animated them) as "phenomena having a merely subjective connection"—that is, as phenomena unified only by "the mind of the observer" (642–43). In this, history was akin to art, for "the way in which the mind is affected by phenomena forms an important branch of the study" (646). However, Boas also insisted that these subjectively determined phenomena be studied inductively, that they were, in fact, "directly and concretely observable and distinguishable" (Stocking 1974a:13). But, again, to observe and distinguish cultural wholes it was necessary to examine culture elements, which meant that "in practice, Boas' historical methodology was perhaps archetypically exemplified by his quasi-statistical study of the distribution of folk-tale elements" (Stocking 1974a:15).

Without attempting to discuss such issues in any detail, let me rephrase them in terms that more clearly relate them to Sapir's concerns. Simply put, then, the contrast between element and whole implies the problem of the ontological status of pattern or structure in human affairs. Are social-scientific laws nothing more than analytic impositions, or do they describe entities or aspects of the real world? What is the ontological status of cultural things— do whole cultures exist (either as things, or as sets of relations) or are there only culture elements in ever-changing associations? Finally, how can anthropologists apprehend the phenomena of culture? Should they work to construct general laws of human history, or ought they to focus "affectively" on the facts themselves? In either case, how are they to go about studying culture, which, whether directly observable or only a product of the observer's subjectivity, nonetheless concerns human subjectivity on a grander, collective scale?

Sapir came rather early in his career to differ from Boas with respect to these questions as they were posed in the study of language. Hymes has written that "Sapir, more than any American anthropologist," realized—as "an empirical fact"—"that the persistence of recognizable form . . . is greater in language than in culture" (1970:259). Behind this realization lay a facility for analyzing linguistic form that made Sapir's doctoral dissertation, a grammar of Takelma, "almost a miracle for its time" (Hymes & Fought 1975:918). But though Boas himself recognized Sapir's linguistic brilliance and even deferred to it at the time of the Takelma work, in his own linguistic practice he "hesitated to carry the reduction to system too far" (Stocking 1974b:462, 479). This was equally true of his approach to culture. In general, Boas' anthropology was "pre-structural" (Hymes 1961:90; Stocking 1974b:478–80). Caught between element and whole, Boas never developed a consistently holistic or structuralist conception of culture. But the questions he raised were to prove so suggestive that "much of twentieth-century American anthropology may be viewed as the working out in time of various implications in Boas' own position" (Stocking 1974a:17). This "working out" was effected by Boas' students. What Sapir contributed, among other things, was a remarkable, and iconoclastic, theory of culture—a theory that is structuralist in its analysis of formal patterning, but transcends structuralism in its concern for individual experience, creativity, and the possibility of change.

At a rather early point in his career Sapir became interested in apprehending subjectivities rather than developing abstracted overviews of some "objective" reality. That is, Sapir sought techniques that would allow an observer to portray from the "inside" the realities that other individuals understand. These interests are expressed most completely in his writings on art. At the same time Sapir elaborated his critique of the "superorganic" concept, arguing that to analyze the social aspects of human behavior did not require the analyst to posit a level of (social) reality that transcends human individuals. These insights are combined in the issue that most interested Sapir at this time, the relationship between individual creativity and given cultural forms. Again this is a theme dominant in the writings on art. Moreover, Sapir's concern with the creative processes of art, as well as his work in linguistics, led him to another realization—the understanding that a cultural pattern, a patterning of values and attitudes, would be something like the formal patterns of art and language (Hymes 1970:260–61). These two sets of insights—concerning the relation of individual and culture, on the one hand, and the nature of formal patterning, on the other—are brought together by the notion of unconscious patterning. It is the idea that individuals "intuit" pattern, and that this intuition allows them to participate in patterned social action without at the same time being coerced by "society"—allows them, in short, to communicate with others in interaction without thereby surrendering the possibility of creativity—that cements a theory of culture accounting both for given form (culture) and the subjective experience of individuals. And though this idea of unconscious patterning is elaborated with respect to an anthropological conception of culture only in 1927, much of it, too, is present in the earlier writings on art. Hence an examination of Sapir's artistic concerns will deepen our understanding of the origins of his mature theory of culture.

It will also show something of how his thought developed. The question of "how" in cultural processes was an important one for Sapir, touching on issues of form and meaning, individuality and creativity. Hymes has shown that Sapir initially separated questions of "how" and questions of "what"—linguistic form (how) merely expressing cultural content (what)—whereas in his later thought he brought them together—form actively shaping content, language creating world view (1970:258–64). But this is only part of the story, for Sapir's mature formulation of these issues grew out of an artistic praxis and the theorizing associated with it. In addition to the questions of "how" and "what," Sapir posed problems in terms directly reminiscent of Boas' dilemmas in the epistemology of science. Sapir sought in art a way to unite form and feeling, cultural givens and subjective experience—a way to reconcile what Boas had called physical science, with its "aesthetic" search for impersonal laws, and an "affective" understanding of individual human hearts. In brief, in art Sapir attempted to come to terms with both his scientific and his romantic yearnings, to reconcile what he portrayed, in one of his poems, as the dainty man and the hungry man within himself. To contextualize this conflict, which for Sapir was both personal and philosophical, we need to know something of his intellectual biography.

The record of Sapir's published work suggests that 1916 was a turning point in his intellectual development. That year saw the publication of his famous monograph *Time Perspective in Aboriginal American Culture,* his last major work purely in the Boasian mold. The same year also produced a paper on the Australian composer Percy Grainger and an essay on American culture in response to one by John Dewey. In 1917, in addition to technical papers and reviews, we find two reviews of psychoanalytic works, reviews of a series of novels and of a musician's biography, and two essays on literary theory, all published in *The Dial.* From 1918 through 1921 Sapir's output of this latter type of writing approximately equaled that of specifically anthropological papers, and during 1922 the number of literary and general reviews, published in such magazines as *The Dial, The Freeman, The New Republic,* and *The*

Nation, far outweighed the number of technical pieces. More important, it is in the non-professional writing—and in the brilliant little book on *Language* he published in 1921 for a general intellectual audience—that we get a sense of inspiration and creativity, as compared to the more routine analyses in linguistics and ethnology. After 1922 Sapir's literary pieces become more and more incidental, his last literary reviews appearing in 1928. The publication of Sapir's poetry follows the same course. His first published poems, and his only volume of poetry (*Dreams and Gibes*), appeared in 1917. From 1918 to 1927 he published a substantial number of poems each year; his last four published poems appeared in 1931. From this "trait analysis" alone, then, we can guess that for Sapir the late teens were a time of shifting interests and even "profound rethinking," as Preston has put it (1980:367; cf. Newman 1951:181–82). What Sapir rethought were some of the premises of Boasian science and his intellectual commitment to them.

Sapir began his graduate training in anthropology under Franz Boas at Columbia University, receiving the Ph.D. in 1909. During his years of graduate study he did linguistic and ethnological fieldwork among several Native American groups, and was affiliated in research and instructional capacities with the University of California and the University of Pennsylvania. After a student career "marked by great phonetic virtuosity, enormous bursts of energy, great hopes" (Voegelin 1952:2), he accepted appointment in 1910 as chief of the division of anthropology in the Geological Survey of Canada, a position he was to hold until 1925.

The record of Sapir's first years in Ottawa shows that he immediately established a Boasian program in ethnological and linguistic research, as well as in his work with the ethnological collection of the Victoria Memorial Museum. During the first years of his appointment Sapir carried out this program without much apparent dissatisfaction. His publications from 1910 until 1916 are primarily concerned with his work on North American languages, as well as ethnological data he had gathered while doing linguistic research. His major theoretical contribution was *Time Perspective,* in which he used techniques developed in historical linguistics to elaborate a methodology for the reconstructive work of ethnology. *Time Perspective* summarized and even exhausted the Boasian paradigm, and, when compared to Sapir's later essays in anthropological theory, seems out of character for him. For example, in *Time Perspective* Sapir claimed "historical understanding" as the "properly ethnological goal," and eschewed the study of individuals for that of "generalized events and individualities" (1916:391–92). He echoed Boas in warning against the imposition of theoretical categories onto raw data where knowledge of historical connections is lacking. He repeatedly spoke of culture in terms of "elements" and "complexes" that have come together in elaborate historical processes to form whole cultures. The "structure" of a "culture complex" was of interest because the analyst could use it to recover chronology, since more loosely "associated" elements could be presumed to be more recent (405). Sapir spoke of cultural survivals and origins, but made only passing reference to the influence of individuals on culture. Though his application of linguistic techniques to ethnological problems took him beyond Boas in methodological daring, the piece remains fundamentally Boasian in orientation and conception. In view of the fact that this monograph adheres so closely to Boasian orthodoxy—indeed, giving it its most elegant expression with respect to the problems treated—we should bear in mind how soon after its publication Sapir was to strike out in new directions.

The first strong expressions of intellectual dissatisfaction on the part of Sapir are to be found in his letters of 1916 to Lowie. We might well imagine that as Sapir came out from under the direct supervision of Boas, and as his comparative analyses of American languages pushed his thinking well beyond what the master would sanction, elements of intellectual rebellion began to crystallize into a new orientation. Preston suggests (1980:368–69) that Sapir was stimulated in this by his friendship with Radin, and reproduces a long letter that Sapir received in 1914, in which Radin castigated Boas for his methodological timidity and lack of historical imagination: Boas was far too concerned with reconstructing chronological accounts of the development of primitive culture, and with "certain general factors, like dissemination, convergent evolution, independent origin, etc." An ethnology exclusively animated by such interests would fail to fulfill its promise; anthropologists should concentrate instead on "sympathetic interpretation" and "intimate" portrayals of daily life (369).

Whatever Sapir's immediate response to Radin's ideas, he began to raise similar doubts in his letters to Lowie. The record of their regular correspondence begins in 1916 (Lowie 1965). According to Lowie, Sapir's position in Canada, "judged purely on its potentialities for scientific research . . . was ideal" (2). However, Sapir felt isolated from the academic and artistic centers of the American cities, and became increasingly dissatisfied with anthropological work. There are indications that he felt himself to have been cast off—presumably by Boas—in his placement in Ottawa. He envied those among his peers who had landed academic jobs in the States, and resented Boas' criticisms of his linguistic work. With the onset of his wife's physical and mental illness as early as 1913, there were also difficulties in his personal life. Sapir's first non-technical publications (in 1916 and 1917) show traces of profound moral questioning in addition to social criticism. He was particularly appalled by the World War and expressed his pessimism and sense of horror in his poetry. The war also affected his research program, the public funding for which was drastically reduced as money was diverted to the war effort (Murray 1981a:65). These troubled aspects of Sapir's situation com-

bined to foster anxiety and resentment, frustration and boredom. He sought
an outlet in musical and literary pursuits. A letter of August 12, 1916, tells
Lowie that "I do practically no anthropology out of office hours, most of my
time being taken up with music" (Lowie 1965:20).

This remark must have elicited a query from Lowie, for in the next letter
Sapir explains his musical interests in a long passage that is worth reproduc-
ing in full:

> Why do I engage in music? I suppose I could call it recreation and be done
> with it, but I do not think it would be quite sincere for me to put off your query
> like that. Whether or not I have "missed my vocation" is not for me to decide.
> I feel I can do not only eminently satisfactory linguistic work but also satisfac-
> tory ethnological work, as I proved to myself in my two Nootka trips. I have
> now an enormous amount of linguistic and ethnological data on my hands from
> various tribes, certainly enough to keep me busy for at least five years of con-
> centrated work. But (and here's the rub and the disappointment) I don't some-
> how seem to feel as much positive impulse toward disgorging as I should. A
> certain necessary enthusiasm, particularly towards ethnological data and prob-
> lems, seems lacking—lacking beyond a mild degree, anyway. I somehow feel
> in much of my work that I am not true to my inner self, that I have let myself
> be put off with useful but relatively unimportant trifles at the expense of a
> development of finer needs and impulses, whatever they are. A chafing of the
> spirit, the more annoying because there is externally so little excuse for it! I
> know, as no one else can, that it is this profound feeling of dissatisfaction and
> disillusionment which hardly ever leaves me, that is mainly (not altogether,
> for I must waste much time on office routine, but mainly) responsible for my
> relatively unproductive scientific career up to date. To amass data, to write
> them up, to discuss "problems"—how easy, but *cui bono?* Do not misunderstand
> me. My "cui bono" is not grounded in any philosophy of relative values. I have
> no theoretical quarrel with anthropology. The fault lies with me. Being as I
> am, for better or for worse, the life of an Americanist does not satisfy my
> inmost cravings. To be frank, I do not believe this discontent is due chiefly to
> the unhuman aspect of our discipline, to its narrow range of appeal. I am afraid
> I may have too much of the "shut-in" personality about me to feel that sort of
> limitation as keenly as a Smith or perhaps yourself. I find that what I most care
> for is beauty of form, whether in substance or, perhaps even more keenly, in
> spirit. A perfect style, a well-balanced system of philosophy, a perfect bit of
> music, a clearly-conceived linguistic organism, the beauty of mathematical re-
> lations—these are some of the things that, in the sphere of the immaterial,
> have most deeply stirred me. How can the job-lot of necessarily unco-ordinated
> or badly co-ordinated facts that we amass in our field-work satisfy such long-
> ings? Is not the incessant poring over of such facts a punishment to the liberty
> loving spirit? Does not one most "waste time" when he is most industrious?
> And yet one always feels relieved and a bit pleased to have done with some bit
> of "scientific" work. I do not really believe that my temperament is so very

unscientific either, for I am surely critical and almost unreasonably analytical. A scientific spirit but an aesthetic will or craving! A sort of at-cross-purposes-with-oneself type of temperament that entails frequent inhibitions, frustrations, anything but a smooth flow of self-satisfied and harmonious effort. Shucks! my self analysis may be all wrong, but the inner dissatisfaction is there.

(Lowie 1965:20–21)

A letter is, typically, spontaneously dictated and thus may reveal, not carefully thought-out analyses, but deeper, more tangled and even contradictory motives. Here are several apparently simple dichotomies—art and science, harmonious form and a formless assemblage of heterogeneous elements, the inner life and the outer—but they cannot be taken as simple oppositions. They cross-cut one another and, as the letter reveals, Sapir was hard put to choose among them. Certain oppositions seem relatively clear—Sapir chafes at the sacrifice of inner needs to outer trifles, he seeks harmonious form and recoils from formlessness, he feels torn between an aesthetic will and a scientific spirit. But what, we might ask, is art, and what is science? For Sapir science is ethnology and linguistics, but he is less sure of his ethnological than his linguistic science, the latter being the more technically precise of the two. Science is also data amassed and "written up," but what good are such activities compared to beauty of form? Yet formal beauty must be discoverable by science as well, for who but a scientist can apprehend linguistic and mathematical relations? Reading from another point of view, we might say that Sapir is here expressing frustration that ethnology is not linguistics: what he can accomplish in the latter—the discovery of form—eludes him in the former. But this formulation is immediately cross-cut by another, for linguistics and ethnology are taken together as science—it is both linguistic and ethnological data that Sapir has "on his hands," ready to be "disgorged." And these two—combined as "our discipline," the science of anthropology— have an "*unhuman* aspect." Is, then, the beauty of form characteristic of such human endeavors as music, philosophy, and mathematics unhuman? Is Sapir at once attracted to it and repelled by it? (cf. 1924b:159).

At this point it might be useful to recall Boas' discussion of the two types of science, physical and historical. Physical science depended upon aesthetic impulses, historical science upon affective ones. "Aesthetic" for Boas meant regularity and generality, whereas the affectivity of history, like that of art, sought uniqueness. Perhaps Sapir's dilemma was that he was drawn to *aesthetic* phenomena (form) in an *affective* way ("what I most care for"). At any rate, Sapir's crisis was not merely personal: he was struggling with implications that contradict one another within a single scientific discipline. Radin also had been threatened by the horns of the dilemma: he yearned for "a real human science instead of one of bones and dust" (Preston 1980:369). Or consider Margaret Mead's recollection of how Boasian anthropology was taught by Boas' students around 1920: on the one hand was Alexander Golden-weiser, "mercurial, excited by ideas about culture, but intolerant of the petty exactions of field work, . . . working on the first book by an American anthropologist which was to present cultures briefly as wholes"; on the other hand, Elsie Clews Parsons, from whom "students learned that anthropology consisted of an enormous mass of little bits of material, carefully labeled by time, place, and tribe—the fruits, arid and bitter, of long, long hours of labor and devotion" (1959:8). Among the Boasians, then, there was the duty to study culture elements and a desire to discover culture wholes—an inhuman science in place and a human science on the horizon. Or, perhaps, there was science and there was art, fighting, as Mead put it, "uneven battles for pre-eminence." To get a better sense of how the match stood with Sapir, let us turn to his poetry and literary essays.

Sapir's poems are short and of the lyric variety. His essays and reviews show that he studied the important American and British poets of his day, but because he experimented continuously with poetic technique he never developed a fixed style from which it would be possible to trace strong influences. As for general content, one finds an intriguing blend of emotion, anthropological insight, social criticism, and a touch of the Orientalism of the period—though Sapir's poetic exotica are drawn more often from the "primitive" peoples of ethnology than from the East of classical and Orientalist scholars.

Many of Sapir's poems reflect great personal anguish and doubt. Sometimes such feelings are unmotivated and unexplained:

> Silence, silence,
> Dearest friend, I pray you—
> For it is not merry in my soul.
>
> (1917a:54)[1]

Other poems imply, or frankly discuss, the reasons for melancholy. There is a general alienation from the "dismal efficiency-mongering" of the modern, bureaucratized world (65), and, related to this, dismay at hypocrisy, particularly that of religion and patriotism. Several poems express horror and outrage at the war, and many suggest the personal tragedy associated with Sapir's wife's illness. What is of most interest for our present purposes, however, is a theme that may be summarily described as the gap between inner and outer human realities.

Dreams and Gibes opens with "The Mislabeled Menagerie" (9–10): the

---

1. References to poems taken from *Dreams and Gibes* (1917a) contain only page numbers. References to poems from other sources are indicated by year as well.

poet visits a zoo and finds himself in a "Topsyturvydom" where the monkey is labeled *Ursus*, the camel ostrich, and so on. His initial suspicion is that some "fussing pedagogue" has attempted a "new labeling scheme," but a zoo-keeper informs him that the animals have been moved so recently that there has been no time to change their signs. The poet then realizes that this mislabeling phenomenon, temporary in the zoo, applies permanently in the lives of many people: the grocer is a statesman, the mayor a grocer, the clergyman a simpleton. Because Sapir felt the arrangement of poems in a collection was significant (cf. Mead 1959:172), we may assume the initial placement of "The Mislabeled Menagerie" announces a major theme in *Dreams and Gibes*. The following sixteen poems (there are fifty-three in the collection) speak directly of people who are not what they seem, and most of the others suggest related problems.

Among those people who are not what they seem, whose inner life differs from their "outward shell" (21), is the poet. Self-doubt and a feeling of being at odds with one's true self are implied in several blunt, sarcastic pieces aimed at academicians. The metaphysician is a dog chasing his tail, the philosopher constructs daily a new system to explain the universe. "Professors in War-Time" chides those who stand aloof, refusing to apply their wisdom and skill "while all the world is soaked in blood and groans with pain" (27). Other poems develop this theme of inner dissatisfaction in more personal ways. "Helpless Revolt" (64) expresses irreducible rebellion against an unyielding reality:

> I have no respect for what is.
> I can not mend and patch,
> I can not bend my soul to the twist
> That will make it fit with the brutal fact,
> That will make it yield to the tyrant world.
> My soul stands firm.
> It would annihilate all in its rage and build anew,
> Rather than bend.
> Therefore it breaks, and the brutal fact remains
> And the tyrant world wags on.

And "Reproof," a beautiful sonnet, has the poet mock his own soul for shunning life and light, losing itself in "endless, brooding self-pursuit" (1918a:102).

Yet other poems go beyond brooding and rebellion to suggest personal approaches that enable one to make sense of, or to come to terms with, difficult human realities. "The Dainty and the Hungry Man" portrays two such approaches: that of the aesthete, for whom beauty alone matters, and that of the Hungry Man who craves "the crassness of life" (35–37). One might guess that the poet sides with the latter, for in the dialogue (which is

the poem) he consistently allows him the last word. But if this poem expresses self-reflection on Sapir's part, as I think it must, one would be nearer
the mark to assume that the two characters represent conflicting aspects of
the poet's personality.

"I distil from the crassness of life / What matters alone—Beauty. / Take
it." Such is the philosophy of the Dainty Man. Yet he is portrayed coldly,
critically, as if he were heartless—the preciousness of his taste suggests a
Byzantine formalism untouched by human passion. Yet despite the pejorative
tone taken towards the Dainty Man, Sapir could not flatly condemn his faith
in beauty. As he had written Lowie: "what I most care for is beauty of form"
(Lowie 1965:20).

On the other hand, the Hungry Man voices passions and themes that run
consistently through Sapir's writing (and not only the literary writing) of this
time. The Hungry Man shuns the delicacies offered him by his opposite,
seeking instead "the thick of life," the tangle of "crowds in the street." This
image of the crowd appears frequently in Sapir's poetry and represents the
exterior surface of the urban world. The poet's typical response to this out-
ward spectacle is to ask what hidden passions animate its participants. Such
is the credo of the Hungry Man:

> And more to me than thoughts serene are the strivings and turmoils of the
> heart,
> And more to me than lovely images is the wayward current of life.

We might summarize his attitude by saying that the Hungry Man seeks to
experience the apparently disorganized, meaningless assemblage of detail and
event that constitutes the surface of human life, yet at the same time to
understand the inner truths of the heart. But the accomplishment of both
aims can be achieved only through a correct appreciation of that which the
Dainty Man worships yet misunderstands: beauty of form. Or, put another
way, to understand formal beauty ought not to be an end in itself, but should
lead to a better understanding of human existence. The Dainty Man and the
Hungry Man must be merged to become the artist, the creator who works
with formal beauty to communicate the truths of the heart.

Sapir's literary essays of this period explore these same issues of outer and
inner realities and their connection to aesthetic form. In this they prefigure
his treatment of such problems in more purely anthropological terms in the
later essays on culture theory. In 1917, the year of publication of *Dreams and
Gibes*, Sapir published two essays in literary theory, "The Twilight of Rhyme"
and "Realism in Prose Fiction." The former counters the preciousness of the
Dainty Man, while the latter addresses the problems of the Hungry Man.
That is, the first essay discusses the relationship of aesthetic form to self-

expression, and thus justifies beauty and art in humanly significant terms. The second proposes a method for achieving both an understanding of human hearts and an objective grasp of the outer surfaces of life.

Sapir's antagonists in "The Twilight of Rhyme" might seem at first to differ from the Dainty Man, for the imperialist orator (who ruins fiery oratory with hackneyed rhyming poetry) and Max Eastman (who campaigns against "Lazy Verse") have passion on their side. But their passion is strangled by the outmoded forms chosen to express it. According to Sapir, Eastman is correct in arguing that the "technical limitations" of an artistic medium have "disciplinary value which is of direct aesthetic benefit" (1917b:99). He errs, however, in valuing a particular technique (rhyme), appropriate in certain cultural contexts but by no means universally, instead of the general principle of the necessity of technical limitations. Sapir then outlines his theory of the relationship between individual creativity and traditional formal means. He argues that a delicate balance must be maintained between tradition and innovation, inherited forms and creativity. Otherwise, formalism and externality overcome sincerity and self-expression:

> Just as soon as an external and purely formal aesthetic device ceases to be felt as inherently essential to sincerity of expression, it ceases to remain merely a condition of the battling for self-expression and becomes a tyrannous burden, a perfectly useless fetter. . . . Perfection of form is always essential, but the definition of what constitutes such perfection cannot, must not, be fixed once for all. The age, the individual artist, must solve the problem ever anew, must impose self-created conditions, perhaps only dimly realized, of the battle to be fought in attaining self-expression. It would be no paradox to say that it is the blind acceptance of a form imposed from without that is, in the deepest sense, "lazy," for such acceptance dodges the true formal problem of the artist—the arrival, in travail and groping, at that mode of expression that is best suited to the unique conception of the artist.
>
> (99–100)

This argument, a cornerstone in Sapir's theory of art, will become central to his theory of culture as well. It brings together two seemingly contradictory forces—cultural form and individual expression—and makes each the condition of the other: given forms are necessary to self-expression, but when the individual works with form instead of merely yielding to it, he changes it. As Sapir says, in true art the formal problem must be solved "ever anew." Thus the pursuit of beauty becomes an attempt to achieve self-expression through creation of form rather than the merely static admiration of beauty espoused by the Dainty Man. That Sapir guided his artistic practice by his theory is evident in his critical judgments, and in the curious fact that most of his poetry before the publication of "The Twilight of Rhyme" is unrhymed, whereas after 1917 he experiments, not only with rhyme, but with such classical devices as the sonnet form (cf. Murray 1981a:67).

The second essay in literary theory of 1917 is "Realism in Prose Fiction." Sapir begins by asserting that "prose fiction is the vehicle *par excellence* for a realistic ideal." He distinguishes two aspects of this ideal, "outer and inner realism" or, in words nearer to those of the Hungry Man, "the flow and depth of life." He then asserts the primacy of the second aspect. The secret of "realistic illusion" lies in the ease with which a given literary form enables its audience to identify with the characters portrayed—"to live through," from the inside, their experiences. In conventional prose fiction the narrator enters the minds of any and all of his characters. In other words, he "claims an unconditional omniscience" that "goes by the name of objectivity." Yet this apparently objective technique threatens the realistic illusion, for it strains the reader's capacity for identification with the characters (1917c:503).

In response to this tension, a newer form of fiction, animated by "a subtler understanding of reality," has emerged. In this technique the author confines his vision to the psyche of one character, leaving the presentation of other characters as a function of this dominant vantage point. This narrative stance involves a trade-off in truth value: what the reader can learn of secondary characters is more frequently erroneous than true. This is because the "inner experiences" of secondary characters "can only be inferred, sometimes truly (that is, in a manner roughly coinciding with the viewpoints of their own selves), more often mistakenly." Yet in spite of this, or perhaps because of it, the technique just described is truer to our experience as we know it and is thus more realistic than that of the omniscient narrator. It follows that the objective and the subjective are reversed—an apparently difficult position that Sapir is prepared to defend:

> At this point the reader may object that while this method pretends to be sweepingly realistic, to aim to grasp a bit of life and imprison it in narrative form, it yet is the merest subjectivism, an egoist's dream in which everything is hopelessly out of plumb, in which the valid relations of the objective world are badly muddled. Nor would he be altogether wrong. And yet, what is life, as we really and individually know it, but precisely "an egoist's dream in which the valid relations of the objective world are badly muddled"? Objectivity, one might say, is romance. But he would need to add that we crave and demand this romantic objectivity, this mad seeing of things "as they really are," and that the literary artist has therefore a perfect right to choose between rigorous realism, the method that is frankly subjective, and objective realism, the romance of reality.

> (1917c:504)

Thus these two techniques, rigorous and objective realism, reveal different truths. Objective realism—which is "romance"—aims for the truth of an overview that tries somehow to account, in an orderly way, for the lives of many people. Rigorous realism—"frankly subjective"—aims at an inner truth, an accurate portrayal of the way one person might see the world. Yet Sapir is not content merely to juxtapose the two. Impelled, perhaps, by his scientific spirit, he offers a third technique for prose fiction that would make possible "a profound and all-embracing realistic art." He proposes that a given tale be told from the point of view of several characters, but each time *completely.* By being subjective in several ways the narrator could at last be truly objective: "for may not objectivity be defined as the composite picture gained by laying a number of subjectivities on top of one another . . . ?" According to Sapir, such a technique corresponds to an inductive process that guarantees "a steadily growing comprehension of the meaning of the whole" (1917c:505). Thus it satisfies the two desires of the Hungry Man, for it brings knowledge both of individual hearts and the collective life. And it speaks to the epistemological dilemmas of Boasian science, for it allows an observer to study subjective phenomena inductively. As such, it suggests something of the "science of interpersonal relations" that Sapir was to envision in his last essays (1939:579).

Thus far, in two literary essays of 1917, we have two elements of Sapir's emerging theory of culture—the question of form and creativity, and the concern for understanding human interaction from multiple "inner" points of view. In the same year Sapir published his famous critique of Kroeber's "superorganic," which gives us a third element in the nascent culture theory. "Do We Need a 'Superorganic'?" is written for a professional audience, but Sapir's concern for artistic creativity, and for "striking and influential personalities" (1917d:443), would seem to motivate the argument. The essay discusses the distinction between the "historical" and "conceptual" sciences, and Sapir cites, not Boas, but the German philosopher Rickert, to whom he acknowledges an explicit debt (447). Sapir argues that individual and social behavior can be distinguished only analytically, for all behavior is the behavior of individuals. Whether or not a particular item of behavior is taken to be social or individual depends upon the interests of the analyst, and his choice is thus "arbitrary" with respect to the behavior in question (442). It follows that there can be no such thing as a superorganic level of reality that coerces individuals and nullifies their creative possibilities: human beings can always change the course of history, can always adapt given forms to their own ends. Thus this essay addresses, from the anthropological side, the issues of culture and creativity that interested Sapir the artist.

In literary reviews and essays of the next several years Sapir continues to work with these issues. Again and again he speaks of true art as subjective truth externalized in unique form, a formula that unites the themes of 1917.

In his critical analyses he sharpens his sense of what this means by examining the degrees to which these elements of art are present or absent in the work of a particular artist or technique. Thus, for example, the "later work" of Edgar Lee Masters is said to lack the technical means necessary to give expression to feeling. The poet is said to have forgotten that "an unembodied conception is, in art, no conception at all" (1922a:334). On the other hand, there are works that are purely technical, that express neither thought nor emotion, and these too are destined for oblivion: "Craftsmanship, no matter how pleasing or ingenious, cannot secure a musical composition immortality; it is inevitably put in the shade by the technique of a later age" (1918b:491). In general, Sapir seems to have won—perhaps in the writing of his own poems—a greater commitment to the notion that technical discipline is necessary for self-expression: "Perhaps it is precisely the passionate temperament cutting into itself with the cold steel of the intellect that is best adapted to the heuristic employment of rhyme. The temperament and the triumphant harnessing of form belong, both of them, to the psychology of sublimation following inhibition" (1920a:498). If we remember that Sapir had previously championed the cause of unrhymed verse, and that he had since begun to use rhyme, it is difficult not to imagine these lines as a bit of self-analysis. They give us a picture of Sapir working out a theory of art, and of culture, as he tried to understand, through introspective analysis, his own artistic praxis. He goes on to call for a new science of aesthetics that will "get down to the very arduous business of studying the concrete processes of artistic production and appreciation" (499).

Sapir's discussions of aesthetic principles were complemented by analyses of particular artistic products, and in these he could develop his technical understanding of formal patterning. It is difficult to tell what effect his previous experience in analyzing linguistic patterning had on his analysis of artistic techniques. However, the theory of unconscious patterning—which he sketched in *Language* (1921a:55–58) and elaborated in a seminal paper four years later (1925)—occupied Sapir as a problem in poetry as early as 1918 (cf. Sapir 1919; 1921b:213).[2] It is worked out in some detail in a remarkable paper on poetic form, "The Musical Foundations of Verse," published in 1921. This paper contains, first, a sophisticated structural analysis of poetic "sectioning," showing how various rhythmic elements defined by mutual opposition, create the "appreciable psychological pulses" of a "rhythmic contour" (1921b:220–21). Second, it relates these rhythmic oppositions to *the ability of the listener to perceive them,* if only intuitively or subconsciously.

2. Murray points out, however, that Sapir may well have thought through the basic argument of his phonemic theory as early as 1913 (1981b:10); and the idea of unconscious patterning is already present in Boas in 1911 (cf. Modjeska 1968).

"Not all that looks alike to the eye is psychologically comparable," Sapir tells us, and thus "the same passage *is* both prose and verse according to the rhythmic receptivity of the reader or hearer" (215–16, 226). Here, then, we have the combination of a structural analysis of formal patterning with a concern for the subjective perception of pattern in the minds of those who use it— the essence, in short, of Sapir's phonemic theory and an important component in his final theory of culture. Thus by 1921 we have the major elements of Sapir's mature theory of culture present in his writings on art.

How were the ideas and insights developed in the writings on art worked into Sapir's more narrowly anthropological writing? We might begin with Sapir's two reviews of Lowie's *Primitive Society*, for these show both the degree to which Sapir remained a Boasian and the degree to which he was reworking Boasian themes to fit his emergent approach. Sapir praises Lowie's book for presenting the "American school" of anthropology to the public. This school is defined by inductive historical research, which it opposes to evolutionary speculation and psychological reductionism:

> We learn to see a given primitive society . . . as a complex of historical processes that is only to be unraveled, and then in insignificant degree, through a minute weighing of the concrete, interacting features of that society and through the patient following out of the numerous threads that inevitably bind it to its geographical neighbors.
>
> (1920b:378)

Though this recalls Boas' distributional studies of folklore traits, or Parsons' "careful assemblage and analysis of details" (Mead 1959:8), Sapir also implies that the historical process is human rather than superorganic: "No one that has watched the gradual, tortuous emergence of a social institution from the warp and woof of circumstance can feel it in his heart to say that he is but beholding the determinate unfolding of . . . whatever psychological concept be accepted for guidance" (1920b:378). The unstated counterpart to this historical critique of various reductionisms would be the role of the individual in the creation of culture. Culture itself is described as "the fine art of living" (1920c:332). And in his approach to culture the anthropologist must maintain, as Lowie has done, that "humanness of attitude" which "is simply a reflection of his human contacts with primitive folk" (1920b:377).

The implications of such an attitude are more fully spelled out in Sapir's review of *American Indian Life*, edited by Parsons. Sapir praises this group of fictional sketches of individual Native Americans precisely because they attempt to portray an exotic way of life from the point of view of the individual who lives it, rather than in an objective overview of the culture. The latter method highlights the traits of a way of life and, in so doing, obscures the reality of that life as those who live it might understand it. Sapir had earlier (1917e:424) denigrated such an approach as "item-listing," and here he spells out what is wrong with it: "It is precisely because the exotic is easily mistaken for subject, where it should be worked as texture, that much agreeable writing on glamorous quarters of the globe so readily surfeits a reader who possesses not merely an eye, but what used to be called a soul" (1922b:570). Writers tend to concentrate on the surface of an alien way of life because immediately palpable exotic externality commands their attention as the proper object of discourse. But stopping there, they fail to explore the "individual consciousness" of those who experience that life, though this is "the only true concern of literary art." The review thus shows how thoroughly Sapir had assimilated the problem of ethnological description to that of "realism in prose fiction." As he himself asks, "can the conscious knowledge of the ethnologist be fused with the intuitions of the artist?" (570; cf. Nyce 1977).

These sympathetic reviews of works by Boasian anthropologists should be compared to the *Time Perspective* essay to gain a fuller appreciation of the development of Sapir's thought between 1916 and 1922. One other paper of this period should be considered as well, Sapir's famous essay on "Culture, Genuine and Spurious." By 1918 Sapir had almost certainly completed it, though it did not appear in final form until 1924. Written for a general audience, it is Sapir's first attempt to present a theory of culture. The essay contains the first rigorous definition of the Boasian conception of culture as the genius of a people, seen in terms of the patterning of values. At the same time, it goes beyond a merely "scientific" definition of culture to include aesthetic and moral considerations. In the discussion of these latter issues Sapir sketches his vision of cultural harmony, thus presenting the first explicit statement concerning what came commonly to be known as "cultural integration."[3]

Sapir begins by considering three common understandings of the meaning of the word *culture*. First, he distinguishes a technical usage in which culture refers to "any socially inherited element in the life of man, material or spiritual" (1924a:309). To avoid confusion, Sapir rejects the label "culture" for this Tylorian assemblage and speaks instead of "civilization." Second, he examines (and finds wanting) the popular notion of culture as individual refinement based on selected acquisitions of intellect and manner. Sapir next goes to some length to spell out a third definition—perhaps because, as he

---

3. I base this claim for the originality of Sapir's formulations on Kroeber and Kluckhohn's study (1952) of the culture concept. The claim of absolute priority is relatively insignificant, for these were ideas "in the air." Sapir's contribution to their elaboration is incontestable, however, as is his influence on colleagues working on the same problems.

says, "those who use it are so seldom able to give us a perfectly clear idea of just what they themselves mean by culture" (310). This third usage—that of the Boasians?—takes from the technical conception its emphasis on the group, and from the popular notion the idea of a selection of those elements that are "more significant in a spiritual sense than the rest." However, spiritual significance is not dependent upon art, science, and religion—as adherents to the second definition might assume—but, rather, upon pre-eminent attitudes and values, drawn from whatever domain:

> We may perhaps come nearest the mark by saying that the cultural conception we are now trying to grasp aims to embrace in a single term those general attitudes, views of life, and specific manifestations of civilization that give a particular people its distinctive place in the world. Emphasis is put not so much on what is done and believed by a people as on how what is done and believed functions in the whole life of that people, on what significance it has for them. . . . Large groups of people everywhere tend to think and to act in accordance with established and all but instinctive forms, which are in large measure peculiar to it.
>
> (311–12)

Here, then, we have the idea that a culture is a patterning of values that gives significance to the lives of those who hold them, and, furthermore, that people's participation in the pattern is "instinctive"—in other words, unconscious. But Sapir does not stop there, for even this third definition is merely "preliminary" (312). What interests him is the "genuine" culture, and this is defined by features that are drawn directly from Sapir's work in poetics and literary theory. First, in the genuine culture the patterning of values is aesthetically harmonious. In other words, like a work of art the genuine culture is formally perfected, or, in a later terminology, "integrated": "The genuine culture is not of necessity either high or low; it is merely inherently harmonious, balanced, self-satisfactory. It is the expression of a richly varied and yet somehow unified and consistent attitude toward life" (314–15). Second, this perfection of form is "expressive"—it is the embodiment of living thought, of values that people practice: ". . . if it (the genuine culture) builds itself magnificent houses of worship, it is because of the necessity it feels to symbolize in beautiful stone a religious impulse that is deep and vital; if it is ready to discard institutionalized religion, it is prepared also to dispense with the homes of institutionalized religion" (315).

There is a significant comparison to be drawn here to a key idea in Boas' work—that of the secondary rationalization of unconscious formal patterns (cf. Boas 1911:67). In his discussions of form and function Sapir follows Boas in this, arguing that actors' appeals to function—or to ultimate truth—are often mere rationalizations for actions whose origins are purely formal. Yet the argument is expanded here to coincide with Sapir's theory of art. What is rationalized, and clung to, is "the dry rot of social habit, devitalized" (1924a:315)—in other words, empty shells of formal patterning that no longer express living values. Just as the genuine poet would discard a formal device once it "ceases to be felt as inherently essential to sincerity of expression" (1917b:100), so the genuine culture discards institutional forms once they have lost their expressive function. Thus it is that the genuine culture "is not of necessity either high or low": as in art, what matters is the embodiment of thought in form, not the sophistication of formal technique as such (cf. 1918b).

Finally, the genuine culture is expressive in another sense. It is "internal," as Sapir says; "it works from the individual to ends." In other words, its ultimate values are built "out of the central interests and desires of its bearers," rather than imposed externally, from history and tradition down to the passive individual (1924a:316). For Sapir this internal quality of a genuine culture manifests itself in the relationship of individual creativity and cultural form. Here the similarity to his arguments on poetic rhyme is apparent. "Creation," he argues, "is a bending of form to one's will, not a manufacture of form *ex nihilo*" (321). A genuine culture provides the context of traditional forms that nourishes each individual. At the same time it allows the individual to "swing free," to express his inner self through the creation of new forms (322). By contrast, the external or spurious culture suffers either from "surfeit" or from "barrenness." In the first case it overwhelms the individual with devitalized forms which, like trite rhyme in poetry, inhibit self-expression; in the second it does not provide the support and stimulation necessary for the realization of the individual will in acts of creativity. The spurious culture is thus a land of tinkers, for it can neither nourish nor tolerate "the iconoclasms and visions" of true artists.

Like the monograph on *Time Perspective*, "Culture, Genuine and Spurious" is in some respects uncharacteristic when compared to Sapir's later essays on culture theory. The romantic formulation of the idea of cultural harmony or integration gave way to the epistemological doubts expressed in his argument against the superorganic. Sapir came to insist that cultural wholes are analytic constructions having no reality, as wholes, as entities, in human behavior. When anthropologists speak of "a culture" they refer to a pattern or system that they themselves have constructed in the analysis of their data. Culture in this sense is a model abstracted from human interaction. But most anthropologists take a further step by reifying this model, treating it as a real-world existent and then using it to explain the very interactional data from which it has been abstracted. Sapir calls this "a fatal fallacy with regard to the objective reality of social and cultural patterns defined impersonally" (1938:576). It is this fallacy which allows theorists to oppose the entities "culture" and "individual" and pretend that the former controls the latter—

that is, that cultural norms constrain individuals, forcing them to behave in socially accepted ways.[4]

In contrast to this position, Sapir was to argue, not that culture does not matter, as Ruth Benedict interpreted him (Mead 1959:201), but that "the true locus of culture is in the interactions of specific individuals and, on the subjective side, in the world of meanings which each one of these individuals may unconsciously abstract for himself from his participation in these interactions" (1932:515). From this it follows that culture "varies infinitely" (518), since each person can interpret any element of patterned interaction in a way that will be psychologically satisfactory to him. Furthermore, because every individual can convince others as to the validity of his interpretation, any such interpretation has, "from the very beginning, the essential possibility of culturalized behavior" (1938:572). It is thus misleading to speak of individuals "adjusting" to culture, for what they in fact do is to bend cultural givens to their own ends, using them for creative self-expression and constructing culture anew in the process.

However inadequate this summary of Sapir's later work may be, I hope that it suffices to show the relationship between Sapir's art and his anthropology. In both, Sapir's first goal is to understand subjective realities, the truths of experience as individuals know them. In both, he concludes that an excessive concern with outer realism—the omniscient narrator or the anthropologist who reifies culture—produces a distorted view of reality, however much it pretends to objectivity. In both, he favors instead a focus on the interaction of subjectivities, on multiple inner points of view. Finally, both treat formal givens—artistic convention or cultural values—as means to self-expression rather than constraints upon individual freedom.

I have tried to show that in the practice of art Sapir worked out ideas that later became central to his theory of culture. Such a presentation raises the larger issues of intellectual influence and personal experience in the trajectory of a career. What, precisely, does it mean to say that Sapir worked out ideas in the practice of art? Did the ideas originate in the praxis, or were they present already, if merely latently, in his mind, accessible through some combinations of experience? How are we to understand Sapir's poetic endeavors in the context of a larger biography? Does his poetry represent a detour, motivated by frustrations and personal anxieties, from an otherwise normal career, or ought Sapir's art to be seen as part of his anthropology?

When I became acquainted with Sapir's poetry I noticed first the thematic

4. Preston (1966) presents a fuller, and somewhat different, exposition of Sapir's understanding of the reality of structure.

evidence of anthropological influence on poetic content. But as this essay has shown, it makes as much sense to seek the influence of Sapir's poetry on his anthropology as to expect to find things the other way around. Only retrospectively can it be claimed that Sapir's poetry was merely a diversion: in actuality, art and anthropology were united in the life and mind of one man, and that life was lived in a particular intellectual milieu, at a time when certain questions and ideas were in the air. In practice it is rarely possible to construct the history—as a unilinear series of influences and events—of a mind, a life, a milieu. The associations are too complex.

Take, for example, the question of intellectual influence, of the "origin" of Sapir's ideas. In addition to Boas, whose influence on Sapir can hardly be overestimated, who were the other thinkers that Sapir responded to? One can, of course, cite Freud and Jung on the basis of Sapir's sympathetic reviews of some of their works. But Sapir rarely acknowledged intellectual debts. Thus it is all the more remarkable that he should explicitly avow a debt to Croce in his book *Language:* "Among contemporary writers of influence on liberal thought Croce is one of the very few who have gained an understanding of the fundamental significance of language. He has pointed out its close relation to the problem of art. I am deeply indebted to him for this insight" (1921a:iii). Both Modjeska (1968:346–47) and Hymes (1969;1970:261, 264) have reasonably suggested that Croce's influence might have been important in Sapir's intellectual development. Yet Hall has argued that Sapir could not have been significantly influenced by Croce—that Sapir merely read into Croce more than was actually there—interpreting him "in the light of his own much . . . deeper knowledge of linguistic structures" (1969:499). But, however useful such an argument is to preserve Sapir's reputation for brilliance, it fails to account for the enthusiasm of Sapir's explicit acknowledgment. I would suggest that the problem vanishes when we understand that influences are rarely specific causal connections. Even in the case of Sapir's debt to Boas, the question is not so much one of where a person's ideas originated but, rather, of why he chose to develop those ideas and not others, and how—under what circumstances and in what directions—he developed them. It is in response to the question of "how" that Sapir's art becomes relevant. He once wrote to Benedict that poetic technique "comes to its own only after great experience in handling words and forms" (Mead 1959:163). That his understanding of linguistic form was intuitive is perhaps true, but the development of his linguistic theory must have depended at least as much on long experience working with particular languages as on native ability (cf. Pike 1967:65). The same may be said of his theory of culture. He had at hand the proto-theory of Boas, his developing understanding of language, and inspiration from people like Croce, Rickert, Freud, and Jung. But it was in the practice of art, where he could experience the living force of the relationship between feeling and form, that he was stimulated to forge ideas—some borrowed, some reformulated, some original—into his own theory of culture.

In light of this argument we are led to reconsider the relationship between Sapir's art and his anthropology. There is a surface plausibility to the claim that Sapir's poetry was a temporary response to the difficulties of a particular phase of his life. But poetry was not merely an outlet, an activity utterly separated from Sapir's "serious" work. Several commentators have pointed out that Sapir's poetry influenced the style of his anthropological writing (Newman 1951:182–83; Voegelin 1952:2). In addition to this stylistic influence I have argued that we should recognize an influence on the substance of his theory. This is, after all, what we would expect if we take seriously Sapir's theory of culture: just as the form of a language or culture cannot be separated from the content or thought that it embodies, so a self-conscious creative praxis, as in music and poetry, must inevitably shape any deliberate reflections on human creativity, as in a theory of culture.

ACKNOWLEDGMENTS

Earlier versions of this paper were presented to the Chicago Group in the History of the Social Sciences (sponsored by the Morris Fishbein Center for the Study of the History of Science and Medicine) at the February 1981 meeting, and at the fourteenth annual meeting of the Cheiron Society in June 1982. I would like to thank the participants in those sessions for their helpful comments. In addition, Franci Duitch, Dell Hymes, Richard Preston, and George Stocking read the paper as it progressed through various versions, and stimulated me with their critical suggestions.

REFERENCES CITED

Boas, F. 1887. The study of geography. In Boas 1940:639–47.
———. 1911. *Handbook of American Indian languages, part I. Bur. Am. Ethn. Bul.* 40. Washington.
———. 1940. *Race, language, and culture.* New York.
Hall, R. A. 1969. Sapir and Croce on language. *Am Anth.* 71:498–99.
Hymes, D. 1961. Review of *The anthropology of Franz Boas,* ed. W. Goldschmidt. *J. Am. Folk.* 74:87–90.
———. 1969. Modjeska on Sapir and Croce: A comment. *Am. Anth.* 71:500.

✓ ———. 1970. Linguistic method in ethnography: Its development in the United States. In *Method and theory in linguistics*, ed. P. Garvin, 249–325. The Hague.

✓ Hymes, D., & J. Fought 1975. American structuralism. *Cur. Trends Ling.* 13:903–1176.

Kroeber, A. L., & C. Kluckhohn. 1952. *Culture: A critical review of concepts and definitions*. Paperback ed. Garden City, N.Y. (1965).

Lowie, R. H., ed. 1965. *Letters from Edward Sapir to Robert H. Lowie*. Berkeley.

➤ Mandelbaum, D. G., ed. 1949. *Selected writings of Edward Sapir in language, culture, and personality*. Berkeley.

Mead, M. 1928. *Coming of age in Samoa*. New York.

———. 1959. *An anthropologist at work: Writings of Ruth Benedict*. Boston.

➤ Modjeska, C. N. 1968. A note on unconscious structure in the anthropology of Edward Sapir. *Am. Anth.* 70:344–47.

Murray, S. O. 1981a. The Canadian 'winter' of Edward Sapir. *Historiog. Ling.* 8:63–68.

➤ ———. 1981b. Sapir's gestalt. *Anth. Ling.* 22:8–12.

Newman, S. 1951. Review of Mandelbaum 1949. *Int. J. Am. Ling.* 17:180–86.

Nyce, J. M. 1977. The relationship between literature and ethnography: The example of Edward Sapir, 1917–1922. Paper read at the 4th Congress of the Canadian Ethnology Society, Halifax.

➤ Pike, K. L. 1967. *Language in relation to a unified theory of the structure of human behavior*. The Hague.

➤ Preston, R. J. 1966. Edward Sapir's anthropology: Style, structure and method. *Am. Anth.* 68:1105–27.

➤ ———. 1980. Reflections on Sapir's anthropology in Canada. *Can. Rev. Soc. & Anth.* 17:367–75.

✓ Sapir, E. 1916. Time perspective in aboriginal American culture: A study in method. In Mandelbaum 1949:389–462.

———. 1917a. *Dreams and gibes*. Boston.

———. 1917b. The twilight of rhyme. *Dial* 63:98–100.

———. 1917c. Realism in prose fiction. *Dial* 63:503–06.

➤ ———. 1917d. Do we need a 'superorganic'? *Am. Anth.* 19:441–47.

———. 1917e. "Jean Christophe": An epic of humanity. [Review of *Jean-Christophe*, by R. Rolland.] *Dial* 62:423–26.

———. 1918a. Reproof. *Dial* 64:102.

———. 1918b. Representative music. In Mandelbaum 1949:490–95.

———. 1919. Review (unsigned) of *The foundations and nature of verse*, by C. F. Jacob. *Dial* 66:98, 100.

———. 1920a. The heuristic value of rhyme. In Mandelbaum 1949:496–99.

———. 1920b. Primitive society. [Review of *Primitive society*, by R. H. Lowie.] *Freeman* 1:377–79.

———. 1920c. Primitive humanity and anthropology. [Review of *Primitive society*, by R. H. Lowie.] *Dial* 69:528–33.

———. 1921a. *Language*. New York.

———. 1921b. The musical foundations of verse. *J. Eng. & Germ. Philol.* 20:213–28.

————. 1922a. Mr. Masters' later work. [Review of *The open sea*, by E. L. Masters.] *Freeman* 5:333–34.

————. 1922b. A symposium of the exotic. [Review of *American Indian life*, ed. E. C. Parsons.] *Dial* 73:568–71.

————. 1924a. Culture, genuine and spurious. In Mandelbaum 1949:308–31.

————. 1924b. The grammarian and his language. In Mandelbaum 1949:150–59.

————. 1925. Sound patterns in language. In Mandelbaum 1949:33–45.

————. 1932. Cultural anthropology and psychiatry. In Mandelbaum 1949:509–21.

————. 1938. Why cultural anthropology needs the psychiatrist. In Mandelbaum 1949:569–77.

————. 1939. Psychiatric and cultural pitfalls in the business of getting a living. In Mandelbaum 1949:578–89.

Stocking, G. W. 1968. *Race, culture and evolution*. New York.

————. 1974a. The basic assumptions of Boasian anthropology. In *The shaping of American anthropology, 1883–1911*, ed. G. W. Stocking. New York.

————. 1974b. The Boas plan for American Indian linguistics. In *Studies in the history of linguistics*, ed. D. Hymes. Bloomington, Ind.

Voegelin, C. F. 1952. Edward Sapir. *Word Study* 27:1–3.

INFORMATION FOR CONTRIBUTORS

Normally, every volume of HOA will be organized around a particular theme of historical and contemporary anthropological significance, although each volume may also contain one or more "miscellaneous studies" on non-theme topics, and occasionally there may be a full volume devoted to such studies. The second volume of HOA, now in press, will focus on the history of British social anthropology. The third volume is tentatively entitled "Displaying Humankind," and will treat historical problems relating to the visual representation of the Non-European Other. Preliminary indications of work-in-progress suggest that it may focus primarily on the history of museum anthropology and material culture study, or, more generally, the role of the "object" in anthropology. In addition to papers on particular institutions, we would welcome historical essays on museum collecting, the criteria of ethnographic "authenticity," the political economy of artifacts and *objets d'art*, the problem of repatriation of native cultural treasures, the changing significance of the object in anthropological inquiry, etc. We would consider also historical essays on the anthropology of world's fairs, ethnographic tourist attractions, or photographic or cinematographic ethnography. The deadline for completed manuscripts will be August 31, 1984.

According to present plans, volume four will focus on the anthropology of a particular cultural moment: the period between World War I and World War II. Although any subdisciplinary aspect of anthropology, within any national tradition, may provide an appropriate focus, authors are encouraged to consider their topics in relation to general cultural trends: intellectual, literary, aesthetic, political, economic, etc.

Among themes under consideration for subsequent volumes of HOA are: "Anthropology and the Humanities in Historical Context"; "Diachronic Perspectives and Anthropological Inquiry"; "The Changing Interdisciplinary Relations and Subdisciplinary Boundaries of Anthropology"; and "The Colonial Situation of Anthropological Knowledge." Since themes may be modified in the light of early response, potential contributors are encouraged to communicate with the editor prior to submitting manuscripts.

All material submitted to HOA for consideration should be typed twenty-six double-spaced lines to a page with one and a quarter inch margins. Documentation should be in the anthropological style, with parenthetic author/date/page references (Boas 1911:120) and a list of "References Cited" (begun on a separate sheet). For exemplification of stylistic details, please pay careful attention to previous volumes of HOA. Note especially that primary published historical sources should be cited by the date of the original or historically significant edition, with the date of the edition actually consulted added in parentheses at the end of the reference list entry. Please note also the abbreviated form for citing "Manuscript Sources" (FBP: FB/F. Putnam 1/20/96), which should be listed separately under that heading, with abbreviations cross-referenced under "References Cited." Please do not abbreviate journal or series titles, which will be shortened as necessary by the copy editor. Manuscripts should be submitted in two copies (original typescript and one photographic copy), and will not be returned unless accompanied by adequate postage. All communications on editorial matters should be directed to the editor:

George W. Stocking, Jr. (HOA)
Department of Anthropology
University of Chicago
1126 E. 59th St.
Chicago, Illinois 60637 U.S.A.

INDEX

Academic anthropology, 4, 10, 72, 73–74, 80, 81, 83, 84, 90, 121, 128, 171
Aesthetics and anthropology, 5, 215, 222, 227–29
Africanism, 122, 126, 152
Alexandre, Pierre, 148
Ambrym (New Hebrides), 175, 178, 189
American anthropology: nineteenth century, 54, 67; contrasted with British, 80; contrasted with French, 126; mentioned, 5, 13, 66, 129
American Ethnological Society, 54
American Indians. *See* Native Americans
Animism, 72, 91
Anthropological Institute of Great Britain and Ireland, 80
Anthropologist as hero, 7, 109
Anthropology: crisis in, 3–4, 126; as universal or particular knowledge, 4; historical approaches, 4; reflexive, 4; reinvention of, 4; synchronic approaches, 4; definition of, 5; national traditions, 5, 54, 70, 80, 87, 111, 126; four-field conception of, 5, 76; as European self-knowledge, 6; methodological values of, 7; and science, 54, 66, 171–74; role in policy formation, 169–71; and values, 173; received understandings of, 196; and practice of art, 208–29 passim; as science and art, 215–16
Anthropometry, 86
Applied anthropology, in Micronesia, 169–74
Archeology, 5, 60, 61, 81, 90, 189
Armstrong, W. E., 176, 177, 185, 189
Arunta, 78–79, 91, 129. *See also* Gillen, Frank; Spencer, W. B.
Australian aborigines: marriage classes, 78; ethnography of, 87, 94–95
Australian National Research Council, 176

Baird, Spencer, 56
Bambara (West Africa), 122, 152
Bandelier, Adolph F., 60, 66
Barnett, H. G.: Oregon fieldwork, 157–58, 168; Salish fieldwork, 160; rejects mathematical treatment, 160–61; Palau fieldwork, 161–69; and cultural change, 168;

and Micronesian administration, 169–73; on scientific aspects of anthropology, 171–72; on science and values, 172; mentioned, 9
Barth, Fredrik, 189–90
Bastian, Adolph, 14, 104
Bate, W. J., 179
Bateson, Gregory, 129–30, 176
Benedict, Ruth, 66, 208, 227, 228
Berliner Tageblatt, 14, 21
Biological anthropology. *See* Physical anthropology
Boas, Franz: on Eskimo migration routes, 13, 15, 34, 49; university studies, 13, 16; early interest in Eskimo, 13–15; preparations for Baffin Island voyage, 14; plan for Baffin Island research, 15, 37; affianced to Marie Krackowizer, 15–16; letter-diary, textual aspects of, 16–17; on "alternating" Eskimo terms, 17; as Doctorā'dluk, 17, 24–25, 36; life ambitions, 17, 37; initial reaction to Eskimo, 21–22; glad Eskimo understand English, 21–22, 42; adaptation to Eskimo life, 21–24, 25–29, 32, 37, 40; refrains from collecting skulls, 23; and Eskimo geographical knowledge, 24, 26–27, 31, 39; surveys coastal areas, 24, 28–29, 33, 39, 43, 50; and death of Eskimo child, 24–25; learns Eskimo games and songs, 24–25; and diphtheria epidemic, 26, 36, 38; inconvenienced by dog disease, 27; irritation with Eskimo taboos, 27; political views, 27, 37, 50; studies Kant, 29; yearning for civilization, 29, 34–35, 37, 42, 44–45; lost in blizzard, 30–32; collects Eskimo artifacts, 33; on truth, 33; on the relativity of culture, 33, 38; on *herzensbildung*, 33, 50; learns Eskimo language, 34, 40; learns Eskimo tales, 35, 40, 42–43; revises research plan, 37, 44; ultimatum to Tyson, 38; iglu described, 40–42; gives food to Eskimo, 42–43; considers his accomplishments, 48; snowblindness, 48; ethnographic and geographical research appraised, 50; on need to preserve Eskimo culture, 50; shift from geography to an-

235

OBSERVERS OBSERVED
Essays on Ethnographic Fieldwork

Edited by George W. Stocking, Jr.

"The new series titled History of Anthropology (HOA), to be published annually under the editorship of George Stocking, Jr., a major figure in this realm of scholarship, intends to provide a central meeting ground for historians and anthropologists to explore questions of mutual concern, with each volume organized around a particular topic. This first volume focuses on ethnographic fieldwork, a keystone of cultural anthropology that is at once a unique means of collecting data (participant observation is often spoken of as an 'anthropological' method) and a crucial rite of passage that transforms novices into professionals. . . . The collection as a whole is of high quality, presenting valuable information and provocative analyses. For an anthropologist, the essays by historians offer fresh perspectives that differentiate this book from others on fieldwork. If this volume is an augury of things to come, HOA promises to be a significant contribution to the anthropological and historical literature."
   —*American Scientist*

ALSO AVAILABLE

FUNCTIONALISM HISTORICIZED
Essays on British Social Anthropology

Edited by George W. Stocking, Jr.

"This volume is likely to prove indispensable to historians of anthropology in general and of British anthropology in particular. There are a wide range of historical skills on display, from traditional textual analysis to historical sociology of the most sophisticated sort, and there is a more or less thorough chronological coverage from the era of classical evolutionism virtually up to the present. One can only hope that historicizing anthropologists will sample some of these wares."
   —*Journal of the History of the Behavioral Sciences*
HOA-2.   1984.   Cloth only.

OBJECTS AND OTHERS
Essays on Museums and Material Culture

Edited by George W. Stocking, Jr.

This third volume of the series focuses on a number of questions relating to the history of museums and material culture studies: the interaction of museum arrangement and anthropological theory; the tension between anthropological research and popular education; the contribution of museum ethnography to aesthetic practice; the relationship of humanistic and anthropological culture, and of ethnic artifact and fine art; and, more generally, the representation of culture in material objects.
HOA-3.   1985.   Cloth only.

The University of Wisconsin Press
114 North Murray Street, Madison, Wisconsin 53715

ISBN 0-299-09454-5

DATE DUE

SEP 0 8 2003		
MAY 3 1 2004		
MAY 2 6 2004		
FEB 1 5 2006		
JUN 0 1 2009		
MAR 1 0 2011		
JUN 0 2 2014		
GAYLORD		PRINTED IN U.S.A.